T0304833

Fly Away Paul

Fly Away Paul

*How McCartney survived the
Beatles, found his Wings and
became a solo superstar*

Lesley-Ann Jones

CORONET

First published in Great Britain in 2023 by Coronet
An imprint of Hodder & Stoughton
An Hachette UK company

2

A CIP catalogue record for this title is available from the British Library

Hardback ISBN 9781399721776
Trade Paperback ISBN 9781399721783
ebook ISBN 9781399721806

Typeset in Plantin Light by Hewer Text UK Ltd, Edinburgh
Printed and bound in Great Britain by Clays Ltd, Elcograf S.p.A.

Hodder & Stoughton policy is to use papers that are natural, renewable
and recyclable products and made from wood grown in sustainable
forests. The logging and manufacturing processes are expected to
conform to the environmental regulations of the country of origin.

Hodder & Stoughton Ltd
Carmelite House
50 Victoria Embankment
London EC4Y 0DZ

www.hodder.co.uk

Two little dicky birds, sitting on a wall,
One named Peter, one named Paul.
Fly away, Peter! Fly away, Paul!
Come back, Peter! Come back, Paul.

Traditional nursery rhyme,
first published in *Mother Goose's Melody*, c.1765

The party is over – but no one really wants to announce the finish of an institution. I didn't leave the Beatles. The Beatles left the Beatles. First Ringo left during our recording of the 'White Album' because he said it was not fun anymore. Then George left because he thought we were not saying enough on *Abbey Road*. John fell in love with Yoko and out of love with the rest of us. I woke up and didn't have a job anymore! Oh Jesus. No band. What do I do? I've got to work out something for myself now.

Paul McCartney

For Brian Bennett and Clem Cattini

IN MEMORIAM

James McCartney Snr, 1902–1976

Mary Patricia McCartney, 1909–1956

Arthur Newton Goldberg: Art Rupe, 1917–2022

Sir George Henry Martin CBE, 1926–2016

Antoine Dominique Domino Jnr: Fats Domino, 1928–2017

Peter William Longland, 1930–2023

The Revd Canon John Oates, 1930–2023

Andrew McLuckie White: Andy White, 1930–2015

Richard Wayne Penniman: Little Richard, 1932–2020

Brian Samuel Epstein, 1934–1967

Malcolm Frederick 'Mal' Evans, 1935–1976

Jerry Lee Lewis, 1935–2022

Glen Travis Campbell, 1936–2017

Allen Richard Toussaint, 1938–2015

Jerry Ivan Allison, 1939–2022

George Reginald Cohen MBE, 1939–2022

Margaret Ann Bennett, 1940–2023

John Winston Ono Lennon, 1940–1980

Linda Louise McCartney, Lady McCartney,
née Eastman, 1941–1998

Neil Stanley Aspinall, 1941–2008

David Van Cortlandt Crosby, 1941–2023

Veronica Yvette Bennett: Ronnie Spector, 1943–2022

George Harrison MBE, 1943–2001

Henry Campbell Liken McCullough, 1943–2016

Christine Anne McVie, née Perfect, 1943–2022

Geoffrey Arnold 'Jeff' Beck, 1944–2023

Michael Ralph 'Mo' Foster, 1944–2023

Steve Gray, 1944–2008

Geoffrey Ernest Emerick, 1945–2018

Gary Brooker MBE, 1945–2022

John Andrew Wilkinson: Wilko Johnson, 1947–2022

Robert Ogilvie 'Rab' Noakes, 1947–2022

Olivia Newton-John DBE, 1948–2022

Linda Ann Fredericks: Linda Lewis, 1950–2023

Andrew Maurice Gold, 1951–2011

James 'Jimmy' McCulloch, 1953–1979

Terence Edward 'Terry' Hall, 1959–2022

Andrew John 'Andy'/'Fletch' Fletcher, 1961–2022

Oliver Taylor Hawkins, 1972–2022

Contents

CHAPTER I

BEFORE

There is timelessness in grief. A dark meandering. The flakes and fragments of longing choke the soul. Memories bleed. Solitude is torture. Sorrow suffocates like leaded drapes, and sets the mind in regret. To remember is a nightmare yet we dare not forget, for fear of losing what's already lost. No prospect alarms more thoroughly than death. No mortal is more aware of death than a rock star.

Paul McCartney has done more than his share of mourning. He has experienced loss in every decade since that of his birth. Of his mother in 1956. The Beatles' manager Brian Epstein in 1967. His father Jim, and Beatles roadie and personal assistant Mal Evans, both in 1976. His boyhood pal, co-writer and sometime nemesis John Lennon in 1980. His first wife and soulmate Linda in 1998. George Harrison in 2001, and road manager and head of Apple Corps, Neil Aspinall, in 2008. 'Fifth Beatle' producer Sir George Martin in 2016. Recording engineer Geoff Emerick in 2018, and his beloved brother-in-law and former manager, John Eastman, in 2022.

On 18 June that year, the day he turned eighty, mustn't he have wondered how, by accident or by design, he had been spared the premature check-out while so many nearest and dearest had been taken? In yet another year that delivered rock deaths by the jetload – Taylor Hawkins, a mere fifty years old; Meat Loaf, seventy-four; Wilko Johnson, seventy-five; Gary Brooker, seventy-six; Ronnie Spector, seventy-eight; Christine McVie and Vangelis, seventy-nine, as well as a host of band members, session musicians and music industry legends – did it ever cross his mind that there but for the grace of . . .?

Or is Paul the kind of guy who stays sane by denying himself morbid thinking and just keeps on rolling, grateful for each new day, as well as for the sixty-year career that has made him a national treasure, a global icon and our greatest living composer? Does he ever dwell on the fact that he has now outlived Lennon by more than the length of John's whole life, or perhaps wonder, as he pondered and penned in 1981, how things would be if his friend were here today?[1]

About rock stars. Do they still exist in the twenty-first century or has that epoch passed but nobody told them yet? I'd bet the latter. I wasn't yet born during the 1950s when popular music divided broadly into jazz and crooners, blues and country, and the new-fangled rock'n'roll – rooted in country or white American folk music, and in the black blues and soul of the formerly enslaved and the racially segregated. Out of rock'n'roll, into the sixties, came pop and the Beatles, swiftly followed by the Stones, the Animals and the Who. A million bands and artists flourished in their images.

Come the 1967 Summer of Love, the hippy movement and the migration west from New York to California, pop had begun an irreversible evolution. It was rock that dominated the seventies, offset by punk, but then it was blindsided into the eighties by the advent of the synth era. By 1985, having been augmented by MTV and corporatised by Bob Geldof's Live Aid, pop was re-invented as big-bucks, bona fide, capitalised 'Rock'. Everyone from Rod Stewart to Tina Turner to David Bowie to Madonna was now a rock star. The epithet 'millionaire rock star' turned into a title, an entitlement and a ubiquitous seventy-two-point headline.

What happened to the Beatles? As a recording and performing entity, by 1970 they had ceased to exist. Which was not to say that we'd heard the last of them.

Without the four boys from Liverpool, who became the greatest cultural and social phenomenon of all time, and whose fame and music affected and continues to affect humans in every nook and cranny of the globe, I would not be telling this story. Not that they are history. Their songs live and breathe. Many of them are as familiar to us as our own names. Apart from a few covers, they wrote and composed their own words and tunes. With little between them in the way of formal music tuition, they all played their own instruments and others besides. They were among the first to launch and run their own record company, Apple, through which they championed other artists.

Of their own musical output, sales exceed a billion units, with more sold via download every day. They notched up seventeen UK Number One singles. They also scored more chart-topping albums than any other act and released more in America than anyone else, ever. The most influential artists in the history of popular music, they continue to inspire more musicians than anyone else could ever lay claim to. Beatles songs have been recorded by singers of all ages, of many nationalities and from every imaginable genre, and perhaps they always will be.

Where did it come from? At the core of the magic of the Beatles were the minds, imaginations and hands of two little boys. John Lennon landed at the Liverpool Maternity Hospital on Oxford Street on 9 October 1940. James Paul McCartney was born at Walton General Hospital almost twenty months later on 18 June 1942. Both were war babies. Both were deprived of their mothers at points in their lives when they needed them most.

John's mother Julia lived an unpredictable lifestyle. She gave little John away to her middle-aged, childless sister Mimi to be brought up strictly and respectably. Julia did maintain contact with her only son, visiting him and contributing modestly to his keep. She also introduced him to music, playing him the records that she collected, teaching him chords on the old banjo that had belonged to John's grandfather and buying him his first guitar. His estranged father Alf also had some musical ability.

3

Paul's midwife mother Mary died from breast cancer at the age of forty-seven when Paul was only fourteen, leaving her husband Jim to raise him and his younger brother Michael. Jim had been a trumpeter in a jazz band, and also played the piano. Family members often came round for sing-songs. He played records on his gramophone, and wired extensions up through the floorboards to the boys' bedrooms, attaching Bakelite headphones to the ends. Paul, already familiar with the BBC's Light Programme, could now tune in to Radio Luxembourg. For his thirteenth birthday, his father had given him a trumpet, as though willing him to follow in his footsteps.

Both John and Paul had caring but dysfunctional childhoods against which to rail. Music, for both, was in the genes. What they did with it, and the great heights to which they soared with it, was down to them alone. John, a fledgling rebel brimming with anger and frustration, also tuned in to Radio Luxembourg to hear the latest releases. Paul was sadder, quieter, more conformist and more reflective, but every bit as open to the call of fifties rock'n'roll.

Paul met George Harrison before he met John, on the bus going to school. George was a year younger, which would normally have precluded a friendship. But the boys had music in common, particularly Elvis Presley. George divulged to Paul that his bus-driver father had learned to play guitar during his years in the Merchant Navy, and that he had a guitar himself. Paul, in turn, was reluctant to reveal that he was having piano lessons, and that he was also learning how to play the trumpet. When the skiffle craze rocked Britain, Paul asked his father if he could return his trumpet to the music shop and swap it for a guitar. In the aftermath of his mother's death, that instrument became both his obsession and his salvation.

On 11 November 1956, eleven days after his mother's passing, the king of British skiffle Lonnie Donegan played the Empire Theatre in Liverpool and Paul was in the audience. Soon after-wards, towards the end of that year or shortly into the next, he wrote his first song. 'I Lost My Little Girl' was a disguised ode to his late mother.

Two friends of Paul's at school, Ivan 'Ivy' Vaughan and Len Garry, played in a skiffle group called the Quarrymen that was led by a local Teddy Boy called John Lennon. On 6 July 1957, the Quarrymen had a gig at a summer fête held at St Peter's parish church in Woolton. Ivy invited Paul to the fête with the intention of introducing him to John; if they got on, perhaps John would let him be in the band.

John and Paul came face to face. Paul picked up one of their guitars, tuned it, and began to play and sing Eddie Cochran's 'Twenty Flight Rock'. To let him into the band, John knew on the spot, would be to put his own nose out of joint. The boy was clearly the superior musician. But to deny the band Paul's talent would be to its detriment. For the sake of the greater good, he let him in.

For the rest of that summer, just before John enrolled at Liverpool College of Art, the two boys wrote songs together, mostly at Paul's home 20 Forthlin Road. Their very first composition was called 'Just Fun'. 'There were a few songs that weren't very good,' said Paul in the BBC Radio 2 special *John Lennon at 80*. 'You know, clearly young songwriters who didn't know how to do it. Eventually we started to write slightly better songs, and then enjoyed the process of learning together so much that it really took off.'

The Quarrymen metamorphosed, via a few name and personnel changes including the arrival of George Harrison, into the Beatles. Local engagements around Liverpool expanded to a few a bit further-flung. This led to them coming to the attention of local impresario Allan Williams, who got them a residency in the German port of Hamburg. It was there that they honed the band, their musicianship and their live performing skills and consolidated their songwriting.

They recorded the song 'My Bonnie' in 1961 with English singer Tony Sheridan, with whom they had performed at Hamburg's Top Ten club. It was released in the UK on 5 January 1962, credited to

Tony Sheridan and the Beatles. The single was noted by Liverpool record store owner Brian Epstein, who went to see the band play live at the Cavern Club and subsequently became their manager. He assumed control over the head of Mona Best, the mother of their drummer Pete, who owned and ran the Casbah coffee club out of her home where the band had played, and who had effectively been their unofficial first manager. Epstein took over from Allan Williams, who told Brian that he could have the Beatles, because they wouldn't pay him his commission from Hamburg. His parting advice was: 'Don't touch them with a fucking bargepole!'

It was Brian who brokered a deal for the Beatles with EMI's Parlophone label, headed up by George Martin. The record producer was blamed for the sacking of drummer Best in favour of Ringo Starr, whom they had met in Hamburg when he was working with Rory Storm and the Hurricanes. But it was never Martin's decision. When he decided to re-record 'Love Me Do' with a session drummer, John Lennon told Brian Epstein that they wanted Ringo instead. Lennon would later declare that 'Pete was a good drummer but Ringo was a better Beatle.'

Their debut release, on 5 October 1962, was 'Love Me Do' backed by 'P.S. I Love You'. It got to Number 17. When it was released in America on 27 April 1964, it went all the way to the top.

Largely thanks to the band's appearance on America's *The Ed Sullivan Show* and widespread subsequent publicity and airplay, Beatlemania soon swept the globe. Between 5 October 1962 and 8 May 1970, a period just shy of seven years, John and Paul would publish around 180 co-credited songs, the majority of which were recorded and released by the Beatles.

The band called time on their touring career in August 1966 to concentrate on studio recording. They released six further albums before going their separate ways. Paul had met American rock photographer Linda Eastman in London in May 1967, and married her on 12 March 1969. John had encountered Japanese American

Yoko Ono at London's Indica Gallery in November 1966, and had married her in Gibraltar on 20 March 1969. Their weddings were separated by only one week. Neither Beatle was in attendance at the other's.

When did it end?

Some would say as early as 1966, when wild applause for the 'more-popular-than-Jesus' quartet waned to an echo after their Candlestick Park farewell.[2] After plugs were pulled and amps were toppled, the bum with the broom scraped the boards. While back-stage, a raucous throng boogied on with anyone who thought they were someone that night in the glittering city of Frisco, plus an overcome Joan Baez and a languid Ronette.

Their seventh studio album *Revolver*, a Promethean effort released in tandem with the double A-side single 'Eleanor Rigby'/'Yellow Submarine', made its debut on 5 August, a little over three weeks ahead of their last-ever touring-band gig. It changed pop in a swoop, and forever. Often hailed today as super-ior to *Sgt. Pepper's Lonely Hearts Club Band*, the magnum opus 'greatest album ever recorded' that tailgated it, *Revolver* was the offering that lifted the lid on who they really were; and why, in the end, they would have to call it a day and walk away.

The year 1966 has been flaunted ever since as the gateway to the modern age. It was a time of people and happenings that sound today like ancient history. A year of youth culture, space races and revolutions. Well, you know. Of Vietnam, Civil Rights, Black Power, and the early simmering of 'women's lib'. Harold Wilson, Indira Gandhi and Chairman Mao, Carnaby Street and Swinging London, and Janis Joplin and Big Brother and the Holding Company. The Stones' *Aftermath*, the Beach Boys' *Pet Sounds*, Bob Dylan's *Blonde on Blonde* and the Kinks' *Face to Face*. The Mamas & the Papas' *If You Can Believe Your Eyes and Ears*, Simon and Garfunkel's *Parsley, Sage, Rosemary and Thyme* and Donovan's *Sunshine Superman*. The

Temptations' *Gettin' Ready*, the Who's *A Quick One* and Stevie Wonder's *Up-Tight*.

It was also the year of Jean Shrimpton, Twiggy and Mary Quant, mini-skirts, flower power and ding-dong bells. Cassius Clay boxing Henry Cooper, Jack 'Golden Bear' Nicklaus bagging all four golf majors, and England beating West Germany 4–2 to win the FIFA football World Cup for the first and only time. A year of hovercrafts, Harrier jump jets and Gemini and Luna space modules; the death of Walt Disney and the birth of *Batman* and *Star Trek*; the Moors murders and Aberfan. It was the year of the Beatles' final British concert, at Wembley's Empire Pool, of John falling for Yoko, and Paul treading water with actress Jane Asher. He would propose the following year, and was accepted by his class-act love, each aware that the other was not the only one.

Many blame Lennon, for dumping his nice, safe, peroxide wife and peeling off with a geek from a gallery; breaking Cynthia's heart, cutting his little son Julian adrift and contaminating the Beatles' chemistry with the meddling of a mouthy upstart. Some cite George for having the audacity to want to contribute songs of his own, corrupting the purity of the Lennon–McCartney collaboration and upturning the status quo. Some even aim the accusatory digit at their minding-his-own-business drummer. When Ringo flared and huffed out on them in August 1968, during the recording of the 'White Album', it was only because he was done with their fussing and fighting. He soon returned with a little help from his friends. But by then, there was crayon all over the control room wall.

The irony can never be lost that, during the most insanely creative, innovative years of their decade together, when they chased *Revolver* and *Sgt. Pepper* with *Magical Mystery Tour*, *The Beatles* (the 'White Album'), *Yellow Submarine*, *Abbey Road* and *Let It Be*, the band was coming apart at the seams. Partly because they were doing drugs, some more diligently and dangerously than others, and they were growing up and outwards, yearning to experiment with other musicians, but also because of partners, children, extended families and mounting responsibilities.

Throw into the mix the ovarian cancer that killed popular singer Alma Cogan, with whom John had been smitten and involved in a clandestine affair; the accidental death from overdose of their manager Brian Epstein; their soul-expanding experiences with Transcendental Meditation guru Maharishi Mahesh Yogi, and their ill-fated sojourn at his ashram in Rishikesh, India.

Then there was the unholy muddle that was their recording, management and cash-haemorrhaging creative enterprise Apple Corps; Paul finding American rock photographer Linda, the love of his life; the arrival of notorious artist manager Allen Klein, whom John, George and Ringo wanted, but Paul did not; and lawyer-managers Lee and John Eastman, Paul's future in-laws, whom he insisted should take control of the mess, but his bandmates said no.

Throw all that up in the air and watch where it lands: in the maelstrom of John and Cynthia's divorce, John and Yoko's miscarriages, their arrest on drugs charges, her abducted daughter Kyoko (whom they never got back), their independent campaigns, nutcase baggings, shaggings and bed-ins, their Gibraltar nuptials and their Plastic Ono Band, not to mention the whole *Get Back* endeavour.

Where, in all of this, were the pair of earnest schoolboys who had first eyeballed each other on 6 July 1957 at that Liverpool church fête,[3] recognising one another as though smitten by a coup de foudre; who became the core of a covers outfit doing the local rounds, harmonising in voices so perfectly matched that they could have been blood brothers, and started to write songs together? The two friends who clocked up their 10,000 hours delivering five shows a day, eight hours a day and night, in Hamburg before consolidating their experience and audience engagement at Liverpool's Cavern, then invaded America and seduced the whole wide world.

We were afforded the briefest glimpse of them again, on 30 January 1969, when the Beatles got up on the roof of their Apple Corps HQ in Savile Row, Mayfair, alongside keyboardist Billy

Preston, to play themselves into history. Whether they knew that or not, it looked obvious afterwards. Traffic, crowds and hearts stopped dead in the streets below. 'I'd like,' said John, 'to say thank you on behalf of the group and ourselves, and I hope we passed the audition.'[4]

Paul married his pregnant fiancée Linda Eastman in March 1969. It was Lennon who announced first that he was quitting the Beatles, on 20 September that year. Because bank accounts, tax returns, contracts and commitments were in disarray, he was dissuaded from going public with his stepping-down until matters could be even-keeled.

In January 1970, John and Yoko chopped off their hair, declaring 'Year One for Peace'. It turned out to be anything but. Come April, John was ensconced in the Los Angeles clinic of Dr Arthur Janov, the controversial, subsequently discredited practitioner of Primal Therapy. Paul recorded his debut, eponymous solo album by himself, secretly, at home in St John's Wood, while in denial of a looming mental breakdown. Just over five months after their wedding, Linda brought forth Paul's firstborn at a private clinic round the corner from home.

On 17 April 1970, Paul released his offering on the Apple label, together with an odd Q&A interview in which he declared his detachment and thus became 'the one who broke up the Beatles'. The album, featuring what is probably his greatest-ever solo composition, 'Maybe I'm Amazed', was almost universally slated for that reason. Paul, Linda, her little girl Heather, their newborn, Mary, and Martha the sheepdog soon absconded to Paul's remote farm on the peninsula of western Scotland known as Kintyre.

'I nearly had a breakdown,' Paul admitted to daughter Mary in an interview filmed for his *Wingspan* project in 2001. 'I suppose the hurt of it all, and the disappointment, and the sorrow of losing this great band, these great friends . . . I was going crazy.'

In that vast, rolling wilderness on the edge of nowhere, Linda coaxed her man back to life. On New Year's Eve 1970, Paul went to the High Court to sue his bandmates and Apple, demanding the dissolution of the band.

'It was a difficult time because it wasn't a clean break,' Paul told an interviewer for NRK in 1989.[5]

'The business difficulties that were created were [are] still going on twenty years later. It's a shame, really. But these things, unless you set it up particularly business-wise . . . and then you get some lawyers on the case and you are really screwed. So it was quite sad . . . they were friends. To see it just fall apart was sad. But the liberation was a personal one. It meant that I didn't have people buying my groceries for me, and my office wouldn't tell me what to do. I could tell myself now what I was going to do. So good personally, difficult professionally.'

Thirty-one years later, in August 2020, he nudged closer to the truth.

'The only way for me to save the Beatles and Apple – and to release *Get Back* by Peter Jackson, which allowed us to release *Anthology* and all these great [subsequent] remasters of all the great Beatles records – was to sue the band,' Paul reflected in an exclusive interview for *GQ* magazine. 'If I hadn't done that, it would have all belonged to Allen Klein. The only way I was given to get us out of that was to do what I did.'

Thus did Paul become the vilified Beatle who destroyed the greatest band in history and broke the heart of Planet Earth. The running media and fan commentary was spiteful and soul-destroying. It couldn't possibly have been his idea, not our Paul, not the cute one, you've only got to look at him, butter wouldn't melt, he'd never have thought of doing such a thing by himself, he must have been driven to it, by that sort he married, look at the brazen hussy now, getting in on the act, never been near a piano stool in her life and now she's 'writing songs' would you believe, she'll be upstaging him next, who the bloody hell does she think she is? And so on. What do you call a dog with wings, ran a popular joke once he had formed his new band. No prizes.

'FUCK LINDA', someone scrawled on a wall opposite their North London home. Imagine yourself in dressing gown and slippers, drawing your bedroom curtains of a morning before going down to make your first cuppa of the day, and having to look out on that. A heartless press appeared to endorse the sentiment, seizing any opportunity to do the young mum down. When Lennon's *Imagine* album appeared in September 1971, the anti-Paul-and-Linda mob revelled in the put-downs.

'The only thing you done was "Yesterday",' bitched a lyric line in the track 'How Do You Sleep'? This was Lennon sneering at his boyhood best friend and former co-composer for having come up with the most covered song in history and implying that the muse had long deserted him. Was John's deep-rooted fear that he couldn't do any of it without Paul?

The McCartneys consoled themselves with the simple life deep in the hundred-acre wood on High Park Farm, with its ancient, ramshackle farmhouse, stone barns, leaking tin roof and dripping taps. Swapping gold-plate-bidet luxury for newspaper squares on a string on an outside lavatory wall – figuratively – they revelled in new-found freedom. They ran and ran with their dogs on wind-swept Westport Beach, where most days they had just the sand, rocks and waves for company, and the landscape all to themselves. They grew food, cooked simply and lived a frugal existence utterly at odds with the cossetted, jet-setting, all-consuming lifestyle of the Beatles.

They looked after the sheep that they would soon be refusing to eat, and began to flirt with the vegetarianism that would one day become Linda's third career. They rode their horses relentlessly, often without saddles; made do and mended, dallying around Campbeltown Loch and the quaint old town at its head, at times in overcoats and scarves thrown on over PJs and wellies. They sniffed the head of their perfect baby and thanked the lucky stars that lit their infinite soot-black nights. Got stoned, made love, strummed chords and scribbled words. Eventually.

That Linda managed to drag Paul from their bed, distract him from drinking, doping and smoking himself to death on filterless fags, showering him with love enough to dilute his lethargy and coaxing him from a terrifying depression, while at the same time juggling and feeding both a newborn and a restless eight-year-old without the most basic of modern conveniences, was Herculean. It was hard, she said, but she had no choice. All she could do was what had to be done. She did it. Credit where due.

'Once it was clear that we weren't doing the Beatles anymore,' recalled Paul, 'I got real withdrawals and had serious problems. I just thought, "Fuck it! I'm not even getting up, don't even ring, don't set the alarm." I started drinking, not shaving, I just didn't care, as if I'd had a major tragedy in my life and was grieving . . . and I was.'[6]

Not until fifty-two years after their break-up did Paul open up to any significant degree about the mental health of the four Beatles at both the height of their fame and at their demise. As Beatles, he confessed in a 2022 interview with *The Sunday Times* ahead of his headlining appearance at Glastonbury, they were more likely to make fun of their fears and concerns, if only to hide them. Did any of them suffer with depression? 'Yes,' he said, 'I think so. But you talked about it through your songs. You know, John would write "Help! I need somebody." And I thought, well, it's just a song. But it turned out to be a cry for help.'

Paul's own mental meltdown came 'mainly after the break-up of the band. All of us went through periods when we weren't as happy as we ought to be. But you know, there were a lot of things we had to work through. You didn't talk about mental health.'

Research has shown that men experience depression differently from women. They often appear angry and aggressive when they are suffering, making it nigh on impossible for their nearest and dearest to understand that they are depressed. Paul said that he suffered the 'classic' symptoms of 'the unemployed, redundant man' during the period immediately after the break-up. 'First, you don't shave, and it's not to grow a groovy beard. It's because you cannot be fucking bothered. Anger, deep, deep anger sets in, with everything. With yourself number one, and with everything in the world number two.'

He felt sad and tearful. Guilty and empty. He stared at walls, couldn't eat or concentrate, and slept too much. He had a lovely young wife, a new baby and a little girl to play with and occupy. But every day, come early afternoon, Paul was out of his skull on whisky and marijuana and was of no use to anyone.

Linda wondered what had hit her. 'We had been married for just seven months,' she said. 'What was I supposed to do with that?' Instead of being able to enjoy her new baby and the little family that she and Paul now shared, she said, she found herself very fearful about her husband.

It was Linda who suggested, in desperation, that he form another band. He wasn't doing it without her, he said. He'd only get back to it if she would. He made Linda agree to cross to his side of the fence. She must learn the piano, he would teach her himself if he had to (although he did arrange a 'proper' teacher in London). He would soon have her writing songs. She would see. The family diverted to the States for a bit. All sorts went down over there. Linda convinced him to clamber back on the nag that had thrown him: to assemble another band, start again from scratch and hit the road in a back-to-basics way.

The foundation of all this, of Wings – the band with the ever-changing line-up that saved McCartney's life – was the marriage they called the tightest in rock'n'roll. An impenetrable alliance that would weather most storms. Until the big one blew in to wrench them apart forever, two more children and almost thirty blissful years later.

One of the hallmarks of the McCartney brand has long been his goofy optimism. How was he ever going to be 'just another guy in a band', when his first band had been the Beatles? Especially when he was the one calling the shots and paying the wages. The very concept of a band, a group, implies partnership – even in set-ups with an indisputable leader, star and paymaster. What McCartney put together and called Wings was never going to be other than the boss, the boss's spouse and a succession of hired hands.

This was evident both in his at times alleged insufferable dominance in the studio, and in shekels dispensed. Being directed by McCartney soon got the better of original Wings guitarist Henry McCullough, who slammed out following an argument, dragging drummer Denny Seiwell behind him. Former Moody Blues guitarist and singer Denny Laine played on, the only one apart from the Maccas who remained faithful to the long-term cause. Not even he would ever attain equality, despite his propensity, in his wind-down years, to sell himself as 'a Wings co-founder' and co-creator of both the concept and the songs.

Seventy smackers a week never did go far. It was galling to note, on tours well into the decade, that Wings support acts were raking in substantially more favourable pay. The backing musicians, for that's effectively what they were who were not called McCartney, arrived and departed with exhausting regularity.

Yet they would last for a decade: two years longer than the Beatles. They would wield such incredible impact and influence that at one point they were hailed as the biggest live band in the world. Via a mere seven studio albums – *Wild Life* (1971), *Red Rose Speedway* (1973), *Band on the Run* (1973), *Venus and Mars* (1975), *Wings at the Speed of Sound* (1976), *London Town* (1978) and *Back to the Egg* (1979) – plus one live album, a pair of compilation LPs, twenty-nine singles and just one UK Number One: 'Mull of Kintyre', still one of the biggest-selling singles in musical history.

Not to forget a Grammy award success record that measures well against the achievements of the Beatles, with twelve nominations and six wins, compared with the Beatles' twenty-three nominations and only one win more from their far greater output of twenty-one studio albums, six live albums, fifty-four compilations, sixty-three singles, thirty-six EP singles and twenty chart-toppers. And breathe. You see?

Despite their momentous, pervasive success, Wings were widely savaged and dismissed, both during their heyday and beyond their conclusion. Even Paul himself has at times been driven to comment that they were 'not very good'. It wasn't true. He couldn't have meant it. The self-denunciation, bewilderingly unlike him, is barely fathomable. Surrendering to public opinion and the derision of a scathing, scornful press unimpressed by his decision to include his unmusical wife in the line-up – if it was good enough for John and Yoko, it was good enough for the Maccas – he failed to defend the most misunderstood group of the seventies. They were victims, yes, of the Fabs' monstrous reach and enduring legacy. But who wasn't?

Paul himself described his efforts to eclipse his first band as 'the impossibility of the universe'. I beg to differ. I must defend the group who made the music that ignited me, even before I left school; the music that led me to go back and discover the Beatles and, going forwards, a plethora of groups and artists who would become the inspiration and obsession of my life and career. Because Wings were an infinitely better band than many remember. Their Bond theme 'Live and Let Die', with its quirky reggae-infused middle eight, outclasses Madonna's 'Die Another Day', Shirley Bassey's 'Goldfinger', Tom Jones's 'Thunderball' and Tina Turner's 'GoldenEye'.

Their late-sixties-inspired 'Jet', the daring blare of 'Band on the Run', and radio perennials such as 'Listen to What the Man Said', 'My Love', 'Silly Love Songs', 'With a Little Luck' and 'Coming Up' sound as vigorous and as relevant today as when they were written and recorded half a century ago.

Wings were also a means to an end. They served a purpose without which Paul may well have lost his nerve, remained buried on his farm and never again have reached for a guitar. His second band were the next logical step in the direction of his eventual emergence as the most prolific ex-Beatle and one of the most successful solo recording artists in history. In Wings, was he re-finding his voice . . . or discovering from scratch what his voice really was? Because during the glory days of the Beatles, he could come to the office with a song as perfect as, say, 'Yesterday', and still have to embrace the input, influence and indifference of three other band members plus producer George Martin and others besides.

How exposed, how lacking in confidence, did Paul feel at this crossroads in his life and career? To what extent were the decisions he made at this point wrapped up in Linda and his passionate love for her? How much of his dilemma was due to a sickness of London, the pressures of the Swinging Sixties, the oppressive vibe of the capital and a culture into which, after all, he had not been born? Because Paul was a Northerner: a plain-talking, provincial, working-class lad from Liverpool, who at twenty-five was living the life of a sophisticated aristocratic tycoon; with his own mansion in one of London's most desirable neighbourhoods, precious artworks dangling from its walls.

The lifestyle was fake. It wasn't him. His retreat north of the border, to that simpler life on that vast wilderness of a farm, seems more than significant. Paul's watershed moment was not merely a matter of taking stock and staking out a fresh musical journey. It was about remembering who he was and about rejuvenating his true self. It was, in the words of one of Lennon's final songs a decade later, just like starting over.[7]

Paul succeeded in reinventing himself. He embarked on a totally new career. It has, to date, lasted for an incredible fifty years beyond the Beatles. He continues to perform and record to this day, beyond his eightieth birthday. On 25 June 2022, having sprung a surprise warm-up gig the night before on an unsuspecting audience at the Cheese and Grain – a not-for-profit 850-capacity venue tucked away in Frome, Somerset, more than a hundred miles west of London and half an hour from Glastonbury – he made a triumphant return to the world-famous festival at Worthy Farm.

Watched live by more than 100,000 fans including Harry Styles, Kate Moss, Spice Girl Geri Horner, actors Lily James and Dominic Cooper and members of his own family, he kicked off with the Beatles' 1964 hit 'Can't Buy Me Love' before ripping through 'Hey Jude', 'Lady Madonna' and 'Something', 'Live and Let Die', 'Maybe I'm Amazed', 'Blackbird', 'Let It Be' and seemingly endless more. He also delivered an emotional duet of 'I've Got a Feeling' with his lifelong friend John, who appeared as a hologram above the hallowed Pyramid Stage.

Foo Fighter Dave Grohl dropped in for his first live appearance since the death of beloved bandmate Taylor Hawkins three months to the day earlier. Dave and Paul belted 'I Saw Her Standing There' and 'Band on the Run' together. Then on wandered the Boss, Bruce Springsteen, who treated the gobsmacked crowd to his own 'Glory Days' before sliding into the Beatles' 'I Wanna Be Your Man' alongside its co-writer.[8] More than two hours after the main man had ambled from the wings as the sun set over Glastonbury Tor, Grohl and Springsteen returned to back him in an emotional finale wrapping with 'The End'.

But we are getting ahead of ourselves. In order to comprehend the wider significance of Wings – as the transition band and training ground for the globally revered solo superstar that Paul didn't yet know he longed to be – we must go back. Ruffle some feathers. Retrace the flight, debrief the crew, locate the lost luggage and get a handle on the period that was crucial to his survival – not only as a musician, composer and performing artist, but as a human.

CHAPTER 2

ESCAPE

The many who have blamed Linda Eastman and Yoko Ono down the decades for the demise of the Beatles were perhaps not far wrong. Not that either woman set out to demolish the band. Not deliberately, nor with malice. They did so simply by being there. Which they had every right to be, given that their respective partners had chosen them and wanted them around. They simply preferred the company of their women, at that stage, to that of their fellow bandmates and of any previous plus-ones.

Yoko was subjected to more than her share of the blame, certainly from the world's media. It was an unfortunate misreading of a situation that clearly played for years on McCartney's mind. In October 2012, during an interview in acknowledgement of the impending fiftieth anniversary of the group,[1] he put the record straight via David Frost for the Al Jazeera English television channel.

'I don't think you can blame her for anything,' he told his interrogator. 'When Yoko came along, part of her attraction was her avant-garde side, her view of things. So she showed him another way to be, which was very attractive to him. So it was time for John to leave, he was definitely going to leave. With or without Ono in the picture.'

Klaus Voormann, artist, musician and the Beatles' old mucker from their days in Hamburg, is more emphatic. He insists that Yoko replaced Paul as John's primary creative collaborator.

'When he met Yoko, it was the start of a new life,' he told me. 'John put the Beatles right behind him. The fans don't want to hear that, but it's true. The band, that music, those years belonged to his past. He wasn't John anymore, he was JohnandYoko: one half of a whole. He stopped trying to be a tough rock'n'roller, which he never really was, and he became himself. I was so proud of him for that, and of course I was happy for him.'

As for the woman who became Paul's first wife, Linda Eastman was a professional rock photographer. She dealt routinely with groups and artists. More than a few of her friends and exes were household names. A respected fixture on the New York and LA music scenes, her reputation had reached London on its own merit. Yet she was newsworthy only as the arm candy of an ex-Beatle. But it was more than that.

The crucial factor underpinning the controversial, oft-dismissed suggestion that Linda and Yoko were responsible for the break-up of the band was that Paul and John had both lost their mothers. Not only was motherlessness a common denominator, connecting them in the suppressed, unprocessed grief that would inform much of their songwriting; it had also created vacancies.

Young men during the forties and fifties tended to leave the family abode only when conscripted into the armed forces or to get married.[2] There were exceptions. My own father, for example, left home at seventeen to live in digs when he started playing professional football. John Lennon's situation was unusual in that he was given up, as a small boy, by his mother Julia to her elder sister Mimi Smith, who ruled her Menlove Avenue, Woolton, roost with an iron fist.

Relations between aunt and nephew became strained after the death of Mimi's husband, John's kind and more accessible Uncle George. They were exacerbated when John's mother Julia was knocked down and killed outside Mimi's house on 15 July 1958, when John was seventeen. Coming a year and nine days after he first met Paul, the tragedy united them. John's bedroom window looked out on the stretch of road where Julia died. He couldn't bear it. He escaped Mimi's relentless micromanaging and that terrible view eventually, to doss in the shared, squalid Liverpool bedsit of fellow art student Stuart Sutcliffe.[3]

He later returned to Mimi's before marrying his pregnant girl-friend Cynthia, to his aunt's disgust, in August 1962. The newly-weds lived rent-free in a Falkner Street flat owned and loaned to them by manager Brian Epstein, until baby Julian arrived in April 1963. The following year, they were installed in a large, grown-up house called Kenwood in St George's Hill, Weybridge, Surrey.

After his mother Mary died on 31 October 1956 when he was only fourteen, Paul continued to live at 20 Forthlin Road, Allerton, with his father Jim and younger brother Michael until he was 'nine-teen or twenty'. After the Hamburg comings and goings, the band's success necessitated a move south. Like John, Paul had been nurtured and influenced by numerous 'aunties' and other extended-family members, many of whom stepped up to help widowed Jim, who 'hadn't a clue' as to how to bring up his sons.

Unlike John, Paul had no 'Mimi', no singular mother substitute. His father did not re-marry until eight years later, when he took as his second bride a widowed mother-of-one, Angela Lucia Williams, twenty-eight years his junior and only twelve years older than Paul. But Paul was now twenty-two. The band had conquered America and Beatlemania was in full swing by the time his stepmother arrived. While he made an effort to have a good relationship with her, to begin with at least, he never got to live with her.[4]

It was not until Paul moved into the grand 57 Wimpole Street, London, home of his musician friend Peter Asher and his actress sisters Jane and Clare that he enjoyed the attentions and mother-henning of a bona fide mother figure. The proper, upright lady of the house, music teacher Margaret Asher,[5] became by default a kind of surrogate mother to Paul. Her beautiful, poised, strawberry-blonde elder daughter Jane, already a successful actress, became his girlfriend. This golden couple enchanted London, the nation and for a while the world.

Soon after Paul acquired his three-storey Regency villa on Cavendish Avenue, St John's Wood for £40,000 in 1965, Jane joined him there. Of course she did. But she was in demand as a touring actress. She made clear to Paul that her career came first. Her boyfriend was never faithful, entertaining gals galore while she was off on the road. Though they did become engaged on Christmas Day 1967, and Jane went with him to Rishikesh, India during the spring of 1968, she severed ties for good that summer. Not only had she grown averse to Paul's enthusiastic use of LSD; she had also found him, on her return from a job, in their bed with another girl. Out she flounced and that was that. Frosty Margaret the mother-in-law-in-waiting pitched up later to pack Jane's bags.

The point being that neither Cynthia nor Jane was a mother figure. Poor, passive Cyn stood resolutely by her man and clung to her married-woman status, probably all too aware that John was never faithful to her. She meekly accepted Brian Epstein's admonishment that she must remain below radar, because Beatles fans would desert their boys if it emerged that one was already a married father. Eppy could be forgiven this apparent callousness. That most feared of fates had befallen 'Endless Sleep' and 'Bad Boy' popster Marty Wilde, dad of future chart poppet Kim, whose 1950s rock'n'roll career with his Wildcats was essentially killed by his marriage certificate.

As for Jane, she was the perfect partner on paper. Educated and refined, she walked Paul into a world he could never have imagined as a half-orphaned scally from Liverpool. Hers was a Beaux-Arts realm of first nights and glittering cocktail parties, fine dining, auction rooms and galleries, pressing flesh with the odd royal, the almost-blue-blooded and plenty with letters after their names. Paul was a sponge. He soaked it all up. He took to literature, art and arty types as though to the manner born. Why not? This was the height of Beatlemania. He was rich, world-famous and walking on water. He had more money than most of them. Just sayin'. But he still had a problem.

The first song that Paul ever wrote for guitar, towards the end of 1957, we have seen, was his deceptively upbeat lament about his mother

Mary, 'I Lost My Little Girl'. Eleven years later, he said, during the stressful period that led eventually to the Beatles' collapse, he had a dream in which his mum appeared and reassured him that everything would be okay if only he would just 'let it be'. The song inspired by his vision, for the album that would come to be released under the same name, was written in 1968, recorded in 1969 and released in 1970.

John, meanwhile, confronted his own feelings of grief and loss in the haunting 'Julia', recorded for the 'White Album' ten years after his mother died. Barely two years down the line, after he had screwed himself up further in Primal Therapy, he penned the infinitely more disturbing 'Mother', released originally on the 1970 *John Lennon/Plastic Ono Band* album. That clutch of tracks concluded with 'My Mummy's Dead', an eerily emotionless number that heaves with psychological paralysis.

'We cannot underestimate the loss of a parent on a young adult,' states clinical psychotherapist Richard Hughes. 'The held view within neuroscience is that the brain does not reach maturity until the mid-to-late twenties. The last part of the brain to mature is the prefrontal cortex, which is associated with reasoning, problem-solving, prioritising, creativity, impulse-control and decision-making abilities. The prefrontal cortex is particularly sensitive to the detrimental effects of stress and trauma. We all know that young people are prone to risk-taking, intense relationship experiences, and suicidal feelings.'

The loss of a primary attachment figure is a significant trauma, Hughes goes on:

'Trauma is the uncertainty of psychological survival. Twenty-somethings, who are essentially soft-shelled adults, still need their mother's love; the hugs, hair-stroking and guidance (as much as they may push away from that). Combine this loss of connectedness with age-appropriate developmental traits, and the emotional impact is devastating to the fragile sense of self. In our early twenties, our "self" is still entwined with our primary attachment figure. To lose this attachment, this source of love, is to lose our "self". The loss of a parent can be the root of both misery and creativity. A motivation to survive and ultimately thrive. Or it can be an entombment that leaves us disembodied and fractured. Of course, human beings have neuro-plasticity. Through connectedness, love and creativity we can heal. Trauma does not need to be our forever narrative.'

The deep, unspoken grief of both Beatles had not been assuaged by the women to whom they had originally committed. What each of them craved, subconsciously or otherwise, was a particular kind of woman to fill the gap. A strong, fertile female capable of giving him a family, while at the same time ensuring that he would always remain her priority. Both Paul and John were crying out for someone to take them in hand and make it all right. Overwhelmed by fame, fortune and fall-out, they were lost boys from Neverland, stabbing in the dark.

Paul had the right kind of fiancée, who was completely wrong for him. He must have known it, which is why he carried on putting it about. John had 'done the right thing' by Cyn when it emerged that she was expecting, but had pulled the plug on his heart. It catches up. He too went on with the shagging; with cocks, as we now know, as well as hens. Both boys needed a mother figure? It's what all men need at that point in their lives. Even the ones who insist they do not. Even those who would race you the 40,075-kilometre circum-ference of the Earth barefooted, to get away from her.

Mother is Mother. The fundamental relationship. The most inti-mate, influential connection in a man's life. A daughter can transfer her dependence on mother love to the babies she births herself. A son's experience of fatherhood is once-removed. His need for Mother is more complex.

A far-fetched variation on the tired old Oedipal theme? It is much more than that. For example, scientists have long recognised the significance of 'sexual imprinting' on mate selection. Humans seem to prefer a mate who is similar to their other-sex parent, either in personality, appearance or both. The phenomenon occurs in every species. Wolves, wallabies, name it. Studies show that the most reliable indication of a male's partner choice is eye and hair colour. If these are similar to his mother's, he is in with a chance.

What's more, men are mostly attracted to women who are similar in age to their own mother when she gave birth to him. In other words, Mother is never far away.

Even if a man goes out of his way to avoid any woman who reminds him too much of his mother, her influence is still in play. He resists the mother/son bond at his peril. A boy who has not been nurtured and protected by his mother into young adulthood will continue to seek those things from another source. Even if he doesn't realise that he is doing it. Every rule has an exception, but this one seems tight. A cold, brutal matriarch, conversely, according to psychologists, will sometimes breed a wife abuser. An extreme trauma pattern, that one, yet more common than we know.

'Every unmet desire in adulthood is laid at the maternal doorstep,' says Natalie Angier, biologist, author and Pulitzer Prizewinning science writer for the *New York Times*. 'If anything, the loss of the larger kinship matrix focuses the fury of our helplessness entirely on our mothers.'[6]

None of which is to denounce Paul or John as a pussy or a mummy's boy. It is simply to remind ourselves that, if the first person who held you, cleaned you, kept your belly full and your body warm and dry was Madre, it stands to reason that you are likely to select a mate who rekindles those sensations of security. Many men are drawn to maternal, nurturing women for precisely this reason. Now here's the bonus ball: both Paul's Linda and John's Yoko had track records as mothers. Each arrived at their Beatle marriage with a small daughter under one arm. They were card-carrying. They came with credentials. Their experience as parents, however, could not have differed more.

Linda was Mom to four-year-old Heather, born during a brief first marriage, when Paul met her in 1967. He was impressed, Paul has said, by her relaxed devotion to her child and by her natural mothering skills. Yoko, like John, was married when they met in 1966. Yoko had three-year-old Kyoko by second husband Tony Cox. John was father to Julian, four months older. Effectively abandoning his own child to care for someone else's, John saw little of Julian after he left Cynthia, but grew devoted to Kyoko.

An awful custody battle ensued, during which Cox abducted his own daughter in December 1971. The pair vanished into thin air. Despite being the most famous couple in the world, as well as one of the richest – they hurled money right, left and centre and did everything imaginable – they never got Kyoko back. Let that sink in. John was long dead by the time Yoko saw her child again. She had been deprived of her firstborn for more than twenty-three years.

All of which informs the relationships created by these two couples. In desperate need of the stability of hearth and home, the love of a good woman and a brood to hang with and raise – fundamentals that he hoped would offset the insecurity that engulfed him during the disintegration of the Beatles – Paul invested himself wholeheartedly in Linda.

Angry, bitter, opprobrious John lost his heart and soul to a seven-years-older, sophisticated, creative female with connections and ambitions of her own, who would raise his game and be the perfect foil; who came prepared to campaign to win custody of her daughter, fearless in the face of agitation, authority, politics and controversy, and who would be the most mega Mother of them all. He even called her that. To her face: 'Mother'. And third-person: 'We'll have to ask Mother what she thinks about that,' when she was standing right there, in front of him. As evidence, it leaps.

For fifty years, American psychologist and educator Dr E. Paul Torrance, 'Ellis' to his friends, pioneered research into the human ability to create. Known as 'the Father of Creativity', his Torrance Tests are used internationally. Identifying the four elements of creativity as fluency of ideas, flexibility in their variety, originality, as in the uniqueness of ideas, and elaboration, relating to the details of those ideas, he aided the identification of gifted individuals throughout the world.

In 1995, Torrance noted that creativity naturally follows when an individual is intrinsically motivated, resulting in stubborn persistence. The Beatles are a prime example of intrinsic motivation leading to extreme creativity, spending countless hours rehearsing, recording and polishing songs obsessively. In interviews, Ringo Starr called Paul 'a workaholic'. What did they make, one wonders, of Paul's diversions into painting and poetry, and of John's own creative journey that began with drawing, painting and cartooning as a boy, launching his own schoolboy newspaper *The Daily Howl* and penning poems and long-form prose well before he awoke to his urge to create music?

Does the multi-disciplinary approach dilute or concentrate the creative compulsion? What about the barriers to creativity? The fear of experimentation, say. The known paralysis that sometimes arises from perfectionism. The fear that others will judge and even ridicule you. Add to that the loss of Mother, the single greatest contributor to the risk of long-term emotional and mental health issues including anxiety, depression and substance abuse, and you have a life-threatening cocktail.

It is significant that both Paul and John were prone to all these potentially destructive forces. Why was the damage not more obvious before and during the existence of the Beatles? Because the pain was deferred. Because they were comfortably numb, and denial is as cosy as a fireside on a filthy night. Why go there if to resist is to spare yourself pain? Think about it. Music invaded their hearts and minds, filled their ventricles, cortices, lobes, lungs and throats to overflowing. The world remains forever grateful that it did. It distracted them and gave us music that is never going away.

The Beatles happened quickly. Success consumed them, changed them, chewed them up, tried but failed to spit them out . . . because by then they were bigger than success. Only once the spell was broken did they come eyeball to eyeball with that old devil called delayed reaction. Uh-oh. Neither Paul nor John grieved for Mother at the time they were deprived of her, for the simple reason that they were not helped to do so. There was no grief counselling in those days. The folks back home tended to leave well alone.

Just as U2's Bono said about the death from a brain aneurysm of his mother Iris in 1974 when he was fourteen, four days after she had collapsed at her own father's graveside during his burial, 'We [father, brother, himself] were three Irish men, and we avoided the pain that we knew would come from thinking and speaking about her.' She was never spoken of again. 'I fear it was worse than that,' he added. 'That we rarely thought of her again.'

'I became an artist through her absence,' he also said. 'And I owe her for that. I thought the rage I had was a part of rock'n'roll, but the rage was grief.'[7]

Consider Madonna, whose thirty-year-old Ma lost out to breast cancer when her little girl was five. Explaining the root of her obsession with control, Madge told *Billboard* in 2016: 'Obviously, you could say it has to do with my childhood, if you're going to psychoanalyse me: my mother dying and me not being told, and a sense of loss and betrayal and surprise. Then feeling out of control for the majority of my childhood and becoming an artist and saying that I will control everything.'

Consider also Tom Petty, who fell into deep depression after Katherine 'Kitty' Petty passed the day after his thirtieth birthday. His major success – multiple hit albums, chart hits such as 'I Won't Back Down', 'Free Fallin'' and 'You Don't Know How It Feels' all came after his mother's death, which for him was a tragedy. Having survived heroin addiction, an accidental overdose reunited Tom with Momma in October 2017, at the age of sixty-six.

Take a look at Beethoven, deprived of his beloved 'best friend', mother Maria Magdalena in 1787, when Ludwig was sixteen going on seventeen. Her loss impacted his sense of self and his personal relationships for the rest of his life. Like his father, he toppled into alcoholism. After Mother's death, he composed himself inside out, a genius possessed.

'Early trauma frequently results in the individual escaping into an inner world of his own making that can be a safe harbour from the perilousness of the outer world,' comments Nancy Swift Furlotti, Ph.D., an Aspen, Colorado Jungian analyst.

'It can be a place of creativity where ideals of freedom and perfection can take hold. This is where Beethoven's genius prevailed. Yet, as he set himself up to aspire for greatness and beauty, nothing less was acceptable. This ideal was projected onto the women he fell in love with, none of whom could ultimately live up to his ideal. He so longed for love and companionship but was incapable of compromise. This resulted in depression, feelings of despair, unrelenting self-criticism, and somatic disturbances such as the gastrointestinal illness that he later attributed to his social isolation. His deafness certainly did not help, but instead pushed him further into his own inner world.'

The greatest composer who ever lived, Beethoven is now believed to have been one of the first composers to express his innermost thoughts and feelings in his music – just as tormented Vincent van Gogh, who was rejected by his mother Anna Carbentus van Gogh and sold only a single work during his lifetime, was probably the first to express the spectrum of emotions, none more so than misery, in paint.

For someone who has lost a parent or has experienced attachment deficits such as poor parenting and deprivation, the world of music and performance can act like an extended or substitute family. According to Richard Hughes, 'It can feel reparative. The music studio and the main stage can be healing. Connectedness, love and creativity are all there. So is the "shadow" of all that. Attachment wounds may end up being medicated with self-limiting coping strategies. Narcissistic behaviour can be destructively seductive. Connection can turn out to be as deep as an empty bottle of Jack Daniel's, and last as long as an encore. None of this is truly reparative.'

In the 2022 Gary Numan documentary *Resurrection*, Foo Fighters singer, guitarist, songwriter and former Nirvana drummer Dave Grohl did not mince his words. 'It's been said that when you experience trauma in early life, you stop maturing emotionally,' he commented. Exactly. As clinical psychologist, trauma specialist and author Dr Carla Marie Manly elaborates: 'When an individual is traumatised, especially early on in life, the memory of the trauma is stored both in the brain and the body. As a result, if healing does not occur, the traumatic incident can impede healthy development.'

Depending on the severity of the trauma, the Sonoma, California-based doctor expands, one's entire way of being may be formed around the traumatic incident. This happens because the trauma is not properly processed on a neurobiological level. It can, she says, rewire your brain in such a way that it continues to influence your thought patterns and behavioural responses as you grow older. Investigation into developmental disorders did not advance significantly before the 1980s. Mental health was a branch of medicine still in its infancy.

John and Paul were both bereaved in the late 1950s. British stiff-upper-lip culture back then encouraged them to buck up, keep going and put on a happy face, there's a good boy. Even if their hearts were breaking, they felt suffocated by grief, could hardly breathe for weeping and could barely put one foot in front of the other. There was no bereavement support for children, either within or outside the family. Formal organisations of this kind did not exist in fifties and sixties Britain. The first dedicated childhood bereavement charity in the UK, Winston's Wish, was not established until 1992.[8]

Dysfunction and abandonment. Fear and frustration. Disruption of the expected, the scheme, the way things 'were supposed' to be, and rage, rage against the dying of a loved one's light.[9] Dead mothers have a lot to answer for. They give rise to rock stars, that's for sure, whatever the profession in which they excel. Mother substitutes, like Linda and Yoko, are more significant than we may previously have believed. Even if they were unwittingly to blame for having shown John and Paul that they no longer needed to be Beatles.

CHAPTER 3
PASSING

The derelict three-room farmhouse on Kintyre, a peninsula of Argyll in the southern region of Scotland's Western Highlands, was incidental. Paul had barely even seen the place when he laid down the dosh to purchase it. How much? It depends on who you ask. Thirty thousand? Thirty-five?

A writer claimed recently that the relevant Land Registry document had published a purchase price of a mere £4,000. Which register did he search? HM Land Registry is responsible only for England and Wales. The Land Register of Scotland, an independent entity, does not recognise the title number they quoted. Nor does High Park Farm appear on the new register. The Scottish register, based on the Ordnance Survey map, was not introduced until 1981. The department is 'still working to replace the old register'.

Still here? Whatever Paul paid is his own business. Suffice it to say that he found himself the outright owner of a 183-acre estate complete with crumbling farmhouse. He did not buy it, however, from the Mr and Mrs Brown usually quoted. That couple, a real-life Janet and John who had managed a herd of twenty-five Ayrshire cattle (the 'ultimate dairy cow') and a hundred Scottish Blackface sheep there for nineteen years since 1947, were not the owners. They were tenants.

Their landlord was the late Charles Noël Beattie QC (1912–1998), a London-based barrister and author of various books including *Beattie's Elements of Estate Duty* (Butterworths, 1963), a guide to inheritance and transfer tax. Beattie had not inherited the estate, but had purchased it from the Trustees of the late ninth Earl of Argyll, Archibald Campbell, to whose clan it had belonged for nearly three hundred years. When came the time for the Browns to retire, Beattie elected to sell rather than save the estate for his children Elizabeth, Patricia, Michael and Lucy (no spouse is declared on Beattie's headstone). From a Beattie to a Beatle, a chunk of Scotland duly passed. Given Paul's penchant for hanging onto his properties, it is likely to remain in the family well past his demise.

What did Paul know about farming? Not a lot. He probably didn't even know, on 17 June 1966, that he had just purchased a 0.0011% share of Scotland's nineteen million acres. He did not buy the farm with the intention of living there, working the land, tending the herd and the flock and getting away from it all in time-honoured tradition. There was nothing fanciful about it. He sought merely to reduce his crippling tax liability by acquiring assets at a time when the highest rate of UK income tax was around 90 per cent.

Paul bought it after a single flying visit, accompanied by Jane Asher – during which the Browns showed them around the small farmhouse, then sat down with the future vegetarian ex-Beatle and the actress/future party-cake queen for bacon and eggs. The property was one of several possibles in a portfolio put before the 25-year-old McCartney. In December 1967, they returned there by road, Paul driving Jane in his Aston Martin with Martha his Old English sheepdog, then still a puppy, in the back. The car began to flag outside Glasgow and had to be checked into a garage for the night for mechanical attention. They resumed their journey the next day.

Paul had no particular Caledonian connection beyond his band's pre-Beatlemania 1962/63 tour of modest venues in small towns such as Dingwall, Elgin and Bridge of Allan, including their only live appearance in Aberdeen at that city's Beach Ballroom; and their triumphant return towards the end of 1964, playing a string of bigger gigs from Glasgow to Edinburgh to Dundee. But John did. The elder Beatle's links to the land of the brave dated all the way back to his childhood. This might have been why Paul chose to purchase property in Scotland.

Lennon spent many a school summer holiday with his maternal 'Edinburgh aunt' Mater, her second husband 'dentist uncle' Bert and his cousin Stanley on Bert's croft at Sango Bay, near the village of Durness. Its sandy cove is tucked into the 'hat' of the Highlands just to the east of Cape Wrath, Britain's most north-westerly point. The cape's Listed granite lighthouse flares nightly between the Minch and the Moray Firth.

Hugged by gorse-patched rocky outcrops, sea cliffs and dunes, Sango is one of the most beautiful beach locations in the Scottish Highlands. It stretched a fifties Liverpool schoolboy's horizons, introducing dolphins, porpoises, whales, seals and many different species of birds to his imagination, as well as spectacular, yawning sunsets.[1] A plaque on a wall and a memorial garden there inform the visitor that 'John Lennon, 1940–1980, Musician and Songwriter, lived here.'

'He felt more Scottish than English and, growing up as he did in a polyglot city, he was comfortable on those holidays with his aunts and uncles and friends,' affirms Beatles author Philip Norman. 'He was always calling himself "Jock" and "Whistling Jock Lennon" and, even when he was living in New York, he was searching for a house that would remind him of the croft where he spent part of his childhood.'

Scotland was so special to John that he returned to Durness just over three months after his wedding in Gibraltar. He took his bride Yoko, her daughter Kyoko and his son Julian. He wanted them to experience and understand the places, people and things, including bagpipe music (he even got there ahead of Paul) that he had adored as a boy. He took the children shopping for kilts, Aran sweaters and pompommed tam o' shanter floppy hats, and dressed the tots identically.

Myopic John, who should never have been driving in the first place, particularly not with children in the car, crashed their Austin Maxi and tipped it into a ditch. They wound up in the tiny Lawson Memorial Hospital in the village of Golspie, Sutherland. Yoko was the more seriously injured. It must have been John's guilt that prompted him to insist that his new wife must have a bed installed at the studio back in London, so that she could observe the band at work on their 'final' album *Abbey Road*. It must have been mischief that made him throw in a live microphone for her exclusive use, 'in case she wants to contribute anything'.

The other Beatles fumed silently. Hostilities simmered. Hubble, bubble, toil.

Bringing us to the point about dentist-uncle Bert's Highland croft. His property was a working farm, on abundant moorland punctuated by peat bogs and streams. It was not dissimilar to the farm that Paul purchased. He might not be able to capture directly John's cherished childhood idyll, but Paul could experience some of that magic by buying into the location. At some point in the future, too, once he had children of his own, he would get to live John's Scottish childhood vicariously.

It could not have been further from his mind, the day he signed on the line, that he would soon escape London, the Beatles and the fall-out of their implosion to seek refuge there; that he would sink into a deep depression there, be nursed lovingly back to life by his wife, and dare to start contemplating some kind of existence beyond the band there . . . which at first he couldn't imagine he would ever find.

Heather and scrub. Bog and stream. Scots pine, spruce and moss as far as the eye could see. Commentators who can't have been there report that High Park Farm 'overlooks' Skeroblin Loch and is on the slope to Ranachan Hill. It isn't. Lying south-west of one and north-east of the other, a prehistoric standing stone marks a roughly equidistant spot between those two. Stand with your back to the imposing nine-and-a-half-feet-tall, two-feet-thick stone, pace a few steps forward and you are on the famous but remote farmhouse's doorstep.[2]

Fly away, Paul, went the nursery thyme. Fly he did.[3] He came here. It became the hideaway in which this battered, bewildered, heartbroken ex-Beatle got himself back; in which he found the strength to discard his sixties persona and drag himself into the next decade; in which he learned how to think, feel, laugh, love and write songs as an individual. Humble though that unprepossessing dwelling may be – even today, with its corrugated tin roof, stone walls, garish red-painted doors and gates, sunshine-yellow-and-scarlet-porch and olive-green partitions – it is almost a holy place. To rock'n'roll fans, to Beatle-lovers, if only they were allowed inside, it is a shrine to the survival of a superstar.

There are no signposts on the road heading inland out of Campbeltown. Nothing official to tell you that 'Sir Paul McCartney lived here'. No tourist information to indicate that he once inhabited these bleakly picturesque parts. Nearly sixty years since he was handed the deeds to the land and dwellings that he owns to this day, and which he expanded over the years with the subsequent acquisition of Low Park Farm, Low Ranachan Farm and other neighbouring properties to create a fiefdom of around a thousand acres, locals are as cagey as ever about their relationship with the man to whom they still refer as 'the Beatle'.

When Paul, Linda, Heather and Mary escaped the fray to hunker down to a hillbilly existence here all those years ago, most Campbeltonians welcomed them quietly and without fuss. They let them be, and simply accepted them. With the exception of the occasional intruder who contrived to infiltrate and track them down, they were left largely to their own devices.

Campbeltown, the only settlement of significance, sits tightly on the eastern side of the peninsula at the head of a loch. It is named after the Campbell clan, who ruled until the seventeenth century and once owned Paul's land, and is part of the council and lieuten-ancy areas of Argyll and Bute.[4] The Ice Age-hewn promontory of Kintyre – from *Cynn-tìre*, a Gaelic name meaning, literally, 'Land's-end' – hangs down on the left-hand side from the main mass of Argyll like an engorged male member. Accusations of gratuitous prurience are overruled.

Legend has it that the British Board of Film Classification main-tains a secret rule known as the Mull of Kintyre Test applicable, in cases of the potential depiction of nudity in videos and motion pictures, to the degree of erectness of the phallus. If it stands at an angle from the vertical greater than that of the Kintyre peninsula – in plain English, 'the angle of the dangle' – then to show it on film is prohibited. The BBFC denies that such a rule or test has ever existed, or has ever been applied. Which is by no means proof that it has not been. The question as to whether the rule was perchance implemented on 1 April one year has yet to be answered. One imagines that mischievous McCartney, like Lennon no shrinking violet when it came to matters erotic, fell upon this information with utter glee.

Although the town lies just under sixty miles west of Glasgow, the region's topography renders a direct route east to west impos-sible. The drive from Glasgow airport is a tedious 140 miles or so north, then west and finally south. It takes, in clement weather on the primarily single carriageway, some three and a half hours. On a dry day, once the mists have lifted, the landscape is breathtaking. You can see summits, sea lochs and ruined castles for miles. If hindered by lashing rain and even hurricane-force winds as you negotiate the bonny shorelines of Lochs Lomond and Fyne, you will definitely miss dinner. Take a comfort break and a stiffener at the Inverary Inn, and proceed with caution.

Some travellers to Kintyre jump on a bus from Glasgow. Most find the mere thought unbearable. Others board a flight out of the Dear Green Place and are down with a dram at the Royal Hotel bar in little over half an hour. The Maccas tended to fly up from London by private jet, a hop of about ninety minutes. But if Paul decided to drive the distance himself, as he sometimes did, he would stop off on Merseyside and spend the night with his dad. That seemingly endless, meandering road out of Scotland's biggest city, down the west bank of Loch Fyne, crossing to the west coast of Kintyre, dipping on the diagonal and descending at last into Campbeltown, inspired his haunting composition 'The Long and Winding Road'.

Paul wrote the song at the farm fifty-five years ago, impossibly, in 1968. He was still a Beatle then. Just about. He had met Linda in May the previous year, but was technically still with Jane. He wrote it in celebration of the majestic, timeless landscape that cocooned and soothed him at the worst time in his life since his mother died, when 'my favourite band in all the world was breaking up'. His suffering throughout that period is evident. He also appears to be peering deep into his own song as though imploring it to show him the way.

'I just sat down at my piano in Scotland, started playing and came up with that song, imagining it was going to be done by someone like Ray Charles,' Paul said. 'I have always found inspiration in the calm beauty of Scotland, and again it proved the place where I found inspiration.'[5]

The railways never made it as far as Campbeltown. The nearest train station, at Oban, is almost a hundred miles away. It must be one of the reasons why this world within a world has remained remote. Most who were born here do not stray far. Many found their life partners among people they went to school with. When unemployment rose with the decline of industry, young, male Campbeltonians took to the high road in search of jobs and a better life. Some emigrated to former colonies. A significant number came back.

Those who did not still return regularly to visit elderly parents and other family members. Some wonder why they ever left the place where everyone appears to know and look out for everyone else, and where a cosy camaraderie prevails. 'When you can check out any time you like,' as one local said to me, 'why would you ever want to leave?'

There is a mythical air to Campbeltown and its loch. Immortalised in an old folk song repopularised in the sixties by 'Tartan Trooper' Andy Stewart,[6] nothing prepares the visitor for its strangeness. Like the Brigadoon of Lerner and Loewe's Broadway musical about a mysterious Scottish village that materialises for only one day every hundred years, you find yourself wondering whether such a place exists. Is it there or does the eye deceive you? It has a surreal, almost Toytown quality. It seems locked in time and untroubled by lost fortune.

The boom years are long gone. Both its fishing industry and its industrial prominence have reduced dramatically in recent times. It is such a sleepy, relaxed little place that it is hard to imagine the period during the Napoleonic Wars when sinister press gangs would hang around its harbour and Old Quay waiting to nab likely recruits from the local fishing fleet.

This once bustling port was also the whisky capital of the world, producing more than two million gallons of the liquor each year. Dozens of distilleries jostled for position, making the town a haven of wealth. Only three remain: Glengyle, Glen Scotia and Springbank. Campbeltown Loch blended malt whisky is made from its five distinctive single malts, and is vatted and bottled at the Springbank Distillery.[7]

The baronial mansions that line the water's edge like the gems of gorgeous necklaces were built on Scotch. My room in the imposing Craigard House Hotel, which in the old days was the town's maternity hospital, was the operating theatre in which many locals were born. The mothers of two of the people I had come here to see, members of the Campbeltown Pipe Band who played on the Wings 'Mull of Kintyre' single and performed in its video, had been delivered of their baby boys in my bedroom. They were sixteen years old when their moment of glory happened upon them. They are sixty-one now, and this is still home.

Images of the happy, carefree McCartneys riding their ponies in the hills and across the moors are enchanting. What a life they had here: swimming and surfing the waves beyond the gaze of the madding media. Checking times of tides to ensure they wouldn't get cut off before dashing to Davaar Island via the Doirlinn, a long, frequently submerged shingle beach that stretches from the shore; creeping into the cave there that contains a fading mural of Christ's Crucifixion by local artist David MacKinnon dating back to 1887.

That islet, at the mouth of the loch, featured on the sleeve of the 'Mull of Kintyre' seven-inch single, with Linda, Paul and Denny Laine in the foreground. Who knows why they chose it as their illustration. Davaar Island is at least twenty miles from the Mull of Kintyre itself, which is not the name of the entire peninsula but only of the windswept headland at its tip. 'The Mull of Kintyre . . .,' muses Kintyre-born Johnny MacKinnon. 'It depends where you're looking from as to where it is.'

It is impossible to drive all the way there. You point your car in the direction of the lighthouse, brake sharply time and again to avoid hitting the stags, does and bambis that bounce across your path, and abandon your vehicle when the road runs out. From there it's on foot, slip-sliding down a steep, zagging path; past a poignant cairn memorial to the twenty-nine lost in the RAF Chinook helicopter crash of June 1994, and all the way down to the lighthouse. I stood and texted my friend the celebrated Fleet Street cartoonist Tom Johnston, who lives in Cushendall on Northern Ireland's Antrim Coast, thirty miles or so across the treacherous North Channel waters.

'Go out onto Red Bay and wave to the Mull of Kintyre,' I said. 'I am here, waving back.'

Paul and Linda often took their children to matinee screenings at the local 'wee picture house', Scotland's only continuously running cinema that had been going since 1913. They also visited the elegant

Burnet Building next door, which houses the town's museum. Across in the main square, beyond the ferries, yachts and pleasure boats in the harbour, they lingered sometimes at the Campbeltown Cross. The eleven-feet-high, disc-headed stone monument some 600 years old is reckoned to have been carved at Iona Abbey.[8] Its surface is a tangle of intriguing shapes, including dragons and mermaids.

All of which are ordinary things that ordinary families with young children do. Aren't they? Perhaps, in a modern-day Grimms' Fairy Tale dimension where families still live in tumbledown cottages without mod cons. Where he chops wood, shapes mangled bits of furniture out of whatever he can find and drives a tractor, while she rustles up scran on a manky old stove, beaming at the kids as they stick their coloured-pencil drawings all over the walls. Look, folks, we are just like you, living our most authentic, meagre life. Leaving aside our lavish mansion and our millions in the bank to get down with the normal people.

The McCartneys were never normal, were they. Not by the 500-mile ride that would whisk them back to London any time they liked. Their austere, no-frills existence on Kintyre was in many ways a fantasy. Wishful thinking. Paul was on the run, both from his surreal existence in the Beatles and towards a life he couldn't yet envisage. In such circumstances, refuge is all. In the isolation of his highland lair, he could and did restore himself. He did so with the help of his wife and kids, living the plainest and most basic life they could make for themselves.

There was a time when I was more convinced by the back-to-nature, born-again-ness of it all. When I was fascinated by the thought of the Maccas forsaking home comforts in the capital for the mists, drizzle and gales of their Scottish nowhere-land. Huddled on a homemade couch and chairs, turning in for the night on damp, sagging mattresses, struggling to get to sleep to the relentless scrabble of rats and mice in the walls, making do with bare-minimum sanitation – there wasn't even a flushing lavatory or a bath when they arrived – they reconnected with the earth, they said. They confined themselves to the things that mattered in life. How marvellous, I thought, how magical. I was impressed by them. I bought it all.

I wonder now, was there something slightly deranged about it? Something off-kilter and weird, maybe even a bit perverse? Because the McCartneys never were and never will be ordinary mortals. They were nothing like their Kintyre neighbours. While plenty up there were doing nicely, thanks very much, those who were living lives of hardship and hand-me-downs in that far-flung corner were not doing so by choice. They did so to survive. The multimillionaire rock star, his lady and their precious brood could come and go as they pleased.

Everyone in Campbeltown was aware when they were 'in'. When they pitched up at the local agricultural fair to show their ponies, they were naturally the centre of attention. When they sheared their sheep of wool for spinning, it inevitably became a photo opportunity. And how private was their 'privacy', really? Whenever Paul zipped the five or so miles into Campbeltown in his Land Rover 'Helen Wheels'[9] to visit the local Chinese, the whole town knew the Maccas were having a takeaway. When he lugged the family linen down to a neighbouring laundress, the women tut-tutted about 'Lady Linda' (as she wasn't yet) leaving chores to her man that she 'ocht be doin' hersel".

'Linda's photographs have made Kintyre and the McCartney's connection to it much more than it really was,' reveals Johnny MacKinnon, a Glaswegian-born, south England-based keyboard player, who grew up in a 'distillery house' in Campbeltown.

'I call it the furthest place from anywhere and the closest to nowhere,' he says. 'Campbeltown has a great sense of community. There are no strangers – or if there are, they're a stranger to everybody. You could never say that the town itself is a tourist attraction.

Absolutely not. But thanks to the McCartneys, you can say that it's on the map. There is a benevolence on both sides, I think. People there are very protective of Macca and of the relationship he has with the area.

'When I was a kid, they called him "the Beatle". "Oh, the Beatle was at so-and-so's restaurant last night," that kind of thing. The family would often come to the "June show", which was usually held in August because of the weather. May to September, of course, being the worst time of all for "the midge". You learn to live with it. Paul, Linda and the girls would rock up, and they'd enter their ponies in the gymkhana. They would pose for pictures with local people, who called them "Paul" and "Linda" to their faces.'

Johnny has wondered down the years why they ever came there in the first place.

'I mean,' he says, 'he had to go somewhere remote, with all that was going on, and Campbeltown's not what you'd call accessible. But when you can afford so much better, why would you reduce yourself to such extreme spartan conditions as they had to endure on that farm? It has always been unfathomable to me. I have sometimes read, "They didn't even have *electricity*!", and, "They read by *candlelight*!" or by oil lamps or whatever it was. It wasn't that bad! Most power in Scotland is underground, even on hill ground, as we'd tend to call their kind of moorland. But even with power, it was primitive.'

Did the presence of the McCartneys ever disrupt the local community?

'No,' Johnny insists. 'No one impinged on them, nor they on the locals. There were only occasional friction points.'

Like what?

'Such as animal welfare. For example, they wouldn't cut the tails of their sheep. Because they thought it was cruel, presumably. Farmers cut the tails to stop the maggots and prevent them from getting infected. So they were all shearing the wool and taking care to cut the tails regularly, and the McCartneys were not. Both sides thought the other side was in the wrong, so there was an impasse there. Different ways of looking at the world, I suppose.'

The Campbeltown of Johnny's childhood was a busier place than the version the McCartneys encountered. North Sea trawler shipbuilding, a large Jaeger garment factory, a model aeroplane factory and an RAF airbase with a 'huge contingent' of Americans were then in full swing.

'There were a lot of well-educated people coming into the area, and generally a huge buzz,' Johnny says. 'The hotels, restaurants and many bars were thriving. This was all good news for local people. But it struck me early on and has stayed with me ever since: if you're not from there but you choose to go and live there, you are running away from something. Which Paul obviously was. When I moved away, to go to college in Glasgow, the shipyard had closed, Jaeger had shut, the model plane factory had burned down, and everything was starting to crumble. So what the McCartneys found there was a place that was on the verge of becoming a shadow of its former self. Its glory days were over. It was in decline. I can well see now why Paul the ex-Beatle would have identified with that.'

For himself, Johnny admits, he had to leave. 'Had I stayed any longer, I would never have gone. I would have got to my autumn years and would have resented all the opportunities I hadn't had in my life. But it was different for them. They came and went as they pleased, and – this is important – they had other places to go. They were up here for long stretches to begin with. Then when they'd had all their children and those kids had to go to school, at least sometimes, when the band was not on the road, they'd come in the holidays and during the summer months. Their permanent home by then was a farm in Sussex, and they used to bring their ponies from there up here with them!'

Was Johnny a Wings fan?

'Oh, yes! I was too young for the Beatles, but my cousin had *Band on the Run* and *Venus and Mars*, which we'd listen to over and over. I thought it really strong stuff. Those albums must have had some bearing on my urge to become a musician.'

In 1977, when teenage Johnny was working as a shop assistant in the sports section of McGrory's,[10] a small, local department store, members of Wings and some session musicians came into Campbeltown from the huge, Art Deco (but Brutalist-looking) Keil Hotel overlooking Dunaverty Bay in Southend, the southern-most village on Kintyre.

'They all came swaggering in looking like rock stars while I was serving,' he recalls. 'At the time, I didn't really know who they were. They were trying to find someone to take them out fishing. The shop hired out boats and did permits for the lochs as well. They wanted to look for sharks. They kept coming back, wanting tackle to go out on the loch with. Bigger and better stuff each time.

'I found them quite intimidating, these guys in their leather jackets and long hair. They had a confidence about them. They were Macca's henchmen. A bit menacing. And they were bored. Living in a remote hotel, drinking themselves stupid all day, looking for stuff to do. I'm sure they crashed the discos, the weddings and the twenty-first birthday parties that they used to have at the two hotels down in Southend, a local beauty spot. I imagined them taking pot-shots at the poor seals basking on the rocks down there. I'm sure they didn't, though.'

One day, Johnny remembers, 'I made a mistake during a transaction, and I short-changed them. It was an accident, but I gave guitarist Denny Laine too little money back. He noticed straight away. Red-faced and very embarrassed, I was. Just a kid up against these scary big men. And of course I gave him the right change as soon as he pointed it out, which he waited for me to count out. Then he just tossed the coins down on the counter and walked out without a word. So he pulled me out for my mistake, then effect-ively told me to keep the change. It was belittling. Actually, to the fifteen-year-old son of a farmer brought up in that part of the world, it was crushing. It has stayed with me.'

44

What Johnny found most perplexing was why anyone would choose to live in a place with such terrible weather.

'It's not nice,' he shrugs. 'Windy most of the time. Trees so wind-blasted that they lean backwards. It does rain quite a bit, too, so there is always mud. Temperatures are relatively mild because of the Gulf Stream [the strong North Atlantic current]. Although palm trees grow there, it's hardly Florida. There is rarely heavy snow or ice. Still, as Billy Connolly says, there is no such thing as bad weather, only bad clothes.'

What about the local food? Might that have been an attraction?

'Hardly!' he laughs. 'Mince. Stewing steak. Cabbage. Smoked fish, and eggs. That's about it. They must have had better cuisine up there on the farm, growing and cooking their own. Linda would later be doing her vegetarian cookery books. I remember when the first Chinese restaurant appeared in Campbeltown, in 1974, 1975. The Golden Ocean. It's still there! That was the most exotic thing available to them. Later on came another Chinese, then an Indian. We didn't know we were born. Other than that, there was fish and chips.

'There were the pubs. Sadly, due to the shrinking economy, a lot of those pubs have now closed down. In the days of Wings, the hotels were busier, and there were lots more bars to frequent. One, called the Kintyre, was *the* place to go. They re-named it Splash, as *Cheers* [the American sitcom] was on television at the time. Paul and his musos would have gone there. And they would have met kids of my generation, working behind the bar.'

As for music in the town, 'We bought records at McGrory's or Woolworth's or in Jenny Strain's. She sold wool, knitting needles, sewing stuff . . . and records. Linda was always in there, buying bits for her knitting, stitching – second-hand clothes, I think, mostly – and mending. Live music was only cèilidh bands and cover bands. I didn't see a proper live band until 1980, when Wings were pretty much over and done with. Peter Gabriel was on at the Glasgow Apollo. I was seventeen at the time, and so I went.'

No one appreciates the remoteness of Campbeltown or of Kintyre unless they go there, he reflects.

'When I think of it now, I think only of one thing: that when the sun goes away and the light fades to nothing, you are always a hundred and fifty miles from Glasgow.'

Quaint sounds punctuate the silence above Campbeltown. The hills, streams and valleys seem to vibrate with voices from days long gone. Rich men who bring their friends here to hunt and shoot, deer-stalk and fish are carried by the wind back through time. Fundamental pursuits in the human quest to survive are now expensive hobbies; the irony is not lost.

For more than half a century now, countless thousands of music fans have made the pilgrimage here, foisting touristic excitement and thudding footsteps on the place to which McCartney came to try and get away. That irony is not lost either. It's the Macca connection that lures them, from as far away as Australia, Japan and China. In 2017 alone, of the 337,000 Chinese visitors to the UK, 62,000 scurried straight for the Highlands.

An attraction that Paul's family never visited, because it was not yet there, is another site that draws visitors to Campbeltown. In the grounds of the local library, the Lady Linda McCartney Memorial Garden features a modest bronze statue of the late Beatle wife, Wings band member, animal rights campaigner and mother of the clan. It was donated by her widower to the Linda McCartney Kintyre Memorial Trust. The life-sized statue created by sculptor Jane Robbins, daughter of Paul's cousin Elizabeth, is of Linda seated, cradling a lamb in her lap. It was unveiled there on Friday 1 November 2002, four years after her death.

Alas, none of her nearest and dearest could make it. Paul and his son James were touring America at the time. Paul was remarried, anyway: to second wife Heather, his bride of five months. His daughters Heather, Mary and Stella excused themselves with work commitments. In a statement read out to those who did make the effort, Stella and Mary expressed their gratitude.

'Scotland was one of Mum's favourite places, and it is wonderful to have a permanent statue to remind us of the great times we spent with her there,' they said. 'We would like to say thanks to the people of Campbeltown for honouring her in this way.'

In 2018, 46-year-old Stella McCartney arranged for some hefty rocks from High Park Farm to be lugged all the way to London. She placed them artfully in the middle of the floor of her new flag-ship store on London's Old Bond Street, piled a few extra rocks from elsewhere among them, and garnished the arrangement lavishly with fragrant moss and thyme. The display could not have been more at odds with the swishing rails of designer garments down either side of the shop, nor with the dinky designer handbags perched on top of them. Stella explained the display as a nod to her remote, organic, rooted-to-the-earth upbringing, which she described as 'idyllic'.

'As you walk in,' she said, 'you get living plants and you get rocks partially from the farm that I grew up on in Scotland. We brought nature into the space . . .' She thought it gave her take on a sustain-able fashion industry 'a level of honesty', she elaborated. Like her parents and siblings, Stella is vegetarian. Her brand is ethical. She won't work with leather. She recycles, she re-uses, she keeps it green.

Four years later, in August 2022, Stella couldn't be more thrilled to be launching her new organic, vegan skincare range. The first recipient of her exquisite new products was her father, who received them as a gift for his eightieth birthday.

'I think my childhood in Scotland was where I felt cleanest,' she told the *Daily Telegraph*.[11] 'It was so natural. We were always naked. My parents didn't even wear deodorant, and yet they never smelled.' Which is good to hear.

'Everything I've done – kids' wear, vegan shoes, mushroom leather bags, organic, certified fabrics – has been because I couldn't find it in quite the way I wanted it,' she added. Her latest range is 'pure, organic, effective, simple. Just three products.' Which ordinary mortals will never afford, so they'll stick with the Nivea.

A bit Gwyneth? A tad Goop? Not quite Smells-Like-My-Vagina zany but on the same spectrum? That High Park rocks-and-roll-on feature felt like nothing if not an *Absolutely Fabulous* publicity stunt; the kind of send-up at which Joanna Lumley and Jennifer Saunders excelled. Enter Eddie and Pats, drunk as fiddlers' bitches, sucking on giant spliffs and with their designer smalls on show. Crawling out from under the stones, failing hilariously to harmonise, they are belting out 'Mull of Kintyre'. Cue cackling.

I couldn't help thinking and I'm still wondering now: what would Linda have made of it?

CHAPTER 4

EARTH MOTHER

The little basement venue that occupied 9 Kingly Street, close to Regent Street and Carnaby Street, started out in the 1930s as a jazz dance club called The Nest. In those heady 'twixt-war days it was owned by Ike Hatch, a lively American singer, pianist and band leader born Isaac Flower Hatch in New York, who reinvented himself in London and answered to 'Yowzah' ('Yes, Sir!'). The Nest became an underground air raid shelter during the 1940s. Post-war, it housed the Downbeat Club on Sunday afternoons.

Brothers Rik and John Gunnell, infamous pop agents and managers, ran it as the Bag O'Nails, known as 'the Bag', during the 1960s. Seven nights a week, the known and the unknown stopped by to hang and to groove. Light suppers were served. Whisky and gin were ordered by the bottle. Members of the Beatles, the Rolling Stones, the Who, the Small Faces, the Hollies and the Animals, Jimmy Page, Jeff Beck and Lulu frequented it. Had Keith Moon dropped a couple of his cherry bombs down one of its lavatories, the sixties music industry might have been obliterated in a swoop.

Its little alcove tables and low, parachute-silk-draped ceiling rendered it a sort of velvet-clad Cavern Club. The Beatles would have felt perfectly at home there, cocooned in music, sweat and the fug of tobacco. Six months earlier, legend has it, Jimi Hendrix had played his first London gig there with the Experience, on 25 November 1966.[1]

Cute chicks caught Paul McCartney's eye all the time. He seldom went home alone. His liaisons, predominantly one-night stands, were facilitated by Jane Asher's frequent professional absences.

'I think inevitably when I moved to Cavendish Avenue, I realised that she and I weren't really going to be the thing we'd always thought we might be,' Paul revealed years down the line in the Beatles' *Anthology*. 'Once or twice we talked about getting married, and plans were afoot, but I don't know, something really made me nervous about the whole thing. It just never settled with me, and [. . .] that's very important for me . . .'

In May 1967, a month shy of his twenty-fifth birthday, Paul was the last remaining bachelor Beatle. John had been the first to get hitched, when he was still only twenty-one, in August 1962 to pregnant Cynthia. The father of four-year-old Julian had already left his wife for Yoko Ono. Ringo, twenty-four, married nineteen-year-old hairdresser Maureen Cox in February 1965. Then in January 1966, 23-year-old George took 22-year-old model Pattie Boyd as his bride.

It would have been the easiest thing in the world for Paul to settle with Jane, who on paper was perfect. But something wasn't right. He kept his options open, oat-sowing behind Jane's back. Until the night a cute, camera-carrying American caught his eye in the Bag, and things got all kinds of dangerous.

The previous month, Paul had taken time out from recording the *Sgt. Pepper's Lonely Hearts Club Band* LP to fly to Denver via San Francisco and see Jane, who was starring in a Bristol Old Vic touring production of Shakespeare's *Romeo and Juliet*. He wanted to surprise her for her twenty-first birthday. Was that the reason? Could it have been a guilt trip? Something was clearly nagging him to hang on to what he had.

He was thinking about making an honest woman of the girl who had inspired such songs as 'And I Love Her', 'You Won't See Me', 'I'm Looking Through You' and 'We Can Work It Out' before some other bloke swiped her. It seems likely that the sweet young lady had eyes only for Paul. From the photographs snapped that night, she was thrilled to see him. They stayed together in a house borrowed from a friend, attended the party thrown for her in a local hotel by the theatre company – Jane's mother Margaret was also present – and then took off for a few days. Just to wander, explore and spend private time together.

The Beatles' old faithful Mal Evans, who had accompanied Paul from London, drove them up through the Rocky Mountains and made himself scarce while the couple reconnected. But for all the Learjets, extravagance and grandiose gestures, something was missing. A mere forty days and forty nights later, in a popular dive beneath a Soho pavement, Paul came face to face with the girl who would change his life.

Twenty-five-year-old Linda Eastman was on a work trip to London. She had been commissioned to photograph musicians for a forthcoming book entitled *Rock and Other Four-Letter Words: Music of the Electric Generation*.[2] She had come to the Bag with the Animals, whom she had befriended after a photo session in New York. Paul had made his way there from a dinner party thrown by Brian Epstein to celebrate the conclusion of the recording of *Sgt. Pepper*, and was seated with friends at his usual 'private' table. Georgie Fame and the Blue Flames had the place alight that night. The scene was set.

'The band had finished and Linda got up to either leave or go for a drink or a pee or something,' said Paul, 'and she passed our table. I stood up just as she was passing, blocking her exit. And so I said, "Oh, sorry. Hi. How are you? How're you doing?" I introduced myself and said, "We're going on to another club after this. Would you like to join us?" That was my big pulling line! Well, I'd never used it before, of course, but it worked this time! It was a fairly slim chance, but it worked.'[3]

If there was anything unique about this one, it may not have been apparent in the moment. Whatever it was, something prompted Paul to ask her. Something made her accept. And something stopped her from making her excuses when he invited her to go home with him that night.

A day or two later, when Linda took her portfolio to show Brian Epstein's assistant Peter Brown, she bagged herself an invitation to the *Sgt. Pepper* launch party. Brian Epstein hosted it at his Chapel Street, Belgravia, home on 19 May, four days after Paul and Linda met. Favoured hacks, snappers, and DJs the likes of Kenny Everett tucked into caviar, salmon and champagne, while feasting their ears on the first media playback of the masterpiece. It was there that Linda shot her first photos of the Beatles, borrowing rolls of colour film from a fellow lensman, because she had come armed only with black and white.

She captured John sporting a Scottish sporran slung through his trouser loops and hanging below his belt buckle, in which, he insisted, he kept his keys (but more likely his stash). It was there that a famous image was taken, of Linda crouching on the floor beside the fireplace, close to Paul, with her face upturned into his like a shining moon.

And that was that. For then, at least.

Linda flew home to her little daughter Heather and their life together in New York. Seven months later, on Christmas Day 1967, Jane and Paul announced their engagement. In February 1968, Jane accompanied her fiancé to Rishikesh, India, for meditation and enlightenment at Maharishi Mahesh Yogi's ashram. That summer, when she returned to the house unexpectedly early from Bristol, where she had been appearing in a production, she found Paul in bed with brisk New Yorker Francie Schwartz . . . a girl who had been around for some time, and whom various Beatles associates believe Paul used to get rid of Jane.

The implication being that he knew Jane was on her way home, and that he contrived deliberately to be found in flagrante.[4] Who knows. Francie was by no means the first. For most of the time that Jane and Paul had lived together, he had been two-timing her with upcoming model and actress Maggie McGivern. He had met and first taken her to bed while she was working as a nanny for Marianne Faithfull and her then husband John Dunbar.

'I haven't broken it off, but it is broken off, finished,' Jane announced live to host Simon Dee on BBC TV's early evening show *Dee Time*, on Saturday 20 July 1968. 'I know it sounds corny, but we still see each other and love each other, but it hasn't worked out. Perhaps we'll be childhood sweethearts and meet again and get married when we're about seventy.'[5]

All of which was jaw-dropping news to Paul, who happened to be watching Jane on telly in his dad's sitting room with his arm around Francie Schwartz.

'I watched the show with Paul and his father,' confirmed Francie. 'This wave of shocked silence went through all of us. It was painful because she was announcing it publicly, and she didn't leave it up to him. That's the one thing Paul never wants to happen. He really is a control person.'[6]

Jane was dignified. There were no histrionics. The emerald and diamond engagement ring was quietly returned.

Linda Eastman came from money. Her parents, New York entertainment lawyer Lee V. Eastman and his wife Louise, had started married life as Mr and Mrs Leopold Vail Epstein and subsequently anglicised their surname. Linda was German-Jewish on her mother's side, Russian-Jewish on her father's, and at one point took advantage of their assumed name by letting it be believed (is that the kindest way of saying it?) that she was an heiress of the vastly wealthy and influential Eastman Kodak company, manufacturers of cameras and photographic film products. She later owned up to the fabrication in an interview, confessing that she had allowed the myth to persist in order to get herself work as a photographer.

She grew up in Scarsdale, an up-market town thirty miles or so north of New York City that could not have been less like Liverpool. Not that Linda was ever a snob. The opposite. Her father had started with nothing but had made it to Harvard Law School. He 'married up'. Linda was open about it. 'He was a very, very bright man. From a wonderful peasant background and yet so astute, so smart.'[7]

The Eastmans occupied a lavish countryside home in which their son and three daughters were doted upon. Many of her father's clients were musical artists and painters with whom they socialised regularly, and the family patronised the arts. But Linda was never into fancy or finery. She felt most at home among horses, and rode obsessively. She also loved losing herself in the woods with her brother John and getting down among the wildlife.

With little interest in school or studying, she found her way into music, worshipped the Everly Brothers and lost herself in her dreams. During the long school summer holidays, the family left town for Wellfleet in Barnstaple County, on the Cape Cod peninsula of Massachusetts: akin to leaving London for a summer in Cornwall. Now a popular tourist and retirement destination, the former whaling port, famous for its annual Oysterfest, clapboard villages, sandy beaches, lobster rolls and art galleries, is where Italian inventor Guglielmo Marconi constructed America's first radio transmitter station.

Those long, hot summers in Wellfleet fostered Linda's love of escapism. The family later upgraded to beautiful East Hampton, Long Island, where she and Paul would later rent summer houses to stay near her family, and where they would eventually own their own home.

The soft spot that Linda retained for Cape Cod was to resurface the first time she visited Kintyre. Because there is something about a peninsula. Bounded by sea on three sides, that sense of being 'cut off' from the mainland, but still with vaguely accessible, remote beaches, abundant wildlife, a back-in-time other-worldliness. Places that 'hang off' the side of a country are places to which to retreat and hide away. From the jagged granite cliffs of the Cornish Lizard to the cracked Kerry coastline of Ireland's Dingle or Halkidiki in northern Greece, the peninsula mentality thrives. It reflected and informed Linda's impressively detached personality.

At seventeen, despite her low high-school grades, Linda gained a place at the University of Arizona to study art history. She relocated to Tucson, where she continued to ride rather than study. She took a photography course, and eventually dropped out. Her furious father made clear that he would not continue to support her financially if she failed to return to school. Linda was considering her options when a plane fell out of the sky, claiming the life of her fifty-year-old mother.

'I had never really connected with my mother,' she commented thirty years after the American Airlines crash, in which a Los Angeles-bound flight dropped into New York's Jamaica Bay and exploded, killing all ninety-five on board. 'But for my father it was a disaster. My parents had been very much in love.' Although she returned to Scarsdale for the funeral, she did not stick around to help care for her young sisters. She practically ran back to Arizona.

'It was a kind of escapism,' she admitted. 'I was very immature. I just escaped.'[8]

Her geology student boyfriend was waiting for her. Whether by accident or choice, Linda was soon pregnant. Three months after her mother Louise's death, twenty-year-old Linda married Mel See on 18 June 1962 – her future second husband's twentieth birthday, and twelve days after the Beatles' historic debut visit to EMI Studios on London's Abbey Road.[9] Not that she would have been aware of any of that.

Their baby daughter arrived on New Year's Eve, and all seemed okay for a while. But by the time that Heather was about to turn two, the wheels were coming off. Mel suggested that they try a change of continents and relocate to Africa. Linda invited him to go alone. Her father had taken his second wife, a rich New York widow with three sons. In 1965, Linda and her little girl made it back home to them, and she divorced Mel that June. Whereupon

55

she became a New York gal about town, a gig-goer, a party chick and a groupie.

Fair? It's how it was. It was the sixties. What's good for the gander. People believed that the Beatles were above and beyond casual shagging. Truth was, they were getting more sex and drugs than anybody. Wholesome innocence was an *act*, dear reader. Don't be surprised.

'I don't care what I'm called, I really don't,' Linda told her close friend and confidant Danny Fields. 'The way I define the word, I wasn't a groupie. There were girls around who were classic groupies; they were very glamorous and often pretty fabulous, I thought. But I did hang out with groups. If that makes me a groupie, so be it . . .'

Linda got herself a little Upper East Side, Manhattan apartment. Some say with an allowance from her late mother's estate, others that she earned it. A receptionist job at *Town & Country*, one of America's oldest and most prestigious magazines, put her in the right place at the right time. On 15 August 1965, she was at New York's Shea Stadium to see the Beatles (as was future Bond girl Barbara Bach, who later married Ringo). When an invitation to the Rolling Stones' press launch for their album *Aftermath* arrived, on a yacht on the Hudson River on 24 June 1966, Linda nabbed it, grabbed a camera and ran on down.

It turned out that she was the only photographer on board. Her pictures were in demand, and she was on her way. She turned pro, focused on rock stars, and photographed numerous future icons including Janis Joplin, Aretha Franklin, Bob Dylan, Jimi Hendrix, the Doors, the Who and Eric Clapton. While she didn't wind up in bed with every one of her subjects, she slept with a fair few, including Mick Jagger and Warren Beatty. Who hadn't?

After their initial hook-up in London in May 1967, Paul and Linda did not see each other for another year. When Lennon and McCartney tripped into New York for four days to launch Apple

Corps in the United States, meet with Apple Records' new chief Ron Kass, submit to press interviews and make a television appearance with Johnny Carson on NBC's *The Tonight Show*, Linda ensured that they ran into each other again.

On their last day, at a press conference held at the Americana Hotel, she joined the throng of photographers. When the press conference was over, she grabbed him. When henchman Neil Aspinall indicated that they had to get going, Paul asked Linda for her number. With nonchalant style, she scrawled it on the back of a cheque. She probably didn't expect him to call. He did, only to explain that time had run out and that they were flying back to London next day. Then he did a weird thing: he asked her to join him and John in the car conveying them to the airport, so that they could chat *en route*. More weirdly, she accepted.

There she sat, wedged between John and Paul in the back, laden with cameras. To have been a fly on that pane. Then it was kiss-kiss, say cheese in the Pan Am lounge, and she was whisked back to Manhattan alongside Neil Aspinall.

Two days after his twenty-sixth birthday, Paul, his school chum Ivan Vaughan and Tony Bramwell, another old faithful who was now deputy head of Apple Films, jetted in to LAX via New York for the Capitol Records convention. With Capitol set to manufacture and distribute Apple's discs, the same function performed by EMI in the UK, it was an important engagement. In New York, Paul managed to take his mind off it long enough to call Linda – was he still carrying around her blank cheque? – and invited her to join him on the West Coast. Her answering service responded. She wasn't in.

He left a message and journeyed on, with no idea whether she would get it or whether she'd come. They checked into their bungalow at the Beverly Hills Hotel and waited. Should I say, didn't wait. Because the bungalow soon filled with swishy, hopeful beauties, as accommodation did wherever Paul went. He returned from the convention to find that Linda had joined them . . . off her head on pot and with further supplies to share. While females were shooed from the premises, an apologetic Paul insisting 'It wasn't me,' he and Linda exchanged the glance that was later interpreted as the moment when they 'clicked' and fell in love.

They went out to the Whisky a Go Go club on Sunset Boulevard to seal the deal. Blow them down if Linda's old mate Eric Burdon of the Animals wasn't in the adjacent booth, in the company of Georgie Fame, who had serenaded them at the Bag the night they first met. Signs everywhere. Back to the bungalow they went. Poor Ivan and Tony had to stay out all night, pretending that they were having a great time at the Whisky. All would have been well and would have danced along, but for the untimely arrival of someone they had not seen coming.

Peggy Lipton, a feisty eighteen-year-old upcoming model and actress (weren't they all), had been Paul's on-off paramour in the States for the past two years. It was a bigger part of her life than it was of his. She was clueless about Linda when she pestered Bramwell to get her in to Paul. Tony could fob her off only for so long. Paul hadn't yet made an appearance, being ensconced in his room with Linda and the bag of drugs. When noise from outside got too much, Paul stepped out wearing only his trousers to strum them a number he'd just come up with and coax them to go away. The song was *Blackbird*. He had written it at High Park Farm. But Peggy wasn't going anywhere. She had convinced herself that she and Paul were destined to be together.

'I was madly in love with Paul McCartney . . . knowing full well that disaster lay ahead,' she wrote in her 2005 memoir *Breathing Out*.[10] 'How could it be otherwise? Every woman wanted Paul.' She fell instantly, she said, for his 'puppy dog, long-lashed, beautiful eyes.'

After meeting him as part of a bunch of like-minded fans, she was invited to attend an event and meet him.

'I arrived almost sick to my stomach with butterflies. I had only lost my virginity six months earlier, and I'd been thinking about

Paul for a year. He greeted me sweetly. He played the piano. The next thing I knew, we were on our way upstairs. The fantasy was playing out a little too fast. Her took me in his arms and kissed me. May I say that this was the kiss of my dreams? As passionate, tender and exciting as I ever could have imagined.'

During their lovemaking, Peggy asked herself how this was making her feel.

'I liked everything about Paul,' she said, 'yet when we walked downstairs together I wasn't feeling too good. I saw myself as just a young girl he had taken to bed, and that was it.'

When Paul called her again the following night, Peggy went back, anxious to turn a one-night stand into a relationship. Once again, she said, it was sexy. But she knew too well that whatever it had been was already over. All she wanted was to get back home as soon as possible. She saw him once more in 1967. In '1969' (she meant 1968), when he called her again ahead of his trip to LA, she was by then the star of TV crime drama *The Mod Squad* and was living unhappily with the record producer Lou Adler. She was keen to see Paul, but made clear that she could not agree to it if he was seeing other girls. Paul reassured her that the only 'person' (he meant 'woman') around was a photographer who was 'travelling with' them.

'Two days later,' she remembered, 'he called in the middle of the night. "Peggy, can you come over to the Beverly Hills Hotel? I really need to see you." What else could I do? I went. It was four in the morning when I got there.'

Either Bramwell or Aspinall told her that Paul was sleeping.

'It was daylight when he emerged. He was strumming a guitar and singing to me. At least, I thought he was singing to me. But as I leapt up to join him, I spotted a woman coming out of the bedroom. Paul and this girl made a dash for the limousine, hiding their heads. I stormed into the bedroom and wrote, "You made your choice" across the mirror in the girl's lipstick. Then I just cried.'

The following year, 'Paul married the girl from the bungalow. Her name was Linda Eastman.'

When Linda Eastman told her girlfriends that she longed to marry a Beatle – preferably John but he was taken, so maybe she'd make a play for Paul – she was only echoing the sentiment of millions of other lust-struck young girls around the world, and could never have intended to be taken seriously. Did anyone take Dora Bryan at her word when she recorded 'All I Want for Christmas is a Beatle'?[11] The fact that Linda did wind up wearing Paul's ring was taken by many, given her early naïve declarations, to indicate that she must be some sort of witch, who had entranced then snared her helpless man as a spider nabs an insect in her web. Paul was emphatic, down the line, once the deal was done. He had, he said, pursued *her*.

Things sped up between them beyond their Beverly bungalow sojourn. Back in London, sick and tired of the revolving-door chaos that his home and life in general had become, he picked up the phone to Linda and asked her to come over.

'It was September,' she said. The month of her birthday. 'I remember Heather was just going to start Dalton, and my parents were so furious with me.[12] She got into Dalton. It would have been great. It was really good for Heather; I wish she had had that kind of life, instead of this crazy life. Dalton and then do well at school, go to university, whatever. But I had no feeling of responsibility, I must have been quite irresponsible to think that a five-year-old kid is starting school for the first time, and I'm buzzing off leaving her. It was one of those, "Oh, can you stay with Ella for a few weeks? And not tell anybody and not talk to anybody and I'll buzz off to London."'

She remembered that her father and stepmother made her feel horribly guilty. But anyway, she did leave her daughter with somebody else, and she went. When she arrived at night at Paul's dingy, squalid, student-like dosshouse, he wasn't there to greet her. He was at Abbey Road, recording for the 'White Album'. When she called him to say she was there, Paul despatched Mal to make sure that she was okay, knowing that his fridge contained no more than 'half a bottle of sour milk and a crust of cheese'.[13] Linda didn't mind. She was in love.

She stayed for several weeks. Venturing into the studio only when the band were mixing, she took photographs. She and Paul painted together. They would go driving through London late at night, at Linda's insistence 'trying to get lost'. Doing nothing in particular quickly became part of their 'thing'. They would do anything, in fact, that would remove him from the Beatle part of himself. Anything to remind him that, deep inside, he was still himself.

If her well-to-do upbringing and comparative gentility inhibited him to begin with, he got over it. This was a girl who had grown up eschewing perceived poshness, who preferred to hang with the servants, who felt most comfortable in the company of animals, who liked cooking, homemaking and other ordinary things from which Paul's life had long been disengaged.

One night, Linda called Heather in New York from bed, and then put Paul on. What on earth was he thinking when he asked the little girl if she would marry him? To him it was a joke. While a five-year-old cannot accurately compute distance, she would have been missing her mother and must have realised that she was very far away. What if she never came back? What if that man in England (wherever that is) decides to keep her there, so she never comes home? A child that young is the centre of her own world. She struggles to understand things from anything other than her own perspective.

For the record, Heather turned Paul down. She told him that she couldn't marry him because he was 'too old'. 'Oh yes, of course,' he responded. 'I forgot that. Well, maybe I should marry your mummy. That'd be good.'

Once the 'White Album' was put to bed, mid-October, Paul took Linda home to New York and to her daughter. And here's where I would give anything for an invisible cloak, and to have been able to accompany them. The world-famous, globally fêted rock star went anonymous to immerse himself in his girlfriend's world. He wanted to see how life worked for her. If they were going to try this, he had to know her, as he had probably never known any girl before.

Paul had never visited New York other than as a Beatle. From the airport to the limo to the luxurious hotel and wherever else he went, he was screamed, hollered and bawled at. He was chased and pinched. He had hands, cheeks and lips, autograph books, programmes and tickets thrust in his face. He was at the mercy of those minding him, and was always trapped. He was conveyed from place to place by security guards or police officers, and was always trying desperately to get away. The relentless attention exhausted him. He had barely glimpsed the city other than through a window, on the run. Now it was time to try things a different way.

With Linda, Paul walked the streets of Manhattan. He rode the subway, boarded buses, and ate and drank in little local restaurants and bars. They went to churches, museums and galleries, and on the Staten Island Ferry. They saw films, frequented the dives, toured iconic neighbourhoods the likes of Greenwich Village, Little Italy and Chinatown. They went out for morning coffee and read the papers, and wandered through Central Park. Linda shared with him her love of second-hand shops, or 'thrift stores' as she called them. He bought a ten-dollar herringbone overcoat in one such establishment on 3rd Avenue, and lived and died in it for years.

How did he go unnoticed? He had stopped shaving. His face was covered by a beard. He wore un-Beatle-like clothes such as military uniforms and other garments that made him look almost homeless. Linda, too, dressed down, in her usual jacket-and-jeans garb. Because nobody was looking for rich Beatle Paul and his glamorous latest love, few noticed them. John Lennon would adopt New York as his home a couple of years later, explaining that the thing he loved most there was his anonymity. Paul had come to that realisation before him. Linda recalled that he *was* noticed on the subway trains. People would follow them occasionally, in which case they'd just hop the next train and shake them off. Overall, Paul came down to her lifestyle, and found that he felt perfectly at home.

In Linda's tiny apartment, on the tenth floor of a building on the corner of 83rd Street, Heather's 'bedroom' was a screened-off corner while her mother slept on a pull-out sofa that had to be folded away each morning. Paul mucked in. He even looked after her daughter when Linda had an assignment. Feeling their way, they got there. Paul reconnected with reality. He returned to London with his instant family on 31 October 1968.

During the first week of November, they got away from it all by decamping to Kintyre.

'It was the most beautiful land you have ever seen,' Linda told Barry Miles. 'It was way at the end of nowhere. To me it was the first feeling I'd ever had of civilisation dropped away. I felt like it was in another era. It was so beautiful up there, clean, so different from all the hotels and limousines and the music business, so it was quite a relief, but it was very derelict.'

That December, they flew on a whim by private jet to crash the holiday in Portugal of Beatles biographer Hunter Davies. While there, Linda discovered that she was pregnant. Her boyfriend proposed, insisting ever after that he had been planning to do so anyway. Back in London, they found Heather a little school near Cavendish Avenue, close enough that they could walk her to and fro.

No announcement was made of their wedding at Marylebone Register Office on 12 March 1969. Still, everybody seemed to know about it. The bride dressed down in a yellow coat. Her groom matched it with his tie. No other Beatle attended the ceremony. They lunched at the Ritz. Then it was back to New York for a honeymoon chez the in-laws. Beatle babes from Cardiff to Canberra seethed with grief.

Somewhere across London, a strawberry blonde beauty must have glanced at the space on her finger where a diamond and emerald engagement ring had glinted. A little over six months had elapsed since Jane Asher revealed the end of her five-year relationship on television. She could not have avoided the headlines. The newspapers said, she'd gone from his head. But had she?

CHAPTER 5

RENAISSANCE

Eastman and Eastman, effectively Paul's new family law and management firm, announced the launch of McCartney Productions Ltd on Tuesday 7 April 1970. The company's debut project was to be Paul's first solo album, *McCartney*, recorded covertly at his Cavendish Avenue home on a four-track tape recording machine during December and January. He'd made it on 'a Studer, one mic and nerve,' he later commented. He might have added, '. . . and on a wing and a prayer, with the encouragement and unfailing devotion of my darling wife.'

He tested his equipment with 'The Lovely Linda', a snippet of a song he had conjured at High Park. It all seemed to hold up nicely, despite the lack of a mixing desk and therefore any visual indication of recording levels. Winging it: exactly how Macca liked to play. The love note to his Mrs became the opener of the album. It fades to childlike chuckles, which feels appropriate. Imagine the exhilaration he must have felt on having mastered the tech; the confidence that it instilled in him. He could now get down to business.

He wrote and composed every song himself; played all the instruments, including piano, drums and guitars as well as his usual bass guitar, and a range of percussive implements and ad hoc appliances. The only other person involved in the process was Linda, who contributed backing vocals to some of the tracks, and who kept him going whenever he panicked and wanted to throw in the towel.

The essence of the album, Paul explained in the ill-advised 'press release' was 'Home. Family. Love.' He had his priorities right. He had survived. There is an overriding sense of emotional rawness to this fourteen-track, unadorned, uncomplicated clutch of pieces. An obvious back-to-basics feel. Garagey and echoey, homely and woolly-socky, it was indie ahead of its time. Yet the listener is left in no doubt that Paul found himself through it. The tracks range from intimate and close to plaintive, bold and silly. The stand-outs, for me, are 'Every Night', 'Junk', 'Oo You' – which throbs with Lennonesque heaviness, and displays a density missing from virtually every other track – and the masterpiece, written and composed for Linda: 'Maybe I'm Amazed'.

'I loved that record because it was so simple,' declared Neil Young in 1999, during his induction speech admitting Paul into the Rock and Roll Hall of Fame. 'There was so much to hear and to see. It was just Paul. There was no adornment at all, there was no echo, there was nothing. There was no attempt made to compete with the things he'd already done. Out he stepped from the shadow of the Beatles. And there he was. It kind of blew my mind.'[1]

The song soars: lyrically, melodically, vocally, instrumentally and emotionally. It has everything, from desperation and sheer misery to triumphant self-assurance and pride. Every flutter of fear felt by a man confoundedly smitten is here. It flares with energy and need. It may be the greatest distillation of love in recorded song. It feels Shakespearian. Over all the musical years to come, Paul never improved on its arresting vocal, its thunderous piano, its glorious guitar solo. Most of those in the know who heard it first, and many millions of fans all over the world since, agree that 'Maybe I'm Amazed' is the finest song he ever came up with. Does it out-do even 'Yesterday' and 'Blackbird', written as and for the Beatles?

Reluctantly, I suspect – because no true artist allows himself to believe that he might have peaked at the tender age of twenty-eight

– Paul thought so. In 2009, while promoting his double live album *Good Evening New York City*, he confessed to the press that 'Maybe I'm Amazed' was the composition he would most like to be remembered for. But it was not released as a single. Despite which, it received endless airplay. By the time Paul conceded his obvious mistake and put out a live version of it from the *Wings Over America* album seven years later, its spotlight moment had passed. While the single became a Top Ten hit in the US, it reached only Number 28 in the UK.

But the original has never worn thin. Essential to its brilliance is the fact that this track was not recorded in the wallow of hearth and home with the kids writhing around on the rug among fallen Christmas tree needles and the wife popping in with mugs of tea. No squeaky doors or background bickering here. Nor was it conjured at Willesden's Morgan Studios that February where, under the alias 'Billy Martin', Paul copied his four-track recordings to eight-track to facilitate a few more overdubs. Work on it was confined to the cathedral of EMI studios, Abbey Road, where he finished and mixed the album, and where 'Maybe I'm Amazed' was recorded on 22 February 1970. He also laid down the side one track 'Every Night'.

The location surely adds to the alchemy. Just as church walls exude the emotion of every baptism, confirmation and marriage performed within, along with the sorrow and regret of every funeral, so the foundations of Abbey Road pulsated with every tune conceived and recorded there by the Beatles. Every drop of their history, hysteria, highs, lows, break-ups, make-ups and the frustration and elation generated by their frequently clashing genius echoes loudly and indelibly through this song.

Exaggeration? Not. It stands as a monument to all that had gone before it. Acknowledging it. Accepting it. Thanking it. Setting itself free from it to surge forth with a new love, look at me now, boys; while revealing, maybe a little, just a whisper of choked-back hope that the Beatles might one day patch up their differences and do it all again. It was all that everybody wanted. But Paul was making this album on his own, behind the backs of the other Beatles, and without input from any of them.

The thing that Paul found hardest about this album was that he didn't get to make it with John.

'Because right up until that point I'd been working with [him], the best collaborator in the world,' he lamented. 'Suddenly that was taken away. It was very difficult. But I thought, well, I'm not going to worry about it. I'm going to sling some ideas down, have a little go on the drums. I had my own stuff at the house for my own fun, I wasn't going into the studio with the Beatles. I wasn't sweating it. Then suddenly, it became something.'[2]

How did it go down? Mostly unfavourably. The best music writers of the day, some of whom are friends of mine now but whom I didn't know then as I was still at school, doused it in scorn. Much of it was vilified and ridiculed. Except that One Song. Despite which, the album went to Number One in the US and sat there for three weeks, giving way eventually and ironically to the Beatles' *Let It Be*. It debuted at Number Two in the UK, but couldn't get the better of Simon and Garfunkel's *Bridge over Troubled Water* and its immaculate moment: the late Hal Blaine's incendiary drum performance.

McCartney did lack sophistication. It wasn't cool. But 'Maybe I'm Amazed' took it almost all the way. It conquered charts across the world. Were the fans buying, not solo Paul but into the dream of a go-again Beatles?[3]

What happened just prior to its release was the cause of much misunderstanding and mayhem. Sick to the molars of journalists and broadcasters, and psychologically wrecked by what could only be interpreted as the impending implosion of the band, Paul declined to be interviewed to promote his debut LP. As far as he was concerned, there was a huge so-what factor. He was not the first Beatle to release a solo album. That honour had gone to George Harrison two years earlier, when Apple announced its debut release:

a collection of pieces recorded in India during January 1968, entitled *Wonderwall Music*.[4]

So Paul asked publicists Derek Taylor and Peter Brown to come up with a bunch of questions that he could scribble down the answers to. His team could then respond on his behalf, thus eliminating the need for tedious time-consuming one-to-ones and press conferences. Whoever had the bright idea of tucking into the sleeve of each advance promotional copy of the album a sheet featuring Paul's completed Q&A, just like a press release, should perhaps have been let go. Recollections vary. Among the flock, the pussies were on the loose. It couldn't end well.

The next morning, 10 April 1970, it was splash-headline-news across the globe: McCartney quits the Beatles! His solo album went on sale seven days later, on 17 April. Paul was almost twenty-eight. He had no way of knowing the ill-fated significance of that date. That same day, twenty-eight years later, the love of his life would die in his arms.

He didn't stick around to pop corks. He would only be bombarded with the same old, same old: when are you boys getting back together? We know you four are only having a little break, so when's the next album? It's been more than three years, when are you going back on the road? *Enough.* On the very day the shattering news broke, he and Linda legged it with the kids back to High Park, to commence what Paul would later describe as his 'hippie gap year'.

The first songs he wrote there during this initial period would lead to the recording of the *Ram* album. The family remained in Scotland for the next four months, taking a twenty-day break to the Orkneys and the Shetland Isles that August. Which was quite the undertaking with two young children and a big, boisterous dog in tow. Nappies, for a start. Disposables were only just coming into mainstream use during the early 1970s. It's hard to imagine proto-eco warrior Linda, a woman well ahead of her time, displaying wild enthusiasm for the throw-away diaper. Hit the road with an infant

69

and a bubba for more than a few hours and nappies, potties and frequent supplies of sustenance become primary, journey-halting considerations.

From Campbeltown to the north-eastern tip of Scotland is a road distance of some 340 miles. They somehow managed to miss the ferry and had to bribe random fishermen to carry them onwards in their boat. Martha the dear mutt had to be winched aboard by trawler net. From the Orkneys, they continued their journey by plane. In the north-eastern isles they found natural wonders in abundance to take their minds off the legal storm brewing 700 miles away in London. That far north, in summer, the sun barely sets. The drawn-out days and milky twilight are known as 'the simmer dim'.

What better therapy than to go poking around the standing stones of Stenness, the oldest Neolithic monument in the British Isles; to take stock at Jarlshof, the preserved remains of a 4,500-year-old settlement, and at the Clickimin Broch, a stone-built round house from the Iron Age? Ancient monuments are not merely curious objects to look at. They have a way of grounding anxious humans. In times of trouble, timeless places can be sources of great comfort, as well as a stark reminder of what matters.

Lost in a land of wild ponies, puffins, seals and otters, porpoises, orcas and world-famous seabird colonies, they distanced themselves from the madness and found perspective. Beyond fixed abode, without landline, unencumbered by mobile phones that were years away from general use, they could not be tracked down.

Mickie Most did his damnedest.[5] The former pop singer turned record producer and founder of RAK Records, who had a hand in the careers of Suzi Quatro, the Animals, Jeff Beck, Donovan, Hot Chocolate, Lulu and more, and who would discover and make a superstar of Kim Wilde, was revealed by the *Melody Maker* to be in pursuit of McCartney to offer him a part in a picture.

On 12 September 1970, the paper reported that Most would 'tak the high road' through heather and glen to tempt McCartney with a contract to play the lead in *The Second Coming of Suzanne*.[6] Before Most even got his wellies on, Macca turned him down. The morning after the report appeared, Apple issued a stern denial. Paul and family beat a hasty retreat to France on yet another holiday, in flagrant disregard of almost-eight-years-old Heather's school term dates. A month later they crossed to Southampton and boarded transatlantic cruise ship the SS *France*.

'We were on holiday in France and thinking about making another album,' said Paul. 'I'd written a few new songs and we thought that for a change we'd go to New York to record. It's a good place, with a lot of great musicians and would give us a different slant. We'd tried the amateur bit with *McCartney*, going back to square one; now we wanted to get a bit more professional. So we took the ocean liner *Île de France* [*sic*] and sailed from Southampton over to New York.'[7]

What prompted them to sail the ocean blue on one of the last great liners of the pre-air travel era, when it was by then so much quicker and easier to fly? Maybe they didn't want to take their chances on one of the new Pan American Airways Boeing 747 'jumbo jet' flights, launched out of London Heathrow to JFK New York nine months earlier. While Learjets had been around by then for about seven years, and though he would make a habit of using private planes in future, Paul didn't own one and never would.

Perhaps they simply decided it would be more relaxing and more fun for the kids to go by sea. There is little privacy on a commercial flight, even for those who turn left. The superstar is still in close confinement with fellow passengers. Not even the purchase of an entire row and all the seats in front and behind, as has been known, guarantees uninterrupted travel or deters autograph-hunters (today, the selfie-seeker). You still have to use the same facilities.

On the SS *France*, passengers were not that way inclined. They oozed wealth and class. Most were unlikely to look twice at a mere pop star when they had Hollywood royalty on board: on that particular voyage, Elizabeth Taylor. The McCartneys could retreat to their suites; seek entertainment in the theatre and cinema, library, reading room, and in the children's playroom and dining room. They could lark in the pool and stretch their legs in the open air. They could go whale-watching and dolphin-spotting up on deck, and maybe even gate-crash the odd wedding. The SS *France* hosted hundreds in her time, in her own chapel.

Not only all that. With its 180 cooks, sauce and pastry chefs, rotisserie chefs, head waiters and wine stewards, the *France* was renowned as one of the finest restaurants in the world. They could afford such luxury. You couldn't get it at 35,000 feet.

Six days later on 8 October, a freshly shorn and shaven Paul, sporting sunglasses and a casual Fair Isle knit possibly purchased during that summer's jaunt around the Shetlands, was snapped carrying his half-naked toddler daughter Mary down the gang-plank onto a New York pier. Linda and Heather were dressed similarly. The image was published by the British *Daily Mirror* the next day. He looked like a man on a mission. Which he was. He had told Linda that he had decided to take her advice and form a band. He had gone looking not for America, but for musicians.

'The *Let It Be* album had appeared in May that year,' remembers former BBC Radio 1 presenter Andy Peebles. 'I had been feeling down for some time about where it was all heading. I never boarded the "This is all Yoko's fault" bandwagon, but I had a very uneasy feeling, as many of us in the industry did. When "The Long and Winding Road", a track from that album, was released as a single, I thought, what an incredibly sad ending to an amazing career. I didn't hold out much hope that they would ever get back together again. All I could do was wait with bated breath to see what James Paul McCartney was going to do next.'

Andy knew enough about the music business during that period to know that interesting people had entered the lives of the Beatles, and that their individual worlds had now become bigger places.

'You just knew that things had gone about as far from that Sunday night in America when Ed Sullivan introduced them on television to seventy-three million people as it was possible to get,' he says.[8] He readily acknowledges that the prospect of no further Beatles recordings was almost unbearable.

'John had always been my favourite Beatle,' he confides. 'To me, he was Mr Outspoken, the politics, the life and soul of the band. There was something raw in him, something that we would all have liked to be. He had the daring and the nerve. He seemed invincible. He was never what Paul had become: the pin-up boy. The combination of John and the pretty radical Yoko was formidable. Paul could never have handled something like that. If I could only have one Beatle, it would have to be John.

'Having said that, I loved Paul so much! Give me an hour with him now, what would I ask him? "Do you really think you should be attempting 'Long Tall Sally' the way you did in 1963?" Because, like Elton John, he has lost the top of his range. His voice has changed. But he was fantastic at it back then, and he was also equalled by John. It's why they were so brilliant. The pair of them together was like a double-sided coin, flipping between them. Two incredible frontmen, sharing the load. Their harmonies were extraordinary. They had this innate ability to harmonise together without even having to think about it. Which is not to be unkind or unfair to George. Or Ringo. Every member could take his turn on lead vocals.'

What Andy knew better than most about Paul was that he was extremely fussy. The choosing of new musicians to play alongside him in new ventures was never going to be an easy task.

'He operated on the theory that they'd better be good because they had to be able to play their chosen instrument better than him,' he points out. 'Paul is competent on a whole range of instruments. So when he selects musicians, they are going to have to be very skilled and demonstrate incredibly high standards. Beyond that, I also knew instinctively, Paul would now be hell-bent on re-creating what he had just thrown away. That's why I wasn't surprised by the rumours that he was talking about starting a new band.'

'When we got to New York, we started to audition musicians,' Paul said. 'I put the word out via a couple of people and some drummers came by to play. Denny Seiwell, who had been working as a session man, was the best. He's a nice guy and we got on well, so we started the *Ram* sessions with him. I also auditioned guitar players, playing a couple of songs together to see if I liked their personality, if we got along. Dave Spinozza and Hugh McCracken emerged from those auditions, really good guys.'[9]

The trials were held in a better-days loft on Manhattan's 45th Street. First up was 21-year-old session guitarist David Spinozza, one of Linda's finds. He was hired. Two days later, Paul put up day rental on a downbeat Bronx basement, where he planned to try out drummers.

'The cream of New York drummers was all sitting around looking nervous,' recalled Denny Seiwell, a jazz turned session drummer. 'I wasn't. To me it was just a possible gig and I wasn't fazed that I was playing for an ex-Beatle. I did my thing. I gave Paul my best Ringo impression; hard snare, some funky rim work and lots of tom-toms. Plenty of tom-toms. Paul smiled. He tells me, "You got the job."'

Seiwell was struck by the fact that the former Beatle did not attempt to join in at any point.

'He didn't even have a guitar with him. He liked my attitude. The other guys were really put out at being asked to audition. Not me. I just sat and played like I'd done at a thousand jazz jobs. I always say, if you can't get it on for yourself, you can't get it on for anybody.'

Paul had 'a certain look in his eye', he says. 'I knew he was looking for more than a drummer. He wanted a character, someone he could get on with. We hit it off immediately.'

According to Paul, 'We found Denny lying on a mattress like the ones in *Midnight Cowboy* where the people just pass them by. We thought we'd better not do that, so we picked him up and put him in front of a drum kit, and he was alright.'[10] Recollections may vary.

The sessions for the album that would become *Ram* duly commenced, with Seiwell and Spinozza – and later, the latter's replacement, McCracken (when the former was contracted elsewhere) – joining Paul and Linda to take tentative steps, record together, and see whether they could be a new band. They collaborated well, sweating songs through exhausting sixteen-hour days, banging out what felt like hundreds of numbers. They seemed to be getting somewhere. That line-up would not last beyond the album, but it was a start.

Only Denny Seiwell stuck around for the initial ride. David Spinozza went on to work with John Lennon two years later, and with Ringo Starr in 1977. Which earned him the distinction of having worked with three out of four ex-Beatles. He would also strum for Billy Joel, Paul Simon and Don McLean, and would enjoy a long association with James Taylor as both guitarist and producer. In 2002, he would join, as first guitarist, the orchestra of the Broadway production of the musical *Hairspray*.

Six-string virtuoso Hugh McCracken, a New Jersey guitarist and harmonica player who had risen to prominence as a member of Mike Mainieri's New York-based, twenty-strong, avant-garde jazz-rock collective White Elephant Orchestra, was in excessive demand. He went on to work with dozens of greats, not least Aretha Franklin, Carly Simon, Roberta Flack, B.B. King, Bob Dylan and Van Morrison. That's him on rhythm guitar on Van the Man's 1967 signature 'Brown-Eyed Girl', and serving up a wailing slide on Eric Carmen's 1975 showpiece 'All By Myself'.[11] He died from leukaemia in 2013, at the age of seventy.

The McCartneys came home for Christmas, which they spent at High Park Farm. They then returned to New York in mid-January to continue recording. Although the eventual album would be credited to 'Paul and Linda McCartney', the only one that ever was, Linda's contribution at this stage was mainly backing vocals. She did share the lead vocal on 'Long-Haired Lady'; and her elder daughter Heather, who was in the studio round the clock with her baby sister (how boring, monotonous and *loud* for those two kids) sang the first BVs of the music career she would never have on 'Monkberry Moon Delight'. Most of the vocals were recorded in Los Angeles.

Considerably more songs had been recorded than were required for the album. Editorial decisions would normally have fallen to producer Jim Guercio, famous for early recordings by Chicago and Blood, Sweat and Tears. But he and Paul clashed. Guercio moved on to a prior commitment, and was replaced by Norwegian engineer Eirik Wangberg. This time, Paul deferred to the expert, and was delighted with the result.

His post-Beatles debut single 'Another Day', recorded in New York the previous October and not included on the album, was released in February 1971 and became a hit in many countries. Quirky and lilting, it benefits from Linda's pleasing harmonies. Its downbeat lyrics contradict its cheery melody. 'Eleanor Rigby in New York City', Denny Seiwell dubbed it.

Linda's co-songwriting credit on the single, and indeed on several of the tracks on *Ram*, led to McCartney being slapped that July with a lawsuit by his music publisher Northern Songs. Paul stood accused of breaking his exclusivity clause by sharing the credits 50/50 with his wife. Mrs McCartney, they argued, had zero previous writing experience. She had no recording track record. How on earth could she be taken seriously as a songwriter? This was, they claimed, obviously a ruthless ploy to con them out of 50 per cent of their due share. Common sense prevailed. McCartney was declared free to collaborate with whomever he chose. But he had known that all along.

Despite its chart success, the single was scoffed at. One critic heard no more in the track than an ad jingle for deodorant. It seemed to its many detractors a flimsy offering in the face of loaded competition. Specifically, George Harrison's profoundly spiritual *All Things Must Pass*, the album of 'My Sweet Lord' and 'What Is Life'; and the Phil Spector co-produced *John Lennon/Plastic Ono Band*, the showcase of heavy, heart-rending laments 'Mother' and 'My Mummy's Dead'. They wanted Paul to hold his own and weigh in with something equally hard-hitting and personal. Not to brush himself off like flakes from a collar with ditties.

The album, same story. *Ram* was rammed. Dismissed. It was nonsense. Some didn't like it enough to hate it, which was worse. Casual indifference cuts more deeply than loathing. Some held it as proof that Lennon had been the more serious, credible artist all along. Paul, they said, was now exposed as the master of muzak. Not everybody went that far. Discerning commentator Chris Charlesworth, who was news editor of *Melody Maker* during the 1970s, assessed *Ram* as 'a good album by anybody's standards, and certainly far better than the majority released by British groups and singers. Trouble is, you expect too much from a man like Paul McCartney.'

So Paul was damned by the paradox of them willing him not to fail, while throwing themselves at him armed with bread knives. He really couldn't win.

'*Ram* is a masterpiece,' asserts Mark Ellen, who should know. The journalist, author, magazine editor and broadcaster, who played bass in a band alongside the future prime minister Tony Blair at the University of Oxford, co-hosted the BBC's *The Old Grey Whistle Test* for five years during the 1980s, and currently co-presents, with long-time collaborator David Hepworth, the popular music podcast *A Word in Your Ear*, is also a highly regarded Beatles expert.

'I direct you to the gorgeous melodies of "Uncle Albert", "Heart of the Country" and "Dear Boy" – which has one of the greatest harmony vocals he ever composed,' he insists.

But it didn't have John. Could each really not do it successfully without the other?

'Just the presence of the other had a colossal effect, whether they co-wrote, advised or merely thought the song met their gold standard and wanted the band to record it,' Mark explains. 'Their solo work proved one thing inarguably: that John needed Paul far more than vice versa.

· 'I adore a lot of Paul's Wings material – "Letting Go", "Let Me Roll It" and "Band on the Run" are all sublime,' he says. 'But I'm not sure it matches anything he recorded during the 1960s. The symphonic majesty of "Penny Lane", its sights and sounds like a three-minute movie? Or the impossibly sweet and tuneful "Here, There and Everywhere"? Or the perfect chords of "Golden Slumbers"? Or the immaculate "She's Leaving Home", told through the twin perspectives of the parents and the narrator? And vocally, I don't think he ever outranked his raw, rock and roll top gear on "Oh! Darling", "Helter Skelter" or "I'm Down". Or, at the other end of the scale, the golden tone of "I Will".'

Did the relentless drive to out-do each other persist throughout Paul's and John's post-Fab solo careers?

'You can only assume that it did,' Ellen says. 'Made worse by John's *Rolling Stone* interviews and very public views about some of Paul's Beatles contributions and records that followed. They both had points to prove, but Paul must have felt he'd won: a higher profile, world tours, hit singles, and big commercial success. And for five years, John effectively bowed out. Though it's hard to imagine that the spells of fatherhood and bread-baking weren't occasionally plagued by what his old rival might be achieving.'

All of which was to come.

CHAPTER 6

RAM

McCartney didn't fancy a supergroup. That's surprising in some ways, since it would have been a piece of cake for him to pull one together. Brian Jones, say people who know, was set on creating one in 1969 after he was forced out of the Rolling Stones, the band he had founded, named and recruited for. He was rumoured to be in talks with John Lennon and Jimi Hendrix with the intention of giving Jagger, Richards and McCartney what-for. It was even suggested that he would retain his old band's name for the new line-up, a move that would have compromised and perhaps even threatened the future careers of Brian's former band mates.

Although the idea has since been dismissed by music writers of the day, it's no more than guesswork. No proof. But if that was Brian's plan, he never got to see it through. On 3 July 1969, he was found dead in his pool. Accident? Asthma attack? Foul play? That jury may forever be out.[1] On 18 September the following year, Jimi apparently overdosed on his on-off girlfriend Monika Dannemann's Vesparax sleeping pills. Did he? CIA hitlists, Mafia debts, paternity claims, suicide and more have been blamed. They're still arguing about it and we will never know, because everyone who was anyone in the set-up is dead. Whichever way he went, Jimi joined Jones in the infamous '27 Club'.

Ten years later, forty-year-old John was gone too, gunned down in cold blood on the pavement outside his Manhattan apartment block by deranged fan Mark Chapman. Or was it someone else? Welcome, suckers, to Princess Dianaland, where fantasy rules, where the notion of mere 'tragic accident' is inconceivable, and where whichever way you look at whatever it happens to be, there must be more to it. More than four decades later, Lennon conspiracy theorists are still arguing the toss. They won't get anywhere.

A supergroup would have been simple for Paul to achieve. He could have had his pick of the best. Any number of acclaimed musicians would have jumped at the chance of joining an ex-Beatle in such a venture. Imagine the energy in a group made up of, say, Steve Gadd on drums, Mick Taylor or Jeff Beck on lead guitar and Danny Kortchmar on rhythm. Then consider the cramping effect of a clutch of huge egos and blinding artistry on Paul's own style.

One of the reasons why the Beatles began to fall apart after the death of Brian Epstein was that Paul assumed creative and commercial superiority. The others grumbled and resisted. They clashed furiously, we know, over future management choices. Paul knew himself too well. He believed in his own approach and the way he did things. He knew that he wouldn't be able to give in to flimsier alternatives. It suited him to be the chief songwriter and decision-maker. Democracy in the recording studio and subservience in general were not his thing. He benefitted from strong managerial back-up by loyal family members. And his primary partner in every aspect of his existence was his wife.

Forging a new path with amenable session men who could do with the work was always Paul's best bet. Spinozza and McCracken hadn't worked out long-term because they were in lucrative demand anyway. They did not need to commit. Drummer Denny Seiwell, already along for the ride, was twenty-seven and just out of the United States Navy Band when the Maccas caught up with him. He was up for the challenge, and stuck around.[2] Paul's new band was a trio so far. Who would be joining them?

★   ★   ★

Pause ... to examine the roles and significance of session musicians. The success of popular music is dependent on fame: that of the artist or band who creates, records and performs it. But we ought to acknowledge at this point that nothing is real. What you see is not always what you get. Most fans are unaware of most of the industry's behind-the-scenes intricacies. Let's call it subterfuge. This was particularly the case back in the day, pre-internet and social media, when what the general public knew about rock stars and the recording process was the tip of a gigantic iceberg.

Many would have been surprised to learn that the recorded output of their favourite groups was often made by, or at least augmented, embellished and improved by, musicians other than the established members of the line-up they knew and loved. I'm not talking about additional instrumentalists, such as a brass section for this track or a keyboard part for that, where the band's standard line-up did not include a trumpeter, horn-blower or keys player. These would be hired in for that specific purpose. I am referring to the phenomenon of 'ghost musicians': those who play in place of official personnel.

A notable example is the late former Scottish pipe band drummer turned session player Andy White, who performed on the Beatles' debut single.

'Love Me Do' was in fact recorded three times, with three different drummers, before its 1962 release. The first version, on 6 June that year, was recorded at their audition for George Martin with Pete Best, the fellow Liverpudlian member of the Beatles who was fired before they became famous. It can be found on *Anthology I*. It is obvious from the lack of drumming competence on this recording why the producer asked the Beatles to drop Best. He plays hesitantly, somewhat erratically.

Three months later, on 4 September, the band recorded the track again, with Best's replacement Ringo Starr. There were fifteen takes. This version is on the Beatles compilations *Rarities* (1978), *Past Masters* (1988) and *Mono Masters* (2014). Its bass drum is light but steady. Ringo and Paul make a tight, credible rhythm section. The boys returned to the studio a week later, on 11 September. On that occasion, session drummer Andy White was recorded on drums, while Ringo was relegated to tambourine. If Beatles aficionados are confused by the various versions, all they have to do is listen for the tambourine. Eighteen takes were made that day. The final take was the one that producer George chose.

The Andy White recording featured on the Beatles' debut album *Please Please Me*. But the UK single, released on 5 October 1962, was the version with Ringo's drumming. The American single release, however, was the one with Andy White. Still with me? Ringo, incidentally, was gutted to be replaced by a studio drummer, and harboured a festering grudge towards George Martin. The mortified producer could only apologise, and promise not to do it again.

'Every drummer is unique and every job is a different story,' says Steve Gadd, the aforementioned (that's his iconic military signature beat, one of the greatest drum intros of all time, on Paul Simon's 'Fifty Ways to Leave Your Lover').

'I've gone on jobs where the drums have sounded fine to me, but the engineer made me change the bass drum head because to him it sounded like a dampener. Then I'll go to another date without changing the head back and the engineer will say the bass sounds like a cannon. I don't argue because it's important to realise that music is a group effort; it's not just about the individual and everyone has got to be out there working together.'[3]

Finalement? To the naked, untrained ear, Andy White's drumming is indistinguishable from Starr's. If 'his' version is a slight improvement on the Beatle's, it can perhaps be put down to Ringo's tambourine.

To confuse matters further, White also drummed on 'P.S. I Love You', the B-side of 'Love Me Do'. But he never got rich on it; nor from the many sessions he played down the years for a string of A-list artists. Session musicians were and still are paid a standard session fee. They do not earn royalties from record sales.

Another prolific example is Clem Cattini, who entered the *Guinness Book of Records* for having drummed on forty-two UK Number One singles. Clem was sixteen when he took to the kit in the early 1950s. He turned pro in 1954, clocked up his first Number One in 1960 with 'Shakin' All Over' as a member of Johnny Kidd and the Pirates, and two years later joined the Tornados. They topped the charts in 1963 with 'Telstar', written by producer Joe Meek.

Clem went on to play on many Meek recordings after that, and on hundreds of other singles throughout the sixties and seventies: for Marty Wilde, Tom Jones, Lou Reed, Cilla Black, Billy Fury, Adam Faith, Dusty Springfield and many more. Whenever a drummer was needed at no notice, they called Clem. He joined the Nashville Teens; and was even, in 1968, offered the drummer's stool in Led Zeppelin. He also played sessions that wound up on recordings by the Beatles, he says. So he has been told. Don't ask him which ones, he has no idea. Because even when specific musicians were credited, it was common for them to be replaced by a ghost player later, often behind their backs.

Clem also drummed for the Rolling Stones. He sat in for Charlie Watts on their 'Heart of Stone' in 1964, with Jimmy Page on lead guitar. This demo recording was not released at the time. The version by the Stones' classic line-up was, and it earned them a hit. The demo went forgotten for a decade, when it resurfaced. It was included on the band's *Metamorphosis* compilation in 1975.

Clem toured with Cliff Richard and Adam Faith, did the honours on Donovan's 'Hurdy Gurdy Man' and drummed on 'Cambodia' and 'Kids in America' for Kim Wilde. Those are his snare and tom-tom fills on Love Affair's 'Everlasting Love' and on 'Jesamine' by the Casuals. Other sessions that he can remember range from Lou Reed's debut, eponymous solo album in 1972 to Paul Weller's 2010 single 'No Tears to Cry'. He was portrayed by James Corden in the 2009 film *Telstar*, and appeared in the same picture, playing actor John Leyton's chauffeur.

In 1971, Clem drummed for Paul McCartney alongside bassist Herbie Flowers, pianist Steve Gray, the Mike Sammes singers and others on an orchestral version of the *Ram* album entitled *Thrillington*. Paul produced the album but did not play on it. It was released six years later under the pseudonym 'Percy "Thrills" Thrillington'.

During the early to mid-1960s, when a band checked into a London recording studio to lay down tracks, there was every chance that their drummer would be replaced by either Clem or Bobby Graham (the Kinks, the Dave Clark 5, the Pretty Things, Herman's Hermits). They were the two most called-upon session drummers of that era. Between them, they played on many if not most of the pop, rock and beat releases of the decade. The reason behind this perceived 'deception' was the necessity for precision; the producer's remit being to refine the quality of the recording to as good as he could possibly get it.

No producer worth his salt would use an untried, untested drummer on an important session. Not even a pretty one who looked decent in the promo pics. While the 'outside world' may regard this as puzzling if not as an outrageous 'con' of the record-buying public, the reasons, if not entirely above board, were practical. Music recorded by bands in the studio differs from their live (or mimed) performance on stage. The two are regarded as separate entities. Responsibilities for each falls to different camps. When the Beatles were in the studio, producer George Martin was in charge. On the road, their management, Brian Epstein and Neil Aspinall, plus the booking agent and promoter, assumed control.

There were occasional suggestions of subterfuge and dishonesty when a journalist got wind of a scoop. So that's not (famous pop star) X or Y on that Number One, but Clem Cattini instead? An outrage!

'The press were sniffing around and calling me up all the time, trying to expose the "scandal" about band members not playing on their own records,' Clem tells me. 'It had been brought to the public's attention, sensationally, by Jonathan King on his TV show [the prime-time Saturday night talk show *Good Evening*, of which the subsequently disgraced King was host]. Whenever a journalist got hold of me and asked me, "Did you play on it?" I was forced to deny it. As much as I didn't want to, I just had to.

'I remember when Georgie Fame was recording "The Ballad of Bonnie and Clyde" in 1967 [the drummer of which was listed as Hayden/Haydn Jackson]. There were some issues with the recording. I had to go in and replace the rhythm section. Mike Smith, the producer, got us in at gone midnight. He'd put the tape in the boot of his car, but the petrol pump had gone wrong or something, and it somehow put an electronic beep all over the track. We had to re-record the lot. It was all very discreet, though. Not even Georgie Fame ever knew about it. I guess he does now.'

Lines of enquiry generally fizzled. It was so often the case that the session men themselves had no idea they had played on a particular hit. Not until they heard it on the radio and recognised the part and their own playing style.

There existed collectives of ghost players, pools of talent who sometimes played together, and from which individual players could be drawn. The most famous of these was the gang of Los Angeles-based musicians who later became known as the Wrecking Crew.

Members of this set-up contributed to literally hundreds of Top Forty hits. Held in high regard within the industry, several went on to become world-famous artists in their own right, including keyboard player Leon Russell, country star Glen Campbell and drummer Hal Blaine – who worked with Elvis Presley, Phil Spector, Frank Sinatra, the Beach Boys, the Carpenters, Neil Diamond, Simon and Garfunkel, the Byrds and the rest. In all, Blaine lent his remarkable skills to 150 American Top Ten hits, forty of which were Number Ones. In the early 1960s, members of the 'Crew' effectively became producer Phil Spector's house band.

Studio time costs. There were neither facilities nor session musicians enough to meet demand. The best were highly prized, not only for their reliability, punctuality and versatility, but for their ability to read music, to interpret a part off the page sight unseen, and to play in a range of musical styles with minimal rehearsal and in the fewest number of takes.

It is worth reminding ourselves here that many rock stars, including McCartney, are unable to sight-read. Indeed, none of the Beatles could read or write conventional musical notation – to which Paul has been known to refer as 'dots on a page'. The band, like so many who made their name in guitar-based pop music, were what Hollywood composers referred to as 'hummers'. In other words, 'you hum it, I'll play it'. They relied on their excellent ears, and on musical memory.

Right from the start, John and Paul applied a 'catchiness test' to their own songs. If they could remember, at their next session, a tune they'd come up with at their last, then it stood a good chance. If they couldn't, they would simply abandon it. They were well aware that nothing but the most memorable tunes would stand the ruthless radio test. In those days, most listening was done via nothing more sophisticated than a transistor radio. The boys' ability to listen carefully was crucial to their craft.

Vocal harmonies came naturally to them, and were sibling-true. What the likes of the Everlys and the Beach Boys, the Osmonds and the Jacksons achieved vocally through genetics, growing up together, a shared environment and virtually identical education – that which we might term 'biological brotherliness' – John and Paul were able to emulate through being attuned to each other as close friends. They may not have been bio-siblings, but they had similar accents, made the same kind of vowel sounds and similar speech patterns and simply favoured the same kind of artists and records. But how much exactly did they understand about musical theory?

'The Beatles started with a pragmatic musical ambition,' observes author and music theorist Keiran McGovern. 'They wanted to learn how to play the songs they liked. Unable to read sheet music

– which was not available for many of their favourites in any case – they relied on careful listening. This enabled them to work out the words, the basic chord progression and the melody. Vocal harmonies always came naturally to them, and this was an area [in which] Paul's father had provided informal tuition.

'Aspiring pop musicians also shared details of chords, words, rhythms, melodies and strumming patterns with their peers. Most of the first meeting between John and Paul was taken up with this. Later George and Paul helped John transpose the banjo chords his mother had taught him to the guitar. Without recourse to textbooks – or YouTube tutorials [unavailable during those pre-internet days] – many musical discoveries were made by chance observation.' For example? 'It was a Slim Whitman concert poster that taught Paul that he could restring his guitar to play left-handed.'

By the early 1970s, advanced recording technology precipitated a decline in demand for the old-school faithfuls. Changing musical tastes, and the expectation that emerging rock groups would naturally play their own instruments on their own records, so would not be in need of ghosts, were factors that contributed to the change.

They were displaced by a cohort of younger, more contemporary session players such as drummer Jim Keltner, who played for all the former Beatles except Paul, for Bob Dylan, the Stones, Pink Floyd, Eric Clapton and Joni Mitchell, and who became an honorary member of supergroup the Traveling Wilburys; and Andrew Gold, renowned for his work with Linda Ronstadt, Art Garfunkel, the Eagles, James Taylor, Jackson Browne and others, and for his own seventies solo hits 'Lonely Boy', 'Thank You for Being a Friend' and 'Never Let Her Slip Away'.[4]

For McCartney, it seems that the notion of 'a band' with a cohesive name, image and identity was from the outset an abstract concept. It may well have been his fantasy, but it was not what he set out to achieve. When he said 'band', he actually meant 'backing band'. Not an alliance of equals, but one designed to lend shape and substance to his own musical progress.

Did it occur to him at the time that it could be a moveable feast, an ever-changing line-up of the best session men according to factors such as availability of musicians and flavour of latest album – allowing him to write (most of) the songs, call the shots, pay the wages and retain control? And in so doing, was he simply trying to avoid another inevitable, eventual collapsing band? If any or all of this was the case, he did not articulate it.

Many industry insiders and diehard fans remain firmly of the opinion that Wings were a 'proper band'. Some argue that it might even exist to this day had it not been for the curve ball that impeded them in January 1980 and the tragedy of John Lennon's murder that December. Others maintain that Wings were a device, a stepping-stone, a construct via which Paul could overcome the huge psychological hit he had sustained after the disintegration of the Beatles, and take his time to find his feet as a solo star. Reconsidered from every angle, both viewpoints must be correct.

Paul was not and never had been a solo artist. Though perfectly capable of achieving sensational solo work, even to the point of writing every song, playing all the instruments and attending to aspects of an album's production himself, he knew in his heart that he was a team player. He liked the vibe of being in a band. That was his comfort zone. Playing off other musicians rather than working by himself was what he knew and loved. Until such time as the other three Beatles might feel inclined to regroup and go again – an unthinkable consideration during the years of spite, recrimination, public slanging matches, insulting record releases, legal crossfire and all-consuming, life-threatening devastation – he was going to have to do his own thing.

With hindsight, Paul does sometimes appear to regard Wings as having been a proper group. On 30 November 1994, in an interview at his own Sussex studio with writer Tony Bacon, he compared his second band to his first in bald terms.

'The Beatles was the best band in the world,' he reasoned, without arrogance. 'It's difficult to follow that. It's like following God.

Very difficult, unless you're Buddha. Anything Wings did had to be viewed in the light of the Beatles. And the comparisons were always very harsh.'

With Wings, he pointed out, he had to perform multiple roles, from band leader to business manager:

'We didn't have Apple, we didn't have Epstein, we didn't have anything,' he said. 'It was me doing it all. That was the biggest headache – that's difficult. In the Beatles, I'd been free of all that. We had a manager, we had three other great guys.'[5]

Interviewed twenty-two years later in May 2016 by BBC broadcaster John Wilson for the Radio 4 series *Mastertapes* at the corporation's Maida Vale studios, before a live audience that included fellow musicians Paul Weller and James Bay and film star Brad Pitt, it was much the same stance.

'We weren't a good group,' he said with an audible shrug. People said, "Well, Linda can't play keyboards," and it was true. But you know, Lennon couldn't play guitar when we started. We knew Linda couldn't play, we didn't know each other, but we learned.' He thus appeared to conclude that the 'band' – by which he meant himself, his wife and Denny Laine, the only other constant throughout its incarnations – came into its own in the end.

Talking his non-musical, non-instrumentalist wife into being part of it was one thing. But while he could devise and show her keyboard parts, teach her harmonies, and tell her precisely what to sing and when, he was never going to be able to bounce off her musically. She was incapable of being his creative equal. He lacked such a person. He needed John. He couldn't have John. Who or what would be his Lennon replacement therapy? Who might he turn to who would be able to anticipate his reactions, read his mind, hear his heart and respond appropriately?

He knew to his deep chagrin that there would never be another Lennon. The unique relationship they had shared since boyhood had spanned his most impressionable years. Through John's eyes he had grown. Through John's ears he had raised his game. To

John's side he was glued for, we might as well say it, eternity. How do you replace that? The realisation would not prevent him from trying. Still crushed by the Beatles' break-up but flaunting his best brave face, he was determined to consign his addiction to John to the past and to find himself another collaborator. Had he been able to admit to himself that John's shoes were unfillable, his relationship with Denny Laine might have survived.

'When I discovered who was going to be joining Paul in his new band, I thought to myself, well there's hope,' says Andy Peebles. 'Denny Laine had been one of my great 1960s heroes. He'd gone from Denny and the Diplomats to the Moody Blues, a pucker rhythm and blues band. With him on lead vocals, that was the best line-up they ever had.'

'I'll Go Crazy', the band's juddering, squealing, electrifying James Brown cover, was the opening track on their first LP *The Magnificent Moodies* (Decca, 1965). It is the only album by the original line-up of Denny, keyboard player and singer Mike Pinder, bassist Clint Warwick, flautist and harmonica player Ray Thomas and drummer Graeme Edge. This is the album that produced Denny's definitive cover of 'Go Now'. The first time I met him, during an early 2000s gig by the Dave Stark Five (the band behind acclaimed tribute act the Trembling Wilburys) at private members' club the Cricketers in Marylebone, London, Denny got up to perform the song with the band. He later told me that he'd written it.

It was in fact the work of US songwriters Larry Banks and Milton Bennett. It had been recorded originally by Larry's ex-wife, soul/R&B singer Bessie Banks, with Dionne Warwick's sister Dee Dee and her aunt, Whitney Houston's mother Cissy, on backing vocals. That version was released on the US Tiger Records label in January 1964. The Moodies added a screamer and put it out that November as 'Go Now!' The biggest hit of their career went all the way. Their failure to follow it prompted Denny to quit and launch the Electric String Band, making room in the Moody Blues for Justin Hayward.

'The moment I first heard Denny's voice, I thought, "Wow",' says Andy. 'When he came into Radio Lancashire where I was broadcasting in 1992, I cued up "I'll Go Crazy" and he looked at me with amazement. "Have we met?" he said. The record played out, and he just sat there with a wonderful smile on his face. This was more than a decade after Wings broke up. He'd gone bankrupt, his marriage had collapsed, his relationship with Paul had disintegrated and he was recording solo again. He was talking about leaving it all behind and making a new life for himself in America.'

All of which was to come when the Romani Brummie-born Brian Frederick Hines took an unexpected call from a Scouser.

'Lead guitarist' is a hot seat. As one of if not the vocal point of any group, he had to look the part as well as play it. An appealing appearance and a winning personality are never mere cake icing. Who would Paul find to fit the bill? Trawling the history, the names, the music, he happened to recall the 1964 Moody Blues hit 'Go Now!' He later identified it as one of his favourite records.

The former boxer's son almost two years McCartney's junior had by then been on the circuit as long as Paul had. A self-taught guitarist, Denny had been inspired by Buddy Holly, and claimed to have given his first professional musical performance when he was twelve. As a teen he joined Birmingham-based outfit Johnny Dean and the Dominators, taking his experience a year or so later into the first band of his own, Denny and the Diplomats. His more stageworthy name, he would explain, was derived from the nickname bestowed on him by kids who used to come to his parents' garden to play in his den. The surname he borrowed from jazz artist Cleo Laine, whose own real surname was Campbell.

The Brumbeat group failed to release a single record. Despite which, Laine, who had a day job in the electrical department of local store Rackhams, was buoyant. The band built an enthusiastic following and Denny started to believe that he was going places.

'John Bonham [future drummer of Led Zeppelin] used to watch me and the Diplomats at the Wednesbury Youth Centre,' he would recall. 'Years later, he stayed at my house and we got drunk. He started singing "Why Cry", "A Piece of Your Mind", and a few other originals we used to do. He knew all the words and everything. Unbelievable!'

With growing confidence came the hair bleach, fancier glad rags and a van, down the side of which they had their name emblazoned. It conveyed them to further-flung gigs, and got them to London. EMI pricked up their ears at one point, but stopped short of offering them a contract. They were then auditioned by songwriter and producer Tony Hatch, potentially for Pye Records. Same deal. Rather, no deal.

But it wasn't all bad. On 5 July 1963, nineteen-year-old Denny and his Diplomats found themselves supporting the Beatles on their second date that year at the Plaza Ballroom, Old Hill, an important venue on the West Midlands circuit that had also hosted the Stones. That afternoon, pre-soundcheck, marked the first time that McCartney and Laine came face to face.

By early 1964, Denny was rehearsing on the side with another new Birmingham blues band, the Soul Preachers, who would evolve into the Moody Blues. Come Easter he was done with the Diplomats. The Moodies signed to Decca, the label notorious for having 'turned down the Beatles' (but didn't really; there is correspondence to prove it),[6] and would by the end of the year be household names.

Denny's tenure was short-lived. Two years. His Electric String Band blew a fuse. He spent a year dossing in Spain, learning classical guitar. Tony Secunda, the Moodies' manager who was looking out for Denny too, managed to secure a decent advance from the Warner Brothers label to launch a new supergroup he called Balls. They were billeted on a farm outside Reading in Berkshire, west of London, where they were supposed to be writing and recording. But, the usual, there was dissent among the ranks. Members came and went. Copious drinking and drugging prevailed.

All that staring at the same four walls pondering the meaning of life brought the ill-fated venture to a head. It fizzled out. Secunda, who had hit the big time with Procol Harum, was now obsessed with his latest protégé, Marc Bolan. He had negligible time to spend on growing Balls. Marc's hit 'Hot Love' reached Number One in March 1971. DJ 'Whispering' Bob Harris remembers T. Rex as '*the* biggest thing in this country since the Beatles, I kid you not. Marc was *it* for that year and a half, spring 1971 into 1973. He was a superstar, a natural.'

Secunda had his hands full with the promotional tour for Marc's album *Electric Warrior*. Denny joined Ginger Baker's Air Force, a jazz-rock fusion supergroup, alongside drummer Baker, bass guitarist Ric Grech, vocalist Steve Winwood and others. They performed their first live shows in 1969 at Birmingham Town Hall and the following year at London's Royal Albert Hall. They also played at Wembley Stadium to mark the start of 1970's FIFA World Cup football tournament.

All of which looked promising. But Denny was still boracic. The homeless troubadour was sleeping on a mattress in Tony Secunda's back office. When the phone rang one day, and the call was for him, and the caller turned out to be Macca, the 'Hallelujah!' choruses must have echoed out of Mayfair all the way to the Birmingham Bullring.

'I'm forming a new band to go out on the road,' said Paul, according to Denny. 'Are you interested?'

He must have been paraphrasing all those years ago when he revisited the phone call with author, film maker, musician and actor Geoffrey Giuliano. Whatever Paul's actual words, the thrust of the statement was loaded.[7]

He was *forming a new band* – dispelling the myth peddled relentlessly by Laine down the years that he and McCartney conceived and launched Wings together. Denny has long maintained that he was a founder member. Clearly, he wasn't. Drummer Denny Seiwell got there ahead of him. Paul and Linda had already agreed together to establish their own new band. The 'Laine' role could have gone to any one of a number of top-notch guitarists. Like 'Denny One', 'Denny Two' was invited on board. There was no 'co-founder' about it.

To go out on the road – implying that Paul was looking specifically for musicians to perform live with him, and maybe undertake formal concert tours. There was no mention, at that early stage, of anything studio-based.

Are you interested? In other words, 'Would *you* like to join *me*? I mean, *us* – Linda and me. Will you come on board? This is *me*, Paul, inviting *you*, Denny, along for what might be a ride. Maybe it won't work. We could fall flat on our faces, but it's worth a try. How about it?'

How about it? With McCartney, one of the richest, most celebrated rock stars on Earth? If he had one, Denny wouldn't have bothered to check his diary. He was stacked to the retinas doing sweet FA. He didn't even have a roof over his head. How do you sleep?[8]

CHAPTER 7
STARTING OVER

A 'John' chapter in a book about Paul? Go with me, here – because all that was happening in John's life at that point affected the progress of his relationship with McCartney, in both positive and negative ways. It is crucial to our understanding of how Paul proceeded.

Where *was* John? What was he up to? Hadn't he and Yoko gone looking for America too? Though it had never been his intention to remain in the States forever, something life-changing was dragging him back there. He even talked about it unprompted on late-night US television, evidently hoping to highlight the horrible situation in which he and his wife now found themselves. It drew negligible attention from the media. Most of those with whom I raised it while researching this book had no recollection of it having happened.

The clue is in the song first released as the B-side of John's 1969 post-heroin second solo single 'Cold Turkey'. 'Don't Worry Kyoko (Mummy's Only Looking for Her Hand in the Snow)' is an eerie prelude of troubled times ahead. Yoko's disturbing, tortured wails and imploring, repetitious lyrics pre-empt her future anguish over the snatching of her child.[1] Both the live and studio versions feature Eric Clapton and John on guitar. The studio recording boasts Beatles buddy and long-term collaborator Klaus Voormann on bass and Ringo on drums.

The track can be found on the Lennons' album *Live Peace in Toronto 1969*, on Yoko's 1971 album *Fly*, and on John's 1972 album *Some Time in New York City*. Why so many outings? It was as though John, who called it 'one of the fuckin' best rock'n'roll records ever made', was determined to prove his point, and wouldn't relent until as vast an audience as possible had heard it.

John and Yoko had spent January 1970 on a remote farm in Vust in the Thy region of Northern Jutland, to which Yoko's former, second husband, jazz musician and filmmaker Tony Cox, had relocated with his new partner Melinda Kendall and Kyoko, his and Yoko's five-year-old daughter. Again, in a prelude of future domestic arrangements, Cox had assumed responsibility for the lion's share of the parenting while Yoko focused on work. A similar set-up would apply down the line when Yoko and John had their son Sean.

Tony and Melinda had absconded with Kyoko without informing her mother and stepfather. Having tracked them down to Denmark, the Lennons were keen to spend quality time with them, in order to negotiate proper shared custody arrangements and to repair the fractured relationship between the couples. At first, things looked promising. Six days of calm exchange and reasoning were then obliterated by a media storm, after a local newspaper discovered the identity of the two strangers lurking among them and blew the Lennons' cover.

In jetted the world's press to scramble for interviews with the pair of 'political prophets' who had been mouthing off and writing songs in opposition to the Vietnam war.[2] They conceded to a press conference to get the pack off their backs. Both had their flowing locks cut short by a hairdresser in Aarlborg to launch Year One for Peace. They gifted the choppings to Michael X, Britain's answer to civil rights activist Malcolm X, inviting him to sell their hair to raise money for the Black Power movement.

All of which alarmed the already skittish and publicity-shy Cox. How could John and Yoko do their share of sane, safe, private parenting while they were preoccupied by such nonsense? Then there was the drugs issue. Cox had seen for himself while at their home Tittenhurst Park that both John and Yoko were using heroin. He feared for his daughter's safety while in the care of druggies. He knew. He'd been there. He had been an acidhead back in the anything-went-and-everything-did sixties.

During the Beatles' winding-down and after his primal therapy with controversial practitioner Arthur Janov at home in Berkshire and in Los Angeles – treatment which involved the re-living of childhood trauma and the resurrection of suppressed memories, another ideology with which he flirted briefly but which he would soon denounce – John made *John Lennon/Plastic Ono Band*. His debut solo album was his most authentic offering yet.

'John expressed his feelings about the world in ways that were so unexpected,' said writer Michael Watts, *Melody Maker*'s US editor during the 1970s. 'That made him a fantastic interviewee. He would say things that opened and stretched your own mind, and which made you consider things in new ways. I think McCartney always felt a bit out of his depth in interviews, because John was so brilliant at expressing himself. Paul was every bit as literate, but he didn't have that gift for animating issues that John had.

'*John Lennon/Plastic Ono Band* is extraordinary. The songs are so naked. They reveal him as so vulnerable. The album stands as the best expression of what he was. He clearly strove to tell things in a completely open-hearted way. It is confessional to the hilt. I thought, and I still think, that it is a great album.'

'Thus began,' Watts told me, 'his campaign to become someone different. Imagine most rock stars attempting such a thing. It wouldn't happen. What he was saying was that the guy they had all fallen for was fake, no good, and now he was going to offer them a different version of himself: a John Lennon whom he himself could love and respect. What a risk that was, because it could have gone completely the other way. He could have lost all credibility.

'He wanted to be someone better. He wished to transcend, and to become a more worthwhile human being. People tend to think that much of what he said was dopey nonsense. Because we journalists are a cynical lot, part of me agrees. But what is in no doubt is that he genuinely believed what he was preaching. He really did want to change the world.'

Much of John's quest for self-improvement was driven by his second wife.

'Yoko was his true love, his genuine soulmate,' Watts asserts. He truly believes it. 'There's no doubt. He found, in her, someone who was completely on his wavelength. Because of all the daft things they did, she was so often dismissed as having led him astray. But the two of them together and she on her own, did very interesting artistic things. The world just wasn't ready for her. She was a true avant-garde artist. Those bed-ins, the bagism, being interviewed in bags, John said, were sort of Dadaist events, and the public hadn't cottoned on to that.

'His fans couldn't reconcile John the pop star with this figure who had begun increasingly to absorb influences from the art world, and was expressing himself in more complex, less conventional ways. What he and Yoko were doing was quite extraordinary, really. Because they were getting audiences of a million times more people than you would get in the art world. Because they were so famous already, before they lifted a finger and actually did anything. He was really enthused by that. He realised and harnessed his power. It charged his batteries beyond his imagining.'

But Lennon's problem was a total lack of subtlety and humility. In this, he differed drastically from McCartney, who had an instinctive understanding of the need for both.

'John was always on it, always rushing towards a gap, to fill a vacuum,' agrees Watts. 'The fact that he had no filter was what made him such an exciting figure. With a little more tact and pragmatism, the Beatles could have progressed to other things, and still have developed their solo careers on the side. But it was all or nothing with John. He was hell-bent on a new career with Yoko, and that is what he went out to get. With him, it was always "on to the next thing."'

It was doubtless inevitable that John and Paul would fail to shake each other off. Each was looking constantly over his shoulder to see what the other was doing.

Paul had realised while still in his twenties that he couldn't carry on putting it about forever. Home and family were what mattered. Those were the things that would give meaning and point to his wild days, his mad existence. They may even, if he was lucky, secure his future happiness. When he fell in love with Linda, he also embraced her daughter Heather. This was crucial to the success of their relationship. Soon after he married her mother, he adopted the child. Before too long, he and Linda had given the little girl two sisters and a brother: a proper family, made with love and care by two motherless, rudderless kids.

Which, leaving aside global fame, fortune and influence, band and business collapse and friendship detonation, and given their tender ages at the time, is all that Paul and Linda were. A little family that they could call their own was the secret, longed-for goal, an almost holy aspiration. It was the dream upon which neither had ever dared to go to sleep, in case that would somehow jinx it and prevent it from coming true.

Other superstar rockers, multiple discarded ex-partners and pinched, borrowed-time wives getting set to haggle over property and pay-outs looked on, open-mouthed. How had the Maccas managed to stick together for richer for richer, fatter and slimmer, better and worse? What sorcery had enabled them to pull off the thing at which so many of them had failed all too hopelessly?

'I knew Linda a long time ago,' remarked eccentric Canadian-born muso Neil Young in 1999, during Paul's induction into the Rock and Roll Hall of Fame. 'We were all very happy when Paul and Linda got together and had such a wonderful family. I felt close to them over the years. I have a lot of respect for Paul McCartney as a man for holding together a great family through the times of rock and roll, and through all of the success, and through all of the swirling. I have a *lot* of respect for that.'[3]

John, who had become a father at twenty-two when his first son Julian was born, had not been prepared for the responsibility. He soon grew bored with his wife, continued to pursue women 'as if Cynthia and Julian didn't exist,' according to *Mersey Beat* editor Bill Harry, and was ripe for the plucking when Yoko picked him. He was content, to begin with, to play happy families and to pretend to toe the marital line.

Julian, born on 8 April 1963, and Kyoko, who landed on 8 August the same year, were as good as the same age. But their instant family wasn't as cosy and as uncomplicated as it may have looked. There were four parents in the mix for a start, two of whom had been abandoned and were disgruntled. Yoko was perhaps jealous of Linda and her lovely brood of girls (to be joined by son James in September 1977). She was desperate for a child or children with John.

In February 1971 she turned thirty-eight, an age at which most women in those days had completed their families (if they were having one) and had resigned themselves to impending menopause. The average age at which women gave birth in 1970 was twenty-seven. Yoko was thirty in 1963 when she had Kyoko. She was also seven years her new husband's senior: unusual at that time.[4]

Her relationship with her stepson was strained. She had no idea, she admitted later, how to bond with little boys. Could she have stretched herself a little and have made the effort to find out? But Julian's presence in her home was an excruciating reminder of the baby son she and John had lost in November 1968, around three months ahead of his expected birth; and of their subsequent miscarriages.[5] She gave birth to Sean in October 1975, giving John the thirty-fifth birthday present he would cherish until his death only five years later.

John's devotion to Kyoko incensed her father Tony Cox. The relationship between the two couples imploded. In August 1970, after John refused to attend Kyoko's seventh birthday party at

Cox's London flat and banned Yoko from going too, Cox, Melinda and the child took off again without letting the Lennons know their destination. When they discovered their whereabouts, John and Yoko rushed to Majorca and abducted Kyoko back. But they were intercepted by police, arrested and jailed. Although a court hearing found in their favour and they were permitted to take Kyoko home, John and Yoko came up with 'commitments' that prevented them from doing so 'just yet'.

By the time they were ready to collect the child, Cox had gone on the run again. Tony, Melinda and Kyoko were American citizens. Intelligence indicated that they had headed home. John and Yoko belted to New York, confident that they would find the little girl in no time. They threw fame, money and influence at a far-reaching investigation. Their campaign drew a blank at every turn.

Back in England, the distraught Lennons immersed themselves in work in their studio at Tittenhurst Park.

'I just wish to mention that my son visits me every weekend at that house, which is a beautiful home in Ascot with eighty acres of ground,' John told talk show host Dick Cavett, when he and Yoko appeared on his ABC late-night talk show on 8 September 1971. 'Yoko's daughter is not allowed to visit us because her ex-husband won't let her see her own daughter. All Yoko wishes is that now and again Kyoko could be brought to that house . . . to spend some time . . .' His voice cracked. John, audibly and visibly upset, paused to compose himself. 'That's the house, waiting for her,' he sighed. 'If you're watching, Kyoko . . .'

Julian's visits tailed off. Because the agony of being deprived of her own child rendered Yoko incapable of being around anyone else's, John effectively lost his child too. Thus began a pitiful estrangement that lasted for most of the rest of John's life. There were brief hiatuses during John's affair with the Lennons' former assistant May Pang, when John and Julian were reunited thanks to May's kind coaxing and colluding. But father and son were already uncoupled when John's untimely death drew the line.

Yoko applied for full custody of Kyoko in the British Virgin Islands. The court granted her appeal on condition that the child be raised in the United States. This was the real reason behind the Lennons' failure to return to the UK. Though it had never been his intention – they still owned Tittenhurst Park, and the place was still filled with their many possessions – John would never again live in England.

As it happened, that suited him. Burnt out by Beatles' break-up frenzy, incensed by the refusal of his fellow countrymen to accept his second wife and enraged by the racism and abuse to which she had been subjected, he was more than ready to try living somewhere new. Like Paul, John was turned on by the prospect of working with American musicians in New York and Los Angeles. Kyoko would come home eventually. Wouldn't she? She never did. For the rest of John's abbreviated life, they never got their daughter back.

Determined that the world-famous, ludicrously rich Lennons were not going to get one over on him, would never deprive him of his daughter or corrupt her with their reckless lifestyle and questionable influence, Cox kept running. The trio pitched up in Houston, Texas, joined an evangelical Christian church, and told Kyoko that she must now answer to the name Rosemary. Moving on from there, they joined Doomsday cult The Walk, which provided perfect hiding places in California and rural Iowa, and where Kyoko acquired yet another new name, Ruth Holman. Cox converted to the religion, and even became an elder.

A further alias would later be recorded, that of Molly Scott, during a period when Cox was calling himself Tony Scott. One enforced name change is going to damage any child, let alone three. The family went to ground, and could not be located. At last Yoko admitted defeat, calling off her private investigators and the FBI. Cox left the cult in 1977, taking Kyoko and leaving Melinda behind. Refusing to quit the community, she divorced her husband and let her stepdaughter go. In 1978, Cox and Kyoko moved to Chicago, where they lingered among the jolly Jesus People USA.

They had the grace to reach out to Yoko after John's murder in 1980. A telegram expressing condolences was signed by both father and daughter, the latter at that point seventeen years old. But they refused to go and meet her, and would not divulge their whereabouts. Yoko took out newspaper ads to wish her daughter a happy life and got on with her own.

Cox grew disillusioned with the cult. It had not brought him relief from the pain caused by Yoko when she left him to marry 'a Beatle'. He had not achieved peace of mind, and remained embittered. In 1986 he and Kyoko co-produced a short documentary, *Vain Glory*, exposing the cult, detailing Cox's escape from it and discussing his relationship with the Lennons. How did he feel about having brainwashed his only daughter into believing that her mother was the personification of evil? He would not, maybe could not, acknowledge the error of his ways. Now in his late eighties, it seems late in the day to see the light.

Kyoko was reunited with her mother only after she herself had become one. In 1994 she took tentative steps towards a reunion that somehow took seven years. In 2001, three decades after they had last set eyes on each other and twenty years on from John's murder, Yoko was spotted one day in Central Park's Strawberry Fields memorial garden, opposite her Dakota building home. She was sitting on a bench with her now 37-year-old daughter, with a tiny Asian child in her arms. That beautiful toddler was her granddaughter Emi.[6]

It was later reported that, shortly after their earlier reunion in a Denver, Colorado park, Yoko quietly deposited £200 million into a trust fund for her granddaughter. Similar arrangements are said to have been made for Kyoko's son.

The Lennons couldn't have left New York even if they'd wanted to. With a historical drug offence on John's record, and with reputations as agitators and aggravators thanks to their politically charged pursuits and zealous campaigning, they were all too aware that the Federal Government wanted rid of them. John was the most dangerous kind of immigrant: an influential one; a subversive criminal with tens of millions of fans.[7]

He fought against deportation, and kept up his quest for the vital Green Card that would grant him the right to remain. He did not dare leave the country for fear that US Immigration might block his re-entry. Yoko couldn't risk leaving with him because Kyoko might one day come back and she wouldn't be there for her. Having undertaken to raise her daughter in America, she had no option but to stay.

John's last ever day in England turned out to be on 31 August 1971. The Lennons began their New York life uptown in the St Regis Hotel, before relocating to a borrowed apartment in the West Village where John felt perfectly at home ... apart from the fact that he knew he was being watched and tailed by the FBI, and that their phone was being tapped. Their final move, for reasons of security, was to the imposing Dakota apartment building on the city's Upper West Side.

They had so far failed to have a child together. Bored in their bed, John was missing the thrill of the free-fall, free-for-all, sexual action of yore. At an early November 1972 party marking Richard Nixon's return to the White House in one of the largest landslide election victories in US history, John spotted a woman sitting alone. He crossed the room, seized her by the hand, marched her past his poker-faced wife into the nearest bedroom – *and she let him* – and had loud, embarrassing sex with her on a bed piled high with guests' hats and coats while the throng stood red-faced and rooted on the other side of the door.

Yoko brooded over the coming days and weeks. She feared that she was no longer attractive to her husband. She believed in their love, and was certain that he would not leave her, but acknowledged that he needed more sex – along with narcotics, a primary rock'n'roll currency – with more partners in greater variety. Rather than turn blind eyes to liaisons conducted behind her back and subsequently denied, Yoko did her controlling thing and took charge. She personally selected a young female assistant from their payroll, May Pang, for John to have an affair with. She was perhaps unaware that John and May, according to May, were already involved. Yoko oversaw the details, established her terms and despatched the hesitant couple to Los Angeles. What she hadn't banked on was the possibility that May and John might fall in love.

Did they? May insists so. Their roughly eighteen-month 'lost weekend' together is still talked about. May wrote books about it and has recently released her own film on the subject: *The Lost Weekend: A Love Story*. It has attracted favourable reviews. But there are, as always, several sides to every story. In this case, John's, Yoko's and May's, as well as the truth.

If it happened today – a 22-year-old daughter of Chinese immigrants ordered by a mega-rich and influential boss eleven years her senior to engage in an affair with the boss's global icon husband – it would provoke outrage. Me Too campaigners would be up in arms and out in force, gluing themselves to things while crying coercive control, arranged adultery and sexual abuse.

But that was then . . . in the drugged-up, knickers-down days of the early 1970s. Everyone was on the Pill, despite health scares. May grew coy at my question when we lunched together in London. Had it bothered her that she might have fallen pregnant?

'It would have been a blessing,' she said. 'John believed that he would have another child. A psychic told him. Yoko was into psychics and fortune tellers, and got John believing it too. Well, I wanted to believe it, but I barely dared to hope. I don't think he thought for a moment that it was going to happen with Yoko.'

She maintains to this day that they shared a love affair. Not that their sojourn in LA was any picnic. John was drunk, violent and uncontrollable much of the time. Most of the rest of the time he was sleeping it off, while she was cleaning up vomit and wreckage. He was not faithful to May. She didn't talk about it with me, but I'm sure she knows. Add to the mix the constant interruptions from Yoko – up to twenty-five calls a day, some days; the intensity of her manipulation now seems extraordinary – and it's a wonder the younger woman didn't crumble and run home to Mom.

When John was on form, he was relaxed, happy, and appeared to be enjoying his freedom. In that town, there was no shortage of musician chums. A gang of unruly soulmates had coalesced. Calling themselves 'the Hollywood Vampires', Monkee Micky Dolenz, Alice Cooper, Harry Nilsson, Elton's lyricist Bernie Taupin and others had got into the habit of terrorising Tinseltown. The Rainbow Bar and Grill on Sunset Boulevard was their HQ. They stumbled from night to day in a fug of self-indulgence and immorality. Not that John devoted himself completely to the pack.

May has her detractors. Of this, she is all too aware. She has frequently been accused of having exaggerated their relationship. But the calendar does not lie. It was on her watch that John rediscovered his musical mojo, and started making great records again; thanks to her that he repaired his relationship with his firstborn; and down to her alone that he made peace with Paul, a reunion that she respected, encouraged and facilitated. She even snapped the last known photograph of Paul and John together, in March 1974.

After which, she and John migrated back to New York – Paul having been 'sent' to LA to talk John into returning (as if anyone on earth could ever *send* Paul anywhere). They moved into an apartment together. There was talk of buying a house in Montauk, a gorgeous throwback village on the South Fork of Long Island looking out across the forever tomorrow sea.

They were making plans to spend time with Paul, Linda and their children in New Orleans, where Wings were recording their fourth album *Venus and Mars* (released the following year), when John visited Yoko back home at the Dakota to 'discuss a cure for smoking'. To all intents and purposes, that was the day he left May. A few close Lennon friends and associates maintain that he had grown tired of her, had come to his senses and had made up his mind to extricate himself from her clutches and return to Mother. Or did Yoko 'turn up the right Tarot cards' or 'put a spell on him'? This was rumoured.

Unable to return to her old job working for the Lennons out of their home, and instructed to vacate the rented apartment after having given up her own previous rental for him, May's love for John left her homeless, penniless and unemployed, and with bits and pieces for a heart.

When word got out, in October 1973, that Lennon was in LA to record an album, every muso within a thousand-mile reach wanted in. That album, *Rock'n'Roll* – a collection of fifties and sixties covers produced by Phil Spector, who turned up each day bombed on amyl nitrate and in fancy dress – proved such a magnet that at times the studio was entertaining thirty plus guests, only some of whom had arrived with the intention of playing music. The process began well but collapsed rapidly, once the booze and drugs kicked in.

Steeped in controversy, delayed by lawsuits, placed on indefinite hold when it came to light that Spector had taken off with the recording masters then crashed his car, had fallen into a coma and was unable to alert anyone as to the whereabouts of the tapes. John's label Capitol had to buy them back eventually, to the tune of ninety thousand bucks. The album wouldn't see the light of day until 1975. Did firearms-obsessed Spector mean to kill John when he pistolled that hole in the studio ceiling?

Rewind . . . to 1971. Reconsider that first full post-Beatles year. Paul, having pulled himself back from mental meltdown, having retreated into the wilderness to find himself and started his own family, makes a fresh start with new musicians in New York and by March has an album, *Ram*, of which he is busting-proud.

And John, spewing his guts and spite into the *John Lennon/Plastic Ono Band* album, mopping blood, trying desperately to get his stepdaughter back and losing touch with his own little boy; hurling himself into the recording of *Imagine* – his signature song and album by which he will forever be defined – at home in Berkshire, in New York, and back again at Abbey Road . . .

Round and round it clangs and drones, the Lennon–McCartney merry-go-round. Churning dreams to dust and pumping steam, to fuel the hope against hope of brand-new magic for old.

Ram was released on 17 May 1971. It reached Number One on the UK album chart and in various countries, Number Two in the US. It is the cherished album of 'Uncle Albert/Admiral Halsey', Paul's first chart-topper in America without the Beatles; and of 'The Back Seat of My Car' and 'Eat at Home'. *Imagine* chased it on 9 September, blowing the charts on both sides of the Atlantic. It is the album of, as well as its title track, 'Jealous Guy', 'Gimme Some Truth' and 'Oh Yoko!' Compare and contrast, we can, we must, but there's no point in it.

Which collection of songs said more about its creator at that stage in the Scrabble? Who was the more content and together, the more optimistic about his own future? Was it Paul or John who was gaining ground? Which of them was in the hottest seat, and stood with the most to lose?

And oh, the aching recollection that Lennon would release only five more albums during his lifetime. All that music that was never to come, swelling inside him fit to burst but lugged unheard to the grave. And what of what we *did* hear?

Some Time in New York City in 1972 was too political, was panned and sold disappointingly. Its reception wounded him. *Mind Games* the following year and 1974's *Walls and Bridges*, featuring 'Whatever Gets You Thru the Night' and '#9 Dream', found greater favour. The *Rock'n'Roll* covers collection of 1975 was John's last before he yanked down the shutters and took a five-year break, to be a hands-on dad to Sean and, so the myth goes, to be the 'house husband' while Yoko bought and sold.

Their collaborative come-back, *Double Fantasy*, was trumpeted across oceans in November 1980. John was murdered three weeks after its release. The album went to Saturn; proving yet again that the best thing an artist can do for his art and his legacy is die. Don't look at me, the world was saying it. Once the prayers had faded and the sobbing was lost to the breeze, Yoko gave us their final collaboration, 1984's *Milk and Honey*.

During John's remaining years beyond the *Ram* and *Imagine* moment, Paul released eight Wings albums: *Wild Life* (1971), 1973's *Red Rose Speedway* and *Band on the Run*, *Venus and Mars* in 1975, *Wings at the Speed of Sound* and the live album *Wings Over America* in 1976. There was *London Town* in 1978 and *Back to the Egg* the year after. In all, he has to date notched twenty-six non-Beatles albums. Post-Wings, the best, for me, are *McCartney II* (1980), *Tug of War* (1982), *Flowers in the Dirt* (1989), *Flaming Pie* (1997), 2018's *Egypt Station* and the 'lockdown album', *McCartney III*. They will never grow old.

We must keep asking it. Had tragedy not intervened, would they have? Could they have? Does even Paul dare to indulge in a little imposter syndrome? Are there ever times when he secretly fears that he might not have had such an overwhelming solo career had John not died? Might they have swallowed pride, buried hatchets and differences, taken back the pointless nastiness, resurrected the old-days rivalry, hugged each other the way they had never dared to as schoolboys, pored over the old photo albums with a pint in each hand and have had another go?

In our many millions we imagine it. We can't not. Countless rockers down the decades have sworn blind that they would never talk to each other again, could never even be in the same room as each other again, that they wouldn't extend a helping hand if the other were being sucked into a swamp or dangling into the dish of Mount Etna – and then have gone on to reap the rewards of longed-for reunions when the time was right. Simon and Garfunkel, anyone?

The bitterness and recrimination that tore the old school chums apart in 1970 was offset only a soupçon by the success that year of the mighty *Bridge over Troubled Water*, one of the biggest-selling albums ever made. Huge solo careers ensued. The pair did regroup a few times. But nothing could compare to their 1981 reunion concert in Central Park. It drew an audience of half a million, one of the greatest ever. Never say never again.

As for the Eagles. When they called it a day in 1980, certain members were set to rip each other's throats out. Cut to 1994, when they recorded the *Hell Freezes Over* album – as in, not on your Nelly, *ever* in a billion – and then regrouped to tour. 'For the record,' deadpanned guitarist and frontman Glenn Frey, during the first gig back, 'we never broke up, we just took a fourteen-year vacation.' He died in 2016, so could regroup no more.

And Oasis? Volatile brothers Liam and Noel had been falling out and in since the pram. After they called it a day most acrimoniously in 2009, Liam launched a new band, Beady Eye, and went solo in 2017. Noel, meanwhile, launched his own new outfit High Flying Birds. Reunion rumours have circulated ever since. In 2015, Noel said for the record on Radio X, 'One should never say never, should we look like a bit of an idiot somewhere down the road, when you're waving a cheque for a quarter of a billion in the *Sun*!' Aye, there is that.

In an interview with *Rolling Stone* in 2012, McCartney revealed that the four *did* consider getting back together while John was still alive.

'There was talk of reforming the Beatles a couple of times, but it didn't jell,' he said, during an interview on 20 December 2020 with US TV's *CBS Sunday Morning* to promote his new album *McCartney III*. But 'there was not enough passion behind the idea,' he explained. 'The reformation suggestions were never convincing enough. They were kind of nice when they happened. "That would be good, yeah." But then one of us would always not fancy it. And that was enough because we were the ultimate democracy.'

'He was showing no signs of slowing up,' said Paul of John. 'You know, he was still making great music. The question is: Would we have ever got back together again? I don't know. We don't know.'

Tomorrow never does.

CHAPTER 8

WILD LIFE

Ahead of Denny Laine went *Ram* collaborators Hugh McCracken and Denny Seiwell to High Park Farm, in June 1971. Accompanied by their respective wives, Californian Holly (who died in 2021) and French Monique (who kept diaries throughout their time with the McCartneys and her husband's term in Wings), they flew in from New York under the impression that Paul had invited them not to work but for a nice holiday.

How the women's faces must have fallen when they were delivered to Campbeltown's stark little Main Street and checked into the Argyle Arms Hotel, adjacent to the modest Town Hall and clocktower. That spartan inn's ancient carpets and curtains, basic and unheated bedrooms, shared toilets and bathrooms, stained tartan upholstery and hairs-on-your-chest fare cannot have wowed them. Nor could the fact that nights were colder than a polar bear's toenails, even though they arrived in early summer.

It was just bad luck that they were there during an exceptionally cold June: the first sub-13°C sixth month since 1928. Scotland may have been drier than average at the time, but sunshine levels were exceptionally low. The only way to keep warm in bed was to retire in one's overcoat (if one had brought one), or to nip down to Reception for a couple of hot water bottles.

Seiwell had never been to Britain before. He had clearly expected balmier days, cosier nights, superior lodgings and an altogether more monarch-of-the-glen experience.

'You flew to that weird airport in Scotland, and Pan Am had us driven down to Campbeltown in a van,' he recalled. 'It was a five-hour trek, and we were dropped off at a local rent-a-car, checked into a typical little Scottish hotel, and set out to find the farm, which was in the middle of nowhere.

'We asked some of the villagers how to get to High Park Farm, and they said things like, "Well, laddie, ye take the wee car . . ." and I'm thinking, what the hell are they talking about? We finally found the right road, and they had said that we'd come to a farmhouse, which was on the edge of the McCartney property, but after that, there was no real road to their house.

'Well, the sun was setting in the black lulls of Scotland and we beeped the horn and this old guy came out, and we said, "How do you find Paul's farm?" and his answer was nearly unintelligible, but he opened this old wooden gate and there were these boulders everywhere. We ruined the car. We ruined about three rental cars; they wouldn't rent us any more cars in this village. Finally, we got to the farm. Two bedrooms in the "main house," a kitchen, the kids, the horses, the sheep. Linda cooked up a dinner that was to die for, real simple stuff, and what we saw was nothing but straight, straight love between her and Paul'.[1]

All four newcomers were bemused by the peasanty quaintness and frugality of it all. A former Beatle with all his wealth, power and influence chooses to bed down with his wife and young kids in the back of beyond with zero in the way of creature comforts? They couldn't fathom it. Nor could Campbeltown and its environs have differed more dramatically from the incoming musicians' comparatively sophisticated dwellings and agreeable lifestyles on the American East Coast.

Further visits would ensue that summer. It was the Seiwells who would box up their lives and place themselves at the McCartneys' disposal; who would turn and face the strange. The McCrackens made their excuses and about-turned. Hugh had young kids of his own back home, from his earlier marriage. To be around the mini-McCartneys would have made him miss them. But in any case, this sackcloth-and-ashes, shabby hair-shirt subsistence was not for them.

We can but wonder again, as his bewildered visitors did, what it was that drew the young, suburban Merseysider turned international playboy, who had already made more money than he would ever spend, who was jaded by life and the disappointments of success, and had seen most of but barely experienced any of the world, to that remote, demanding wilderness of do-without. Had the first, gasping glimpse of his own personal nowhere all those years earlier sparked something deep within him, which reconnected Paul to the distant past? Maybe the act of stripping-back to bare necessities and the simplest, homeliest existence fixed a broken thread. Was there Mother in them there hills?

Paul's dependence on High Park speaks for all of us in a way. It says much about our need for home, both the physical refuge and the sacred space within us where we can lose ourselves when required. Some therapists call it 'centering'. There is a sense that Paul had reached a state of extreme numbness. That he wasn't able to get in touch with his own feelings until, in those remote hillsides away from everyone else, he was secure enough to let them in.

'As a psychotherapist, I am always interested in what *home* means to people,' says clinical practitioner Richard Hughes. 'Home is one of those archaic concepts that has appeared in stories since man first sat around a campfire. From Homer's epic poem *The Odyssey* to the 2020 musical comedy *Eurovision Song Contest: The Story of Fire Saga*, the hero of the story must go on a journey to discover the meaning of home, and ultimately learn about himself.

'Home can be a "secure base" or a "safe haven". It is also a fundamental "need". The French philosopher Simone Weil, who was forced to leave France during the Second World War, wrote:

"To be rooted is perhaps the most important and least recognised need of the human soul." Another twentieth-century philosopher, Martin Heidegger, explored this theme in his writing too. He concluded that all philosophising was about "homecoming", which he defined as the search for "truth and meaning".'

The hero's journey, explains Hughes, represents the part of them that yearns for excitement and self-discovery:

'In Freudian terms, "Ego",' he says. 'But the ego is fragile. Vanity and hubris are the hero's shadow. Of course, the journey is just as important as the destination. But as we lose ourselves in the journey, we risk losing what is important to us. When I first read *The Odyssey*, I questioned whether Odysseus even wanted to return home. After all, the poem reminds us, "a man who has been through bitter experiences and travelled far, enjoys even his sufferings after a time."'

The Portuguese writer Fernando Pessoa captures this in his posthumous work *The Book of Disquiet*:

'The feelings that hurt the most, the emotions that sting the most, are those that are absurd, the longing for impossible things, precisely because they are impossible; nostalgia for what never was, the desire for what could have been; regret over not being someone else; dissatisfaction with the world's existence. All these half-tones of the soul's consciousness create us in a painful landscape, an eternal sunset of what we are.'

'This feeling,' says Richard Hughes, 'which does not have a direct English translation, can be found in many cultures. In Welsh, the word *Hiraeth* has been likened to homesickness, tinged with a yearning for the land and culture, a longing and nostalgia, for something that no longer exists.'

There it is. Paul and his fellow Beatles had obtained the ticket to ride. They had been on the global magical mystery tour. They had traded their privacy for adoration across the universe. They had *made it* – making music that had spanned and united generations, that had spoken to and enlightened the world. In the process, they had lost their own selves. Of the four, Paul and John were the most acutely aware of the need to get back. To what? Lavish lifestyles and spend-spend-spend turned out not to be the answer. A life partner, a soul mate and the creation of personal dynasties became their new obsession. They provided endless material to write about and to inspire new music. But the fundamental need remained.

They emerged from the Beatles as spent forces, empty husks. They had to fill themselves with themselves again. John's and Yoko's heroin addiction, the miscarriages, the loss of Kyoko, the interminable legal battles and hiccups in their relationship were almost insurmountable distractions. Paul's way forward was more user-friendly. The hero had completed his journey and had come full circle.

No one but Paul could say whether he found his soul in the soil and his heart in the heathery highlands. While many fans lamented that his new music was 'pathetic', 'inferior', that he didn't 'sound like Beatle Paul anymore', he was ecstatic. He had offloaded himself. He had found himself. He was free. The music he conjured going forwards was the truest expression of what made him McCartney. It no longer mattered what anyone thought of it. It was for him.

So far, so not quite a band. They had a former Beatle, admittedly, and they now had a drummer. They boasted a complete novice in the shape of a non-keyboard-playing, non-singing Linda, who couldn't give a rat's ass about being in it but at the same time wouldn't dream of disappointing her husband, nor of being left behind. Still post-Beatles fragile and lacking in confidence, Paul needed her there for psychological support. Of bold, brazen, puppy-eyed Paul, at whom the world had screamed undying love, that was a stretch to believe.

Denny Laine was supposed to be Paul's Lennon substitute. He would jump on a plane before Paul could change his mind. He would join them in the shed that the Maccas had dubbed 'Rude

Studios', keep it low, do their bidding, hang out 'til the herd loped back from the hills and never ask stupid questions about the Beatles. Denny didn't need to. He had been there and known them. To a limited extent, he had seen behind the magic curtain. He knew Paul well enough: bank balances aside, they were kindred spirits.

Say what you like about Laine, and many did, at least he was cool. He knew which side his bread was buttered. He was realistic. He'd been broke on a mattress. Thus did the sleeves-up stereo Denny-ohs join in the reggae dabbling. Having sojourned a few times in the Caribbean, Paul and Linda fetched the holiday vibe home with them and were keen to explore island music further. Perhaps because it was as distant from the Beatles as they could get.

It does seem extraordinary now, the amount of criticism and abuse meted in Linda's direction for what was basically a set-up of her husband's, in which he was the architect, decision-maker and final-sayer. It wasn't her idea. She never pushed for it and could well have done without the aggro of it all. It had only ever been about what Paul wanted, which was the hallmark of their marriage; of many marriages, half a century ago. 'The wise wife places her own needs to one side and always puts her husband first,' was the sort of thing our mothers advised, because those were the ways they knew. It worked for Linda. Her devotion and deference were the secret of their success.

Like Yoko Ono, in certain quarters, the mere mention of Linda's name provoked hostility. She was a pretend musician, a charlatan, a fake. The wicked witch had pulled the wool over her saintly husband's eyes and was hell-bent on leading him down a self-destructive path. Mark our words, she will prove his undoing! Look no further than the *Ram* album, her critics sneered. How dare she insist on her name appearing alongside his, as if she could possibly be equal to him? *Rolling Stone* went so far as to damn *Ram* with a killer kick: 'The nadir in the decomposition of sixties rock thus far.'

The criticism dripped with misogyny. It was the seventies, sure, but why so spitefully predictable? Were the boys really still spitting blood, so personally wounded that their four beloved Beatles had gone their separate ways? Did they really still regard Linda and Yoko as the cause, as well as the impediment to their idols' reformation? Couldn't they concede the possibility that all things Wings-related in which Linda was involved might just be Paul's idea?

'Well, we laid ourselves open to that kind of criticism,' admitted Paul during an interview given by the couple to writer Joan Goodman for the December 1984 edition of *Playboy* magazine. 'But it was out of complete innocence that I got Wings together and naively said, "Come on, Lin, do you want to be in it?" I showed her middle C, told her I'd teach her a few chords and have a few laughs. It was very much in that vein. But then people began to say, "My God! He's got his wife up there onstage . . . he's got to be kidding!" And so forth.

'I think she came to handle it amazingly well. She has fabulous showbiz instincts, and by the time it came to the 1976 tour of the States, she was handling an audience better than any of us. But looking back on it, I can understand the criticism. It was as if we were putting her up there to top the Beatles or something. There was never any thought of that. If we were doing it again, we just might be more thoughtful. But I'm proud of her. I really threw her in the deep end.'

As for Linda, publish and be even more damned. Perhaps the most ill-advised professional remark she ever made appeared in the same feature: 'I think Paul felt very frustrated,' she said. 'He wanted it to work with Wings. We just picked the wrong people. He needed the best to work with, but he had to carry almost all the weight.'

When the interviewer leaned in to jog their memories that some of the former members of Wings had said some frankly rude and unpleasant things in print about the McCartneys, including that Paul was a tyrant to work with, Linda was unfazed.

'It's part of the same problem,' she reasoned. 'Paul is such a good musician, and none of the Wings were good enough to play with him . . . including me, for sure. They were good, not great . . . As for all the other stuff that's been written about the two of us, so much of

117

it is rubbish. Former Wings guitar player Denny Laine wrote two articles. One said I led Paul around totally, the other that Paul totally dominated me. I thought Denny came off badly. I could see some girlfriend or an ex-chauffeur writing such rubbish, but a musician?'

That crisp Scottish summer faded and crumpled into fall. When the McCartney roadshow returned to London, Heather ambled back to school, the fledgling band that didn't yet have a name convened at Abbey Road Studios to lay down tracks for their debut album, and heavily pregnant Mrs McCartney set about preparing to be delivered of her thirdborn.

Not even a Beatle's wealth can make much difference when a birth fails to go according to plan. How they wound up at King's College Hospital, a sprawling, dilapidated NHS facility close to Denmark Hill, south-east London, when their home in the capital was at least an hour's drive north and almost eight miles away, was not explained. It can only have been because that was the nearest health service emergency unit with a bed available. An unplanned Caesarean section now faced Linda. It would certainly have necessitated such a move.

On 13 September, following a frightening, tortuous labour during which Paul feared that he would lose both his wife and their child, the couple's third daughter was born. Gowned up ready to assist but shunted out of blood's way when came the surgical moment, Paul found himself alone in a corridor, terrified, practically on his knees and reaching for God, his mother Mary, anybody else out there, seeking words of wisdom, a sign, whatever you've got up there. In desperation the poor man sobbed, he snotted, he prayed. Alone with his fear, in the depths of despair, he was amazed by a heavenly vision. His mind's eye filled with the soft, feathery spread of an angel's pure white wings. On them, he implored the Almighty, please let our little baby be born. At which, his terror subsided. He felt peaceful.

Did that really happen? Did he imagine it? So what if he did? The name of his new band had come to him. Mother sighed, baby cried. Linda and their newborn, who would all too soon be travelling the world with her sisters, was named after Linda's grandmothers, both of whom were called Stella. Back to High Park and out of harm's way the growing family fled. Mother still healing, father still reeling. Back to work.

Their debut album *Wild Life* seems a softly defiant curiosity now. Whatever it was at the time, it drew a line under something dispensed-with. It shed baggage and cleared the lungs. Between this and the Beatles' final long-player, comparisons could not be drawn. It could have done with the guidance of an experienced, even-handed producer, but Paul insisted on steering it himself. Despite having been recorded at the Beatles' old studio (apart from the tracks laid down earlier during *Ram* sessions in LA), this was markedly different. A first-take hotch-potch virtually devoid of audio effects and trickery, its sound was raw, it rocked, it was blue.

Every track was credited to Paul and Linda with the exception of the cover 'Love Is Strange'. Written by Mississippi bluesman Bo Diddley using the name of his second wife Ethel Smith, and previously recorded by him, Buddy Holly and various others, it had been a 1956/57 hit for US R&B duo Mickey and Sylvia. Its inclusion on *Wild Life* was allegedly accidental. Having jammed up a reggae-infused instrumental, it occurred to the minstrels to try playing that song over their tune for an unexpected blend. It worked.

The title track, lamenting the plight of endangered species, started out with sound intentions but failed to progress. The concluder, 'Dear Friend', was immediately seized upon as an entreaty by Paul to John. If it was that, Paul didn't try hard enough. The song's dirge-like melody and bland, repetitive lyrics convey no need, desire or message. It just sits there, as though waiting to be interpreted, wallowing in its own hidden shallows. Was it no accident that the announcement of Wings as the band name was made on 9 October 1971, Lennon's thirty-first birthday?

It was among the first albums I ever owned. That original copy still sits on my shelf. I play it often. The vinyl disc is still protected by the same old plain yellow paper sleeve. I'm very fond of the bucolic image on its familiar cover. There are the two Dennys and Linda, sitting on a low-lying branch across a pond. Paul stands thigh-deep in the water below them, his shoulders in line with the branch, wearing a swirly shirt and waistcoat and strumming a guitar. Linda's right hand clamps his shoulder. Her long, brown legs dangle, her toes trailing in the wet. Her beautiful pale blue, patterned dress falls open way above her knees. Laine is in clown-like tartan trews. Lanky Seiwell sports rolled-up jeans.

Paul and Linda look like the coolest, most natural and happiest couple in rock. Forget Mick and Bianca Jagger, whose complicated wedding in St Tropez the McCartney family had attended on 12 May, travelling from High Park via Gatwick and back in little over a day; a ceremony at which Paul and Ringo had to be seated separately, as Beatle and Apple lawsuits were ongoing; and when Linda and Bianca were both coyly concealing baby bumps, Stella arriving four months later in September and Jade Jagger that October.

Forget, also, George Harrison and Pattie Boyd. The model wife, humiliated by Harrison's outrageous seduction of Ringo's wife Maureen Starkey, would dump her former Beatle for his best friend Eric Clapton before the decade was out. And forget Rod Stewart and his latest blonde Dee Harrington. Glamorous, glossy, *Vogue*-cover couples all, they outshone and outstyled the Maccas in spades. Who cared? They could all see who was genuinely in love.

Were the McCartneys making a point with Linda's bare-faced, let-it-hang bra-less-ness and Paul's threadbare corduroy slacks with a tartan patch on the bum? Ridiculed throughout the seventies for their don't-care scarecrow appearance, they had eyes only for each other. By the end of the decade, they were the only rock superstar couple still married to each other.

It was a long time, it occurs to me now, before I even noticed the doves on the *Wild Life* album cover. Years more would pass before their significance dawned. Look, a little white dove appears to alight from the forefinger of Seiwell's extended left hand as Laine looks across, amused. Another pauses calmly on the branch beside Laine. A third bird appears to be perched on Paul's left shoulder, and a fourth flutters, blurred, to the left of Linda's face. It went over my head at the time, but the symbolism now seems obvious. Intentional or accidental, it was not spelled out.

In the Bible's Old Testament Book of Genesis, a dove was released by Noah after the Flood to find land. It returned with an olive leaf in its beak, proving that the waters had subsided and that the Earth would survive. In the first book of the New Testament, the Apostle Matthew quotes Jesus: 'See, I am sending you out like sheep into the midst of wolves; so be wise as serpents and innocent as doves.'[2] Could his placement of doves in the image have been an obscure reference to a sense of foreboding that Paul may have felt, ahead of the music industry and former Beatles fans receiving and reacting to his new band and album?

The dove is also said to represent love, peace and freedom. It can be a symbol of the human soul. It is used, most significantly, to represent the Holy Spirit. Its white wings, just like those Paul saw or imagined in his vision, mirror the angel wings upon which he asked for his infant to be borne. And to see such a bird in the wild is believed to herald new beginnings, and even prosperity.

Although that shoot by photographer Barry Lategan[3] took place quite late in the year – on 1 October in the west London country estate Osterley Park – the picture is dappled with sunshine. On that bright, dry day, there are mellow tints of autumn among the green above their heads. The four are wearing light summer clothes. Enjoy happiness, the image appears to urge us, while the going is good.

Wild Life launched Wings in the UK on 15 November 1971, and it would make its appearance three weeks later in America. The band threw their album launch party a week ahead of its British release, on Monday 8 November at London's Empire Ballroom, Leicester Square. It was a traffic-stopper. Paul, Linda and the kids travelled down from Scotland the previous evening on the sleeper train. After depositing their young family with Rose the housekeeper back at Cavendish Avenue, they prepared themselves for their quaintly old-fashioned bash.

It turned out to be Paul's biggest night since Beatlemania. He had written all the children's-party-style invitations himself. He wore an unfinished checked suit for the occasion, with the tailor's white tacking stitches and chalk marks still visible all over it. A green polo neck and black sneakers completed his circus-clown look. From the pictures, he seemed to revel in his ridiculousness. Linda teamed her voluminous, long-sleeved, red patterned maternity frock with thick black tights and white trainers, and spent most of the evening gripping Paul's arm.

Many of their 800-plus guests made infinitely more effort with their attire, including shiny members of the Who, Led Zeppelin, the Faces, Deep Purple, a pink satin-clad Elton John, Gilbert O'Sullivan, Ginger Baker, and Apple songstress Mary Hopkin and her new husband, Bolan/Bowie producer Tony Visconti. Paul's dad Jim was in attendance, as were the two Dennys. The press contingent included Chris Charlesworth and Ray Coleman from the *Melody Maker*, and in the famous-DJ corner lurked Tony Blackburn, John Peel and Johnnie Walker.

Conspicuous by their absence were all the other Beatles, and cherished friends from the old days such as Neil Aspinall and Mal Evans. Paul really was proving a point. 'No more looking back, if you don't mind,' appeared to be his message. 'Because *I'm* bloody not.'

Thanksgiving 1971 was spent with Linda's family in New York. The family then came home for Christmas. Early into the New Year, Paul expanded the Wings line-up on a recommendation from Denny Laine, with Irish guitarist Henry McCullough. The

28-year-old long-locked Ulsterman was a maverick appointment in many ways. Often outspoken, less easy-going and less pliable than the Dennys, he and Paul were always likely to come to blows; especially over Linda's limited ability on keys, and over the general Wings leaning towards pop rather than rock. Laine, too, was desperate for a rockier and more bluesy vibe.

Having sealed his reputation in the industry with Spooky Tooth and Joe Cocker's backing group the Grease Band, with whom he performed at Woodstock in 1969, Henry became an in-demand session musician. He served as lead guitarist on the cast studio recording of Tim Rice's and Andrew Lloyd Webber's 1970 rock opera *Jesus Christ Superstar*.

Why did Paul want him? Because he had a plan in mind to mount a rock-up-and-rock-out tour of British universities. Unannounced, here we are, yes it is me, fancy giving us a gig in your hall? It's only him from the Beatles out there on the quad in the van. Yes, way. For such a caper, he needed a fuller live guitar sound. McCullough's first contribution to Wings, fittingly, was on Paul's post-Bloody Sunday protest song 'Give Ireland Back to the Irish' in February 1972. Banned by the BBC for being overtly political, it would become one of his most popular live numbers during the Wings University Tour.

Over the following year, Henry would strum on a number of further singles, including the risqué 'Hi Hi Hi', also banned by the BBC, this time for erotic content and/or drug references (they couldn't decide which?); and the James Bond theme 'Live and Let Die'. For Paul's second greatest celebration of his love for Linda, the song 'My Love', McCullough challenged Paul's autonomy in the band to create, off his own back, the perfect guitar solo. Completely unprepared and unrehearsed, he improvised it on the spot at Abbey Road in front of an orchestra, in a single take. It became his defining moment, his musical legacy.

'With music,' he remarked in an interview with the pennyblackmusic website in 2011, 'sometimes you come across something and it's a gift from God and it's channelled through you. I swear, I never heard those notes before that way.'

'My Love' was the lead single from the much maligned at the time but nowadays cherished album *Red Rose Speedway*. Henry was to walk out in August 1973, just as the band were about to begin sessions for their next, career-defining album *Band on the Run*. He would proceed to work with Pink Floyd, the Frankie Miller Band, and as a session guitarist with a string of artists including Roy Harper, Marianne Faithfull and Donovan. In 1975 he worked with George Harrison's Dark Horse label, to produce his own solo album *Mind Your Own Business*.

Henry would return to Ireland in 1980, recorded many sessions and worked extensively in Europe for the next thirty years, and in 2012 would suffer the heart attack (a stroke was also rumoured) that left him debilitated for the rest of his life. When he died in 2016, he was seventy-two.

Perhaps none of Wings really believed that Macca would go through with his madcap scheme to take his new band out on the road to play venues previously unannounced. Few knew at the time that this had long been his dream – ever since the dwindling days of the Fabs when he tried desperately to persuade the other three that the answer to all their problems was to get back to what they did best. Which was to perform live before an audience the act that they had perfected over thousands of hours in Hamburg, before they hit the big time.

But as Linda knew better than anybody, once he got a wasp in his cap about some scheme or another, it was pointless trying to change his mind. Her job was to keep him happy. That way, she was happy too. Thus did the band convene at London's Institute of Contemporary Arts for a week at the beginning of February 1972, to rehearse for their roadshow that would take off on the eighth of that month, in rented truck and van, from Cavendish Avenue.

Band, kids, dogs, roadies, all piled in meekly alongside a jumble of provisions, instruments, stage gear and kitbags. They sat back, settled down and perhaps even thought of England.

It seems a preposterous idea now. A classic Macca whimsy. The idea that an artist of his stature could simply sling his young family over one shoulder, hit the road and return to his troubadour roots accompanied by professional musicians who must have expected better, now feels a bit daft. To this day, more than half a century later, people are arguing passionately on internet forums about dates, locations and venues; moaning that the band didn't have enough songs; disputing which haircut Paul had on such and such an occasion; clashing over whether Linda forgot the chords at so-and-so hall, and didn't Paul go over to help her only to find that he had forgotten them too – to the point that some students present assumed their fumblings and mumblings to be part of some comedy dimension to the act.

'Yes, it absolutely happened at the [Leeds] Refectory one cold February in 1972,' states one. 'I was there. 50p. Definitely.' Others remember having paid 40p, but hey.

'It was definitely on a Wednesday,' asserts another. 'I should have been playing football that afternoon, in the Wednesday league. A fellow student (who was on the Ents committee, I think) told me and friends to turn up at the Union Building with 50p. He absolutely would give us no details. It was longer than just a sound check. He may have played 'Ireland' three times even! He said they had run out of tunes. I did not take drugs, so did not imagine any of the above.'

Onwards the roadshow ploughed, playing eleven shows in all between 9 and 23 February. From Nottingham to York to Kingston upon Hull, from Newcastle upon Tyne to Lancaster (on St Valentine's Day) to Leeds, Sheffield, Salford (Greater Manchester) and Birmingham, on to Swansea and wrapping in Oxford. With barely a brass razoo to show for it at the end. But profit had not been the object of the exercise. Not for some.

Well. I think back to the hazy gig-attending days of my own undergraduate years. Notes were not taken. Diaries were not kept. Memories are vague. A lot of the gigs we went to happened up the road at the LSE, because that college had better live music facilities than most. We also frequented the Marquee, the 100 Club and the Lyceum. George Melly and John Chiltern's Feetwarmers, Caravan, Ultravox, T. Rex, Dave Edmunds' Rockpile, Jethro Tull, Argent and the Damned were the kind of bands we saw and rocked out to. I can barely remember any of them. I would have remembered seeing Wings, had they still been gigging around the London unis at that point.

It is true that a number of 'big' British rock bands yet to achieve the epithet were in the habit of performing at universities during the early Wings tour era, including Led Zeppelin and the Who. But it is likely that such outings were tightly scheduled. To turn up out of the blue on the off-chance that an educational establishment might fancy you strumming and humming them a few tunes was not the norm. Still, they did it.

On Paul's first tour for six years, his first live performance since the Beatles' 1966 San Francisco live-touring farewell (not counting the ad hoc rooftop concert at Apple HQ, Savile Row in January 1969) took place at Nottingham University.

Had he intended to keep it that long, Paul Gambaccini asked him the following year.

'Oh, no, no, no,' Paul insisted. 'With the Beatles we did a big American tour, and I think the feeling, mainly from George and John, was, "Oh, this is getting a little bit *uhhh*" . . . but I thought, no, you can't give up live playing, we'd be crazy to. But then we did a concert tour I really hated and I came off stormy and saying, "Bloody hell, I really agree with you now."

'I can't remember [where] exactly. It was raining and we were playing under some sort of big canopy and everybody felt they were going to get electric shocks and stuff. We were driven off in a big truck afterwards, and I remember sitting in the back of the truck saying bloody hell, they're right, this is stupid. So we knew we were going to give up playing, but we didn't want to go and make some big announcement . . . so we just kind of cooled it and didn't go out.

'. . . I remember at the end of the Beatles thinking that it would be good if I just went out with some country and western group,' he told the Professor of Pop. 'To have a sing every day surely must improve my voice a bit. Live shows are a lot of what it's all about. If nothing else, you get out there . . .'[4]

If the students flooded in expecting a slick Beatles experience, they were disappointed. Paul wouldn't go there. There were old teeth-cutting favourites including Elvis Presley and Little Richard numbers, and the smattering of Wings songs the band had under their belt to date. That was the size of it. The other musicians are said to have been deeply resentful of the way they were treated: put up in mouldering guest houses and put down with pennies and pound notes in lieu of proper pay.

Bully for Paul and Linda and their (albeit frozen) millions. Not so bully for session guys with a living to make. It is easy to see why the others found the experience insulting. Here were the McCartneys and their brood as good as playing at being in a band on the road. What fun, Mummy and Daddy getting up to plonk about together while the kids looked after each other backstage. It must have felt like the last straw when Paul composed a variation on the traditional nursery rhyme 'Mary Had a Little Lamb' and put *that* out to confound the censorious BBC.

What on earth was he playing at? Denny Laine, for one, was mortified. Perhaps not so mortified, although he wasn't on a share of the royalties of course, when 'Mary' got to Number 9 in the UK and Number 28 in the US. In his interview with *Sounds* in 1972, Paul revealed that he didn't much care for the song himself, but that his kids (especially Mary) absolutely loved it . . . and that that had been the point.

'The great thing about "Mary" for me . . . was that when we took it on tour, it was the song that got the audience singing along on the "la las",' he said. 'That was fantastic because it saved the number for me. And kids loved it. Pete Townshend's daughter had to have a copy. I'd never realised there was a four-year-old audience. Whilst toymakers have got that one sussed around Christmas, no one outside the business short of the Osmonds and the Jacksons cater for it.' Yet another bulb had gone on.

What was 'clear' to all who were exposed to the McCartneys during that period was the extent to which Paul was warming to Linda's passions and interests, especially when it came to her love of animals and wildlife. They did him an injustice. Circumstances were not nearly so cut and dried. I did not have a hands-on father. Neither did my own kids. Paul was an unusually immersed, devoted dad, which has to have been down to Linda. He adored his children and relished his paternal status.

He was, at a time when it wasn't yet 'fashionable', a man who enjoyed the vicarious thrills of parenthood. Partly because he got to relive aspects of his own childhood in the process. Not that the childhood he had shared with his brother could be compared even remotely to the eccentric, peripatetic existence of the Macca brood. He now had the perfect excuse to indulge both them and himself, while at the same time introducing Linda to some of the treasures of his own infancy.

Rupert the Bear, for one. The star of the world's longest-running children's comic strip in the *Daily Express* newspaper, a kind and thoughtful little soul with his distinctive red jumper and yellow checked trousers and scarf, Rupert had been going for more than twenty years when Paul was born in June 1942. There has been a *Rupert Annual* every Christmas since 1936. He and Mike had grown up on the bear's adventures with his pals, Algy Pug, Bill Badger and Pong Ping.

Paul's company, which would become McCartney Productions Ltd and later MPL, had acquired the rights to Rupert the day after the Beatles broke up. His magical song 'Little Lamb Dragonfly', recorded in 1971 and one that many perceived to be about John, had been intended for a Rupert film. In the end, Paul included it on the second Wings album, *Red Rose Speedway*. Not until 1981, post-Wings, would he get around to writing and producing his animated short, *Rupert and the Frog Song,* which features the voices of late actors Windsor Davies and June Whitfield as well as his own.

Directed by Geoff Dunbar, it was released in November 1984. Ridiculed throughout the rock world, it won a BAFTA for Best Animated Short Film, became the biggest-selling video of 1985 and was nominated at the Grammys. The song from the soundtrack, 'We All Stand Together', made Number Three on the UK chart.[5]

Some expressed offence at what they perceived as arrogance on Macca's part. As in, he thinks he can put out whatever he likes because the public will buy it, however stupid or inappropriate it is. But enough were in his thrall to make whatever he was enthusiastic about worthwhile.

Wings had taken flight. Paul had proved to himself that this line-up had definition, had gelled and could perform live together. Their next venture would be a European tour of low-profile locations. A rehearsal tour of sorts, to tighten the band ahead of proposed excursions to the USA and Japan. For which Paul, possibly still hankering after *Magical Mystery Tour* days and long enchanted by the red London Transport bus used in the Cliff Richard and the Shadows' 1963 romantic comedy film *Summer Holiday,*[6] got hold of a 1953 Bristol double-decker.

Originally green, the vehicle's upper-deck roof had been removed in 1966 and the whole thing had been resprayed cream with a neat green trim. As such, it had served on summer pleasure trips around seaside towns in the east of England. It had subsequently under-gone various colour-scheme updates until it wound up on the books of Halls Coaches in 1972. It operated as part of the Valliant Silverline transport business, from which Paul appears to have leased it. The company was credited in the tour programme, and the bus was returned to them afterwards. It was widely believed for years that Paul had purchased it. He had not.

Its next paint job would be its most elaborate yet. Psychedelic colours soon brightened it on both sides, a summery alpine scheme prevailing. The band's name appeared in a beautiful blue sky above snow-clad mountains, the logo was painted above the windscreen and the full names of the band members were stencilled across the back, in the all-important pecking order: Paul, Linda, Denny L, Henry and Denny S.

The seats in the top deck were ripped out and replaced with mattresses and beanbags. Not that Paul intended for the bus to be their lodgings. They would be booked into quite luxurious hotels *en route* (where room 'extras' cost the musicians more than he was paying them). But it made a fun place for the band and kids to hang out in, and it played along with the *Summer Holiday* vibe. Children's bunk beds, a double bed for Paul and Linda, carpeting, a kitchen and Hi-Fi equipment were also installed.

Nine countries, twenty-five cities and as many gigs throughout July and August ensued. That converted geriatric vehicle, accompanied on its travels by a tour bus for the crew, clocked up around 7,500 miles more than it should have done on its Wings charter. There were times when the wheezing crates looked in danger of not making it as far as the gig that night, and cars had to be despatched to ferry in the entourage. Paul, undeterred, kept on winging it. He was determined to keep the show on the road. A lumbering, over-loaded bus was suddenly the least of his worries.

CHAPTER 9

NARCISSISMA

'Visits to Paul and Jane Asher were . . . a bit uptight, and there were constant little frictions, but that's what happens when couples start to come apart,' recalled Marianne Faithfull in 2007. 'In any case,' added the former actress and singing star, Jagger consort and Beatles contemporary, 'I was in a very different position from the one that Jane found herself in. I'd done what Paul wanted Jane to do, and given up my career. I wasn't going on tour with the Old Vic; I wasn't taking any more movie roles and very few parts in plays. Jane was a serious actress and wanted to continue her career, but Paul had other ideas.

'That's why Linda was so perfect for Paul. She was just what he wanted: an old-fashioned Liverpool wife who was devoted to her husband. Whatever we thought of Linda – and she didn't make that great an impression on me – I think it was a credit to Paul that he didn't marry a model. Because that's what all the others have ended up doing, they've married these models. And they have children who also become models.'[1]

Jerry Hall, a subsequent Jagger partner, often quoted her mother Marjorie's famous formula for keeping a man: '"You must be a maid in the living room, a cook in the kitchen and a whore in the bedroom." I said I'd hire the other two,' retorted Jerry, 'and take care of the bedroom bit.'[2] Was that where she went wrong? Did Mick, like Paul, secretly long for the traditional fifties housewife and mother figure to take over where his mother Eva had left off? Did he too crave a woman who would mother him as well as their children; run his household, organise their lives and assume responsibility for all things domestic?

Marianne, the former sexy, pouty pop chick and heroin addict, expressed disdain for dowdy Linda. Unimpressed by her lack of glamour and style, she sniggered along with many of their acquaintance at her clingy, yes-woman wifeliness.

Linda would not have given a toss. She continued to cut her own hair with her nail scissors, throw on her mismatched garments, go make-up-free, neglect depilation, retain her man regardless and have the last laugh. She was a good deal cleverer than her detractors, to revisit a theme discussed earlier. In 2019, eHarmony conducted a survey concluding that 64 per cent of men are married to women remarkably similar to their own mothers in terms of personality traits.

'With mums as our primary caregivers in life,' said the dating site's relationship expert Rachael Lloyd, 'it's no surprise men are attracted to women who possess similar values . . . This study indicates that much of who we are – and who we choose to love – stems from our earliest life experiences.'

Paul lost his mother in October 1956, when he was fourteen years old. Linda had never met Mary McCartney senior. She could not have known much about her beyond what Paul, his brother Mike, father Jim and the brilliant aunties may have told her. But she had perceived what Paul needed; refashioned herself from zippy New York City photographer and, yes, by definition *groupie* to devoted Earth Mother of her husband and their children.

There are countless images and endless footage of Linda with her head on Paul's shoulder, clinging to his arm, clutching his hand, her hand tucked into his armpit or resting on his forearm, leaning over him from behind or seated as though glued to his side. There is almost invariably physical contact between them whenever they are captured. They are joined at the hip literally as well as figuratively.

In one black and white shot, for example, they are seated side by side, Stella on Linda's lap, Mary sitting next to her mother and Heather standing beside her. Over the head of her yawning youngest, Linda holds a camera to her face with both hands. Paul clasps a package. So their arms and hands are not free to hold each other's, but his left leg and her right leg are clamped together so tightly, you couldn't get a twenty-pence piece between. His thigh is even raised as though to ensure complete contact with hers.

In another, colour picture featured in the Linda McCartney Retrospective exhibition at the Walker Art Gallery Liverpool in 2020, before it went on tour, the couple stand or are seated against an ancient, saltpetre-stained brick wall. Paul, wearing a beige polo neck, is behind his navy-clad wife, his right arm wrapped across her front at throat level and connecting the other side with his left. His two arms encircle and protect her. Bearded Paul stares confidently into the lens.

Linda's head is turned away from the camera and inwards, towards his neck. Her open lips reveal her teeth. The body language is clear: parted, non-smiling lips showing that she is relaxed and completely at ease. 'We are most at home in each other's arms,' it says. We knew that.

Many have wondered: how exactly did Macca go from what Mick Jagger was and has continued to be – a world-class shagger – to faithful and devoted husband? Never for his fiancée Jane Asher did he curb his enthusiasm, but there has not been any evidence to suggest that Paul was unfaithful to Linda. Have we grown so cynical that we can't get our heads around the thought of a one-woman rock star? So it would seem. Because it's a paradox. It is not the norm.

I have had enough conversations with philandering rockers and long-suffering rock wives to know that the vast majority of travelling minstrels do not sit around in their hotel suites watching sub-titled soaps, sketching their bedrooms (as Rolling Stone Charlie Watts and Shadow Brian Bennett did) or playing Solitaire. The majority of wives appear to turn a blind eye and enjoy it for as long as it lasts, expecting to be traded in for a younger model. Their collective attitude being, 'I don't care what he does on the road as long as he comes home to me.'

Linda was no fool. She had been with enough rock stars herself to know their wily ways and means. When she hit the big one, she knew that she must play things differently. Her trump card, we have seen, was her little daughter Heather. She wooed Paul with her maternal instincts and loving tenderness. When he crumbled, post-Beatles, she put him first, nursed him like a child and led him back towards the thing that would reignite him. We have seen that he claimed it was his idea that she should be in his band; his idea to show her chords, teach her how to harmonise and to become part of his line-up. Let's challenge that.

What if it were the other way around? Paul was whimpering under the eiderdown when Linda yanked it off him and insisted that he get his kecks on and get back to it. It is perfectly plausible that she might have volunteered her services on backing vocals, and perhaps even have suggested that she could learn to play keyboards for him. How hard could it be? To include herself in his new line-up would have been the next logical step. That way, as things progressed, she would naturally belong in the studio and on the road with him. Where she could watch Paul with a beady eye and keep him out of harm's way.

Maybe, as has long been speculated, her inspiration was Yoko – who was making her presence felt at Abbey Road before the Beatles had even disintegrated; getting up the nose and under the skin of the other three in the process. Should Linda have been more assert-ive at that stage, and have thrown her own weight around a little more too? Not her style. There was time. She bided it.

It hardly matters who said what when, or who suggested what to whom at any precise moment. It is simply that, having met and worked with Linda, I know first-hand that her devoted-wife pose concealed something more iron-clad. She was no shy wallflower. There was a serene ferocity about her. She was intense, direct, no-nonsense. She focused pointedly on your face, and looked you in the eye when she was talking to you. She was fair and was unswayed by ornament and fakery. Shamelessly a natural woman, but one who would get out her balls when required.

People spoke ill of her all the time. She was rumoured to be unpleasant, unkind and dismissive. She was none of those things to me.

I first met her in 1987, during the eighth month of my first pregnancy, at Great Ormond Street Children's Hospital in London. I was, at that time, a reporter for the *Daily Mail*. I had been sent to cover the opening of a new facility there, following the hospital's highly successful Wishing Well fundraising appeal. Linda was a patron, hence her presence.

I remember standing among a handful of fellow fidgety journalists behind a temporary barrier in the reception area. A flurry of activity erupted as Linda was ushered in. She wore a beautiful blue and green silk summer dress and low-heeled court shoes. She was blonde and luminously beautiful in ways that eluded the camera. Sweeping a glance across at the Fleet Street pack, she saw me. She could hardly have missed my huge bump. She stopped and marched over to the barrier. Lifting the rope, she said, 'Hello, I'm Linda,' grabbed my hand and instructed, 'You're coming with me!'

Her maternal instinct had tuned into my condition. She had read my anxiety. It had not been the best editorial decision, despatching a heavily pregnant hack to meet terminally ill children. Hand in hand we walked the wards. Later we shared a sodden handkerchief.

Linda was not known for her goodwill towards the press. She had suffered the headlines, the cruel put-downs, the unfortunate 'what on earth does he see in her' photographs. The stern protector of her family's privacy, she put her husband and her children first.

I found her very easy to talk to that day, and only later realised why. She didn't make it about her. Her focus was always the other person.

As we made our way around the hospital, she couldn't stop quizzing me about my pregnancy and the impending birth. She talked about people we had in common, suggesting names of some I should meet. She could not have been kinder nor have shown more interest. Journalists grow used to and tend to be cynical about that tactic: the full-on ardent attention of a celebrity during an interview, when they come on like your long-lost best friend, fake an affiliation in the moment and, with their eye on a sympathetic write-up, promise faithfully to keep in touch. They rarely do.

Linda did, astonishingly. Post-birth, I was invited several times to conduct interviews with her, both at their Sussex home and at the MPL offices. She always seemed pleased to see me, and we would sit and have a good laugh. She never forgot to include me on guest lists for openings and launches, at which she would welcome me personally. When her first vegetarian cookbook was published in hardback in 1989, she sent me a copy by post. She had inscribed it, 'To Lesley-Ann and lovely Mia, stay veggie! Love, Linda.' The dots of all her 'i's were drawn as hearts.

I bumped into her unexpectedly in Los Angeles that November, during my extended stay with the late film star Raquel Welch, who put me up at her home when I arrived in Los Angeles to work as a West Coast correspondent. We had been introduced by a close mutual friend. Paul and Linda were in the middle of the McCartney World Tour. They had been in Spain, France and the Netherlands earlier that month, and would finish the year with four gigs at New York's Madison Square Garden. The tour would end in Chicago in July the following year.

Paul and Linda were staying with their family at the luxurious Four Seasons Hotel. At forty-seven, this was Paul's first-ever tour under his own name: 103 gigs in thirteen countries to more than a million fans, including one performed to what at the time was the biggest stadium audience in the history of rock'n'roll

– 184,000 people at the Maracanã Stadium in Rio de Janeiro on 20 April 1990.

It was his first *world* tour since the Wings Over the World outing of 1976; his first tour of any kind since the Wings UK tour of 1979; his first since John was murdered in New York in December 1980, nine years earlier, and his first concerts in America for thirteen years. It was also the first in which Paul, at last, acknowledged his Beatles history. As well as the dozen Beatles hits performed throughout the show, his entire encore was made up of Fabs numbers. Jaded old Hollywood is rarely impressed by anything, but the whole town seemed a-buzz at this. And yes, Linda was still a firm fixture in his band: on backing vocals, keys and percussion.

She and I almost fell over each other in the hotel lobby, where I had arranged to pick up my tickets to their 23 November gig at the CA Los Angeles Forum from Geoff Baker. An old Fleet Street rival from his days on the *Daily Star* while I was on the *Daily Mail*, Geoff was working for Paul at that point, as his tour publicist. He would proceed to become McCartney's right-hand man for nearly thirty years, until they suffered a terminal falling-out.

Linda, then forty-eight, was looking girlish. She was dressed in shabby cut-offs and a stained white tee shirt. Her brown calves were unshaven. Her face was devoid of make-up, and her hair was all over the place. She smacked a big kiss on my cheek and said, 'How's Mia?! Why didn't you bring her! What are you doing for the rest of the day? Why don't you go up to the pool here and just hang out? Spend the day, order whatever you like, charge it to Paul – here, this is the room number, we won't tell him! Just put whatever you like down to him.' She sniggered conspiratorially at the mischief.

I phoned a friend to come and share the day on the pool terrace of one of the best hotels in Hollywood. We ordered champagne and all-day lunch on Paul McCartney's room, and called chums back in London on the pre-mobile plug-in, rotary-dial phone brought for my personal use by the pool attendant, whispering, 'Guess where I am . . .'

People never expect to hear than Linda had a playful side. She told me candidly that she set her cap at Paul the first time they saw each other in London's Bag O'Nails. 'I knew I wanted a rocker,' she said. 'That was my world. Those were my people. More than anything, I wanted a Beatle. *That* Beatle. So I let him chase me and chase me until I caught him. It took a while, but I knew it would happen.'

She admitted that she ruled the McCartney roost; that in their marriage, she was the stronger of the two, that Paul was often in awe of her, and that she never, ever held back when she felt that he could do with a telling-off.

In 1991, I trained it north to interview her at rehearsals for Paul's debut classical work, *Liverpool Oratorio*. When I joined her 'backstage' at the venue, Liverpool Cathedral, she was with her close friend and collaborator, the writer and animal welfare activist Carla Lane. Carla's mother Ivy, Paul's brother Mike and the photographer Terry O'Neill were also there. Linda held court, reminiscing about the Beatles' break-up twenty-one years earlier. On a whim, I stuck my neck out and asked her about the near-nervous breakdown that Paul was supposed to have suffered at that time.

'It's true, it happened,' she nodded. 'I calmed him down after all the Beatles madness, and I think I must have been the only one who could have done that. He used to thank me all the time for "putting the sense" back into his life. He still does. All we really want now is to grow old together and be there for one another. We talk about it all the time. We look forward to it, actually. We'll stay in bed all day, eat dinner and make love. Yes, even as old people.'

She knew, she said, that it was her who gave Paul confidence and repaired his self-esteem. She didn't demand credit for it. She didn't need to. It was just the way it was. She said she couldn't imagine her husband with any other woman if, God forbid, anything happened to her. She was matter-of-fact about it. She wasn't saying that Paul shouldn't marry again; simply that she couldn't imagine him doing so. Little did she know that summer that she would be diagnosed with breast cancer four years later. Nor that she had only seven years left to live.

Linda mulled over those long-ago days when she got Paul to 'quit famous-ing so much' and live a simple home life; when she got him 'back to basics'; reminded him of the importance of respecting family traditions such as birthdays, anniversaries and Christmas, and to live by proper values. She had even taught him to bake, she confided. There was 'always' a birthday cake around. Especially during the summer months, she meant, when they celebrated Paul's birthday in June, Mary's in August, and Stella's, James's and her own each September. Heather's always doubled as a Hogmanay knees-up, given that it fell on New Year's Eve.

Paul was especially adept at baking bread, she revealed . . . echoing John Lennon's own new kitchen skill acquired during the mid-seventies, after Sean was born. And yet, Linda had to concede, Paul almost always got his way about 'the big stuff'.

A couple of years down the line, she and I were chatting in a back office at their MPL HQ on Soho Square, and melting Hobnob biscuits into our mugs of lapsang souchong tea. She revisited her pre-Paul years as a single parent, and remembered being spat at and called dirty names by his heartbroken fans on the steps of Marylebone Register Office on her March 1969 wedding day. A few of the bolder bitches later broke into the Cavendish Avenue house and stole her photographs. She hadn't let it rile her, she said.

'I got used to all the slagging off years ago,' she shrugged. 'It doesn't bother me in the slightest. If they're crucifying me, they're leaving someone else alone, right? What's new? You become immune to it, you know? In the early days, I was so blindly in love with Paul that I missed most of it anyway. Or else I just shrugged it off. I've always rubbed people up the wrong way. Even teachers in school used to get on my case. I assumed it was my face. I've always had this long, stern look.' She didn't, particularly.

When we lunched at London's Hard Rock Café, I was struck by the fact that she couldn't have looked less like a rock wife had she tried. Apart from her trim figure and luminous skin, there were no clues. No Spandex pants, peroxide locks or Empire State heels. The 'plain' preppy girl who had married the world's most eligible bachelor was still homely and low-key, even in a rock-centric setting. She didn't try because she didn't have to.

When I visited her at home in Sussex, she greeted me in a huge, chunky-knit sweater yanked on over a tired cotton frock. She'd had it for donkey's years, she said. She liked to hang onto her clothes. Paul, she laughed, was a far worse hoarder than she was. He still had 'practically every garment he's ever worn, including his *Sgt. Pepper* outfit.' When she went out, she usually wore frayed old waistcoats and ancient denim. She often sported a pair of leather cowboy boots, apparently compromising her no-cruelty-to-animals principles, but assured me that they were 'at least a hundred years old, and at least second-hand.'

She had never feared that Paul would leave her for another woman, she said, when I asked her. Since she so rarely let him out of her sight, this was no kind of challenge to believe. No other female had ever come between them. Many must have tried. I am thinking of one in particular who had decided McCartney was the man for her. She was not the only one. But this one got close. Too close. Linda could do little to prevent her from entering their lives. On her guard from day one, Linda had the measure of this particular rock chick. She had been her. She knew what was coming.

On 9 July 1972, the first night of the seven-week Wings European tour, Linda experienced a complete meltdown. It was assumed that she had suffered what was either a bad panic attack or a case of sheer stage fright. She quivered backstage before the band went on at the Théâtre Antique Châteauvallon, a canopied countryside amphitheatre near Toulon, on France's Côte d'Azur. She was so afraid that she was shaking and sobbing uncontrollably. But the two thousand or so enthusiastic fans, tourists and locals present had not rocked up to poke fun at a weeping wife. They were there for 'le Beatle'.

Anyway, she had the best in the business to reassure her. Unbeknown to most, because he kept his Achilles heel under wraps in those days, Paul had suffered extreme stage fright since his earliest days with the Fabs. He knew exactly what she was going through, and took time to reassure her and talk her out of it.

Forty-four years later in 2016, during an online conversation with a Russian fan via his website, he said, 'I remember nearly giving it all up when we were doing a concert in Wembley – which was a Poll-Winners concert – in the really early days of the Beatles. And I remember feeling physically sick with a knot in my stomach, thinking, I should give this up, this is just too painful, what am I doing? I got over it.' With the patience and support of her husband, Linda did too.

On with the show. The British press pack managing to miss the first half as they couldn't find the venue. Robin Denselow was one of them. 'It was a surprising event simply because it was small-scale and peaceful,' he wrote in his *Guardian* newspaper review. 'The sound mix was rough and the films projected behind the stage (of High Park, random animals in the wild and scenes of human urban madness) were amateur and irrelevant . . . Wings make a ridiculous comparison with the Beatles. But at least McCartney was back playing – and it *was* their first concert.'

The road show shifted ninety miles east, for their next gig in the fragrant jet-set enclave of Juan-les-Pins. Where the beautiful people wafted in colourful kaftans, smoking themselves into other dimensions on exotic substances. And where an American beauty with a long-held dream spied a golden opportunity and seized her chance. Remind you of anyone?

This one called herself 'Jo Jo'. A lusciously endowed nineteen-year-old model, who claimed to have graced the catwalks of Parisian A-list couturiers, she said that she was in the South of France on holiday. Right place, right time, boop-boop-a-doop. There being no such thing as coincidence. It could be no accident that her child-hood pop idol had landed in town and was about to give a perform-ance there. She had been writing to her favourite Beatle for years, signing herself 'Jo Jo' in homage to a favourite Beatles song, 'Get Back'. Now here was her god, within arm's reach. She would do anything to get him.

It seems obvious now that Jo Jo played the long game. Worming her way into the after-show, focusing her attention on a humble roadie whom she would remember later only as 'Mick', spending the night in bed with him and getting herself onto the Wings tour via the roadies' bus; and ultimately moving in on an unattached musician who would be her conduit to the inner circle. That unsus-pecting minstrel was Denny Laine.

Dark auburn-locked, big-faced Jo, with her sexy, flaring nostrils and Mahjong-tile teeth, had been born Joanne Alice LaPatrie (sometimes Patrie) in Boston, Massachusetts on 13 July 1953. As one of ten children, she had always been an attention-seeker. At sixteen, she claimed, she yielded her virginity to Jimi Hendrix at the Woodstock Festival in August 1969. 'Those were wild times,' she would recall. 'Everyone was tripping. I was introduced to him in his dressing room and then he shooed everyone out and locked the door and we started kissing. He started singing "Foxy Lady" and then we made love.'

She sidestepped to LA in 1970, when she was seventeen. Her stunning looks and figure opened doors. Immersing herself in the West Coast haze of sex, drugs and rock'n'roll, she worked as a cover girl, a fashion model and in TV commercials. The Doors' frontman Jim Morrison fell for her charms, as did Rod Stewart, whom she said that she saw casually but regularly for around two years. It was rumoured that the parrot-plumed rocker penned his hit 'You Wear It Well' for her. Bet he said that to all the girls. He wrote an affec-tionate tribute for her unpublished memoir, as did Cream and Blind Faith drummer Ginger Baker. And she made up her mind that she was going to marry Paul McCartney.

You see what Linda was up against. The two Americans could not have differed more. To look at, the sloppy, braless 31-year-old mother of three was outdone to kingdom come by this upstart glamazon. Linda was fearful of the havoc this woman could wreak. Especially now that she had her claws into Denny. Laine was deeply offended when the McCartneys dared to express their misgivings about his chosen love. Their objections must have deepened his ardour, for he was not in the mood to let go.

All of which was precisely what Jo Jo wanted. Softly, softly, catchee monkey. The ruffled Mrs Mac was now in danger of falling victim to a self-fulfilling prophecy. The thing that she feared could influence her behaviour to the extent that it could increase Jo Jo's chances. Complain enough to Paul about Denny's squeeze and she might put ideas into his head. But this she knew, which was something. How Denny must have swaggered about the camp with his raving, pneumatic beauty. What he lacked in terms of fortune and fame, he made up for with his looks and his musical talent.

Ya think? McCartney: seventy-one Beatles songs as main composer and about five hundred more beyond the Fabs. Twenty-two British Number Ones including his collaborations with Linda, Wings, Michael Jackson, Stevie Wonder, his own Frog Chorus, and with Rihanna and Kanye West. Laine: known for the Moody Blues' cover of 'Go Now', for having written 'Say You Don't Mind', his own recording of which failed to chart but a cover by former Zombie Colin Blunstone went Top Twenty in 1972; and for his co-writing credit on the Wings Number One 'Mull of Kintyre'. Compare, contrast.

Things might have got snippy had Macca been on a longer leash. Which is not to disrespect the marriage. Immensely attractive and clearly a virile guy, who among us would have been surprised had he fallen for the sizzler under his nose? Rock stars do. The fact that he didn't scoff it when it was sitting there on the plate makes him all the more remarkable. He didn't stray because of the kids? Yadda. That has never in rock history been a deterrent. A rocker gets his way. You only have to look at Laine himself, who would leave five offspring by four different women to fend for themselves.

Later that month, Wings played the fabled L'Olympia, the original music hall in Paris, where the Beatles had spent three weeks in residence eight years earlier. They proceeded to Munich and Frankfurt, Zurich and Montreux (where the reviews were belittling), after which they took a short break and the McCartney clan withdrew to the States. On 1 August they reconvened in Copenhagen; moved through Finland, Sweden, Norway and back into Sweden, circled back to Denmark, then onwards to West Germany, the Netherlands and Belgium, and wrapped back in West Germany on the 24th, at the vast, sinister 25,000-capacity Deutschlandehalle in Berlin, the venue once used by Adolf Hitler for his youth rallies.

How tempted might Paul have been to journey the extra 180 miles north-west to Hamburg, to check out his old Beatles haunts? At that stage, while he was doing everything in his power to distance himself from the past? Not very.

'Everybody was expecting great things with it being the last night, but it just didn't come off,' guitarist Henry McCullough told *Sounds* that October. 'But last gigs aren't always that good anyway. I was talking to some people and they said that when Joe Cocker played the same hall, half the people got up and left. It's a bloody weird gig.'[3]

Robin Denselow had been present at the opener. Back he came for the tour's farewell, and was relieved to find that Wings had got their act together.

'Seven weeks on the road and Paul McCartney's new band . . . is dramatically improved since the first performance,' he wrote in the *Guardian*. 'Trailing across Europe and playing every night has transformed the band from weak apology to an excellent vehicle for McCartney's, at last, revived talent.'

Alas, he didn't go a bundle on the lovely Linda, whose singing was 'still substandard with a tendency to go flat as soon as she moved away from the piano.' Ah, love.

She knew herself that the criticism was fair. But she was defiant. As long as Paul wanted her up there under the spotlight beside him, over her own dead body would she refuse. 'In any case,' as she said to me, 'who cares if I'm out of tune? I *like* out of tune!'

Always the last to know. Hapless Denny Laine would find out only years later that Jo Jo had used him to try to get to Paul. He had known nothing of her fervent love letters to her idol over the years, nor of her cunning master plan. Humiliated in hindsight, he was at least happy at the time. He and Jo Jo stuck together, had two children and eventually got married – on a boat in Massachusetts in 1978. None of which changed Linda's opinion or brought down her guard. Most tellingly, she banned Jo Jo from appearing in the video for the 'Mull of Kintyre' single, perhaps fearing that, in her own pregnant state (she would soon be delivered of baby James) she would be outshone.

Life never quite worked out for Jo Jo. During the early 2000s, I got to know her musician daughter from her marriage to Denny, Heidi Jo Hines. Heidi's a lovely, talented girl with the same big, oval face, generous mouth and glossy locks as her mother. With her effective rock voice, she should have had a bigger career and greater opportunities. The same could be said of both parents, and for that matter her musician brother Laine Hines too. One would almost suspect, if one didn't know better, that falling short of the mark was in their DNA.

As for Jo Jo. 'She told me that the moment she met my dad, after a Wings concert, she knew they were soulmates,' said Heidi. Her mother was clearly economical with the truth when it came to the route that she had stalked.

'She fell in love with [Denny], even though he was just a waged member of the band with little money,' Heidi told *Mail on Sunday* feature writer Angella Johnson in November 2006. 'My brother Laine was born within a year of them getting together [in 1973] and I followed eleven months later [in 1974]. They were the happiest times. My earliest memories are of my eldest brother and I being surrounded by love and laughter. Even when finances were tight, she would find enough to see that we never wanted for anything. To the rest of the world she might have been the ultimate rock chick, but to us she was just the best mum. She was always there for us. No matter what was happening in her life, we always came first. We were very close.'

The family lived together on a houseboat before Denny's ship came in. 'Mum was always in the kitchen cooking,' said Heidi. 'She liked us to sit down to meals together, even if Dad was away on tour. It was a fun house and she was always smiling. She used to dress us up in colourful, fancy-dress costumes and we would role-play.'

Instead of conserving his wealth and setting up his family for the future after 'Mull of Kintyre' became a huge and lucrative hit, Denny splashed out on a lavish Grade II listed detached house in Laleham near Spelthorne, Surrey, known as Yew Corner, which was said to have inspired A.A. Milne to write his Winnie-the-Pooh stories.[4] The house became Excess All Areas Central. The couple were known, for the rest of the decade, as wild boozing and drug-taking party animals.

The money, of course, trickled away. Jo Jo and the kids moved into a flat, then back to America. They returned eventually to London, to live in the same shabby, two-bedroom St John's Wood apartment a stone's throw from the Maccas' home on Cavendish Avenue. I went there with Heidi, her dad and a gaggle of mates in the 2000s. Denny fathered other children – Lucianne with Helen Grant, daughter of Led Zeppelin manager Peter Grant; Damian James with model Catherine James, and Ainsley Laine-Adams with Gilly Adams – but was never much of a father. He headed into the sunset in the mid-nineties.

In 1978, the year that Wings recorded their sixth studio album *London Town* at Abbey Road and on a yacht in the Virgin Islands, by which point the band had gone through several line-up changes and was back to the core trio of Paul, Linda and Denny, family tragedy struck. Jo Jo's drug-addicted, schizophrenic brother Thaddeus fell out terminally with their father and shot him in their Florida home. Dad survived, but was paralysed for the rest of his life.

Under the strain, the Laine marriage crumbled. Denny began an affair with his wife's best friend. Jo Jo succumbed to alcohol and antidepressants and divorced him in 1980, the same year that her father finally died from his injuries. It was a doomed year from beginning to end. The year that began with Paul's arrest and imprisonment in Japan, and ended with the murder of John Lennon. The release of a Denny Laine album seemed superfluous to requirements among such upheaval. It remains notable not only for its McCartney contributions, but for Jo Jo's haunting lead vocals on the prophetically entitled 'Same Mistakes'.

Because the lady had always longed to be a singing star. Another move to try and out-do Linda, or a genuine lifelong yearning as yet unfulfilled? She must have had something. Sting and Andy Summers of Police would not have recorded with her otherwise. Which they did, for a single released under her name on Pye Records entitled 'Hulk', with the B-side 'Dancing Man'. She also tried launching a raunchy girl group, Jo Jo Laine & The Firm. Mercury Records released their single 'When the Girl's Happy (the Boy's Happy Too)'. Labels don't spend money releasing music without potential. So Jo Jo must have had something.

She continued to hang with musicians. Led Zeppelin, duh. That band's Jimmy Page. Aerosmith's Steven Tyler had the hots for her. By 1986 she was managing a group called the Mannish Boys and singing with a band from Boston called Gear.[5]

Her rebound love after Denny was Black Sabbath's tall, handsome 25-year-old guitarist Randy Rhoads. But in March 1982, only six months after they had met, Randy went down in a plane in Florida and Jo Jo fell apart. She rebounded again, with heavy-drinking partner Jimmy Miller, between 1986 and 1988.

147

Her torrid extra-marital affair with the celebrated producer, famous for the Stones' albums *Beggars Banquet, Let It Bleed, Sticky Fingers, Exile on Main Street* and *Goats Head Soup*, was clearly a move to get him to make her a star. He did record her, notably on a remake of the Herman's Hermits hit 'I'm into Something Good', which they restyled for Jo Jo as 'I'm in for Something Good!' Fame and fortune remained beyond her reach. The married man declined to leave his wife. Nothing to see here.[6]

Rarely sober, Jo Jo continued to make ill-advised life choices that impacted on her children. She became involved in a brief, violent relationship with builder Peter O'Donohue that led to the conception of a third child, Boston, born in 1984. Donohue was tried at the Old Bailey and sent down for eleven years in 1988 for his involvement in a £40m armed raid on a Knightsbridge safety deposit centre.

Desperate for money, Jo Jo sold her story to the *Sunday People*, kissed and told on reluctant benefactors the McCartneys and betrayed them to the world. However shaky their relationship had been over the years, the couple had always been good to her. They had, asserted Heidi, treated Jo Jo's children kindly. They had welcomed them to their Cavendish Avenue home and up to High Park Farm. Heidi and Laine remained firm friends with Mary and Stella.

Jo Jo met the infamous Alexander Thynn, seventh Marquess of Bath in 1991, at an art exhibition. In a blink he enticed her to become one of his harem, known as his 'wifelets'. She lived happily with her children at Longleat for several years in a small estate cottage, servicing her master as and when required. That move, and the consequent financial relief, empowered her. Back in the photographic studio, she posed naked and writhing on a tiger skin for men's soft porn rag *Playboy,* in the presence of Conservative MP Sir Antony Buck and his notorious then wife Bienvenida.

The thing with Thynn didn't last. She was back in London and skint again within five years, only to receive, in 2003, a diagnosis of

20 Forthlin Road, Liverpool: Paul's childhood home, where he and John Lennon wrote around thirty of the world's most famous songs.

The first known photograph of Paul and John performing together as the Quarry Men (also Quarrymen) in 1957. Most sources agree on 23 November at New Clubmoor Hall, Liverpool. L–R: Colin Hanton, Paul, Len Garry on tea-chest bass, John, and Eric Griffiths on guitar.

ginal programme
the Woolton
where John
Paul first met.

STALLS   SIDESHOWS   ICE CREAM   LEMONADE

Teas and Refreshments in large Marquee situated behind the hut.

2.00 p.m. PROCESSION leaves Church Road, via Allerton Road, Kings Drive, Hunt's Cross Avenue; returning to the Church Field. Led by the Band of the Cheshire Yeomanry. Street Collection by the Youth Club during the procession.

3.00 p.m. CROWNING OF THE ROSE QUEEN (Miss Sally Wright) by Mrs. THELWALL JONES.

3.30 p.m. FANCY DRESS PARADE.
Class 1. Under 7 years.
Class 2. 7 to 12 years.
Class 3. Over 12 years.
Entrants to report to Miss P. Fuller at the Church Hall before the procession.

3-30 p.m. MUSICAL SELECTIONS by the Band of the to Cheshire (Earl of Chester) Yeomanry. Band-5-00 p.m. master: H. Abraham. (By permission of Lt.-Col. G. C. V. Churton, M.C., M.B.E.).

4-15 p.m. THE QUARRY MEN SKIFFLE GROUP.

5-15 p.m. DISPLAY by the City of Liverpool Police D By kind permission of the Chief Constable Watch Committee.

5-45 p.m. THE QUARRY MEN SKIFFLE GROUP

8-0 p.m. GRAND DANCE in the CHURCH HALL
GEORGE EDWARDS BAND also The Quarry Men Skiffle Group
TICKETS 2/-

GARDEN FETE
ST. PETER'S CHURCH FIELD

WOOLTON PARISH CHURCH   Rector: M. Pryce Jones.

Saturday, 6th July, 1957
at 3 p.m.

ADMISSION BY PROGRAMME
CHILDREN 3d.

PROCEEDS IN AID OF CHURCH FUNDS

Otherwise engaged . . . Paul and his first fiancée, actress Jane Asher.

Linda Eastman kneels at McCartney's feet on 19 May 1967 at Brian Epstein's London home during the launch of *Sgt Pepper's Lonely Hearts Club Band.* Three months later, Epstein is found dead there from accidental overdose.

Paul marries Linda at Marylebone register office, London, on 12 March 1969.

The Beatles give their final public performance on top of the Apple HQ building in London, 30 January 1969. The microphones wore ladies' stockings to protect them from the winter blast. Ringo sported his then wife Maureen's rain mac, while John wore Yoko's fur coat.

Main Street, Campbeltown during the 1960s, as it looked when Paul acquired his estate.

Westport Beach, Kintyre, where the McCartneys ran their dogs.

Paul, Linda, Stella, Mary and Heather, September 1974.

The author at the Standing Stone in Paul's High Park Farm backyard.

Campbeltown Sheriff Court where Paul was tried for growing cannabis plants on his farm. He pleaded guilty and escaped with a £100 fine.

High Park farmhouse on Paul's estate on the Kintyre peninsula.

Little house on the prairie: the tiny cottage, with no mod cons, a lengthy trek from Paul's main farmhouse. Denny Laine and Jo Jo lived there while Wings recorded in Scotland.

Linda, Paul and Old
English Sheepdog Martha
at High Park Farm.

Double-decker . . . In 1972, it traversed 9 countries, visited 25 cities and
clocked up 7,500 miles to earn the title 'Most Famous Bus in the World.'

Wings and the Campbeltown Pipe Band in Lower Ranachan Studio on Paul's estate, after the recording of 'Mull of Kintyre'.

Pipers, drummers and Wings at Saddell Bay on the east side of the Kintyre peninsula, October 1977, filming the video for 'Mull of Kintyre'.

Hot-water bottles at the height of summer . . . The Argyll Hotel, Campbeltown, where the McCartneys billeted their guests.

Piper Ian McKerral, who played on 'Mull of Kintyre' and performed in the video, demonstrating how it's done.

Linda takes tea with 16-year-old piper John Brown.

The Laines: Jo Jo, Denny, Heidi and Laine.

Andy Peebles with Paul after one of their 1980 interviews for BBC Radio 1.

Paul and his dad, Jim, speaking to the press outside his home in December 1967.

John and May Pang at the opening night of *Sgt Pepper's Lonely Hearts Club Band on the Road* at New York's Beacon Theater, 17 November 1974.

e Aid, Wembley Stadium, 13 July 1985: George Michael, promoter Harvey Goldsmith, U2's Bono, Paul and Freddie Mercury.

Bronze statue of Lady Linda McCartney in her Campbeltown memorial garden.

The paperback writer and the writer of 'Paperback Writer': the author with Paul at the LIPA graduation, Liverpool, 26 July 2019.

Paul addresses his graduates at the Liverpool Institute of Performing Arts, Liverpool, 2019.

Paul headlines the Pyramid Stage at Glastonbury, 25 June 2022. I Fighters frontman Dave Grohl and Bruce Springsteen return to the st together for the finale of the three-hour set, during which they deliver classic closer 'The End' from the Beatles' 1969 album *Abbey Ro*

liver cancer. Determined to live her life to the full until the bitter end, she rocked up one night at a book launch in the Cabinet War Rooms, and engaged in a sex act with transexual performer Sasha de Suinn in front of the outraged assembled guests. Unembarrassed by her conduct, she made no excuses and left, quipping on the way out, 'I can't believe he was a she.'

Jo Jo's final fall from grace was literal. When she was only fifty-three but looked much older on account of her reckless lifestyle, she was invited by the house's new owners to stay at her beloved Yew Corner. She took a tumble down the stairs, and died in St George's Hospital Tooting, south London, on 29 October 2006. Like Eleanor Rigby she had lived in a dream, and was buried along with her name.

CHAPTER 10

METAMORPHOSIS

The music papers and the national press were not the only ones baffled by McCartney's new venture. Music industry executives were scratching their heads, not least the movers and shakers at EMI. The parent record company of the Beatles, whose division Parlophone had made them stars, was still distributing Apple product. Contractual obligations meant that Wings continued to release their albums on that label and the individual Beatles remained under contract to EMI for solo work as well as group output until 1976. Paul's new records would be released by Parlophone in the UK and on the Capitol label in America until 1978.[1]

David Ambrose was one of the few EMI chiefs who 'got' Wings. The musician and trained fine artist who had served as Fleetwood Mac's original bassist, played with Jeff Beck, Ray Davies, Rod Stewart, Cat Stevens and more, who made stars of the Sex Pistols, Duran Duran and the Pet Shop Boys and who became Director of A&R (Artists and Repertoire) at EMI, was to all intents and purposes (despite the fact that the former Beatle's relationship with the company preceded his own) responsible for McCartney.

'Being the icon that he is, he was treated there with great reverence,' remembers Ambrose. 'He wielded so much power and influence that whatever he wanted, he got. If you decided to remove the cobwebs from the EMI studios at Abbey Road and McCartney said you couldn't, those cobwebs would remain in place forever.

Why shouldn't he have whatever he wanted, given the vast amounts of money he was generating for the company? We were all living off Beatles and Macca royalties. EMI made so much dosh out of them, it was ridiculous. Our expense accounts were beyond imagining. We owed him.

'He could be unbelievably arrogant at times, but you just had to put up with that. He was above criticism. You could never say, "That bridge section in such-and-such a song is a pile of crap." You couldn't tell him, as I did, that his "Frog Chorus" was rubbish. I got hauled up before the board for that one. "*Ambrose!* What on earth are you doing telling Paul McCartney how to write songs?!" That was a big, personal message to me directly from McCartney himself. It translated as, "Right, go fuck yourself."

'That aside, I admired him enormously. I was very impressed by him. Not only because I had expected him to emerge as the best solo artist of all the Beatles. Which he did, despite the fact that he wasn't the best musician in the Beatles. George Harrison was. George could play a diminished chord, but he couldn't sing. Paul and John were basically art school students [John attended art school, Paul didn't], who weren't that interested in the nuances of music-making. George was the nerd, the scientist, the techno-man. He did know his stuff. But he sang like a goat. Nothing unusual there. There were a lot of stars from that era who lacked a singing voice. They got away with it because those times were more about look and attitude.

'What I really applauded him for,' reflects Ambrose, 'was his personal life. He did an incredibly wise thing. He married Linda. She was a lovely lady and a true inspiration. I remember being in Hyde Park for something or other with Mick Jagger and Jerry Hall, and Mick asked me for my advice. I told him straight: if you want to keep your marriage together, take her on tour, man. Look at McCartney, touring the world with his wife and family. People think he's nuts, but it's the only way to do it. Hotel rooms, loneliness, groupies, booze, drugs, it's all so horrible and destructive.

'Paul sussed that. He knew, he'd lived it. He didn't want to live like an alley cat forever, he wanted to settle down. So he made Linda and the kids part of it. He was ridiculed for it, but he didn't care. He was right. He saved himself by getting the right woman, making a little family and keeping his loved ones close to him. All those people who tried to slaughter him for having Linda in the band were missing the point. She wasn't there to be a musician. That was more a pose, a by-product. She was there because he needed her to be.

'He couldn't have done it without her. He would have gone off the rails, the sad ex-Beatle who'd had it all, whose number was up and who lost it all spectacularly. He progressed to his extraordinary solo career that has carried him into his eighties thanks to Linda. She was the life-saver, the stepping-stone. She deserved her place in the spotlight.'

Ambrose had been a massive fan of the Beatles during the 1960s. 'I learned all their songs on the bass. I was trying to emulate Paul. I have huge admiration for his bass-playing, it's very melodic and creative. Bass lines today are much simpler, more riff-orientated. Songs in general are much more straight-forward than they were. Paul's origins were in trad, in jazz, and were infinitely more complex. He was drawing from the 1940s, the music his dad had listened to and played, and from all his singing, dancing, knees-up aunties on New Year's Eve. We should never underestimate the family influence. The music we grew up listening to is key. He has a fantastic imagination, too. He brought all of that to play. I couldn't help but hero-worship him. He was everything I wanted to be.'

David also admired Paul for having brought Denny Laine into his new line-up. 'I knew Denny pretty well,' he says, 'and thought he was a wonderful human being. He came to see me at EMI. I should have signed him, but I couldn't find the right record. He was a big talent and I would have made him a star. I regret that.'

But McCartney, he agrees, was in a different league:

153

'He was and is a monumental talent. Great bassist. Considerable pianist. The *Let It Be* film was clearly the beginning of the end, you can really see how it all unfolded and played out. It is very apparent that Paul had become the dominant force. John was a casual, cheery bloke at that point, before things got complicated. I always thought the A&R guy didn't get enough credit. George Martin, I mean. People tend to think that he was this all-powerful individual calling all the shots, but in reality he had no say whatsoever. You bend over backwards to get great records out of your artists and you get nothing in the end. I sympathised hugely. That was *me!*'

Wings failed to grab David by the balls until 1973. 'A lot of it was breezy and cheerful. Some of it was sweet. But it didn't quite gel. Not at first. I couldn't figure out why. All the ingredients were there. Paul is fundamentally a brilliant songsmith. Maybe it all sounded a bit too optimistic for me. I come from a different background. I hail from the blues, in which you celebrate sadness and negative emotion. Paul seemed to be all about the opposite of that. Lennon was better at misery. Heartache has always been cool. It crossed my mind a few times, could McCartney actually be too happy to be a musician?'

David disagrees, controversially, with the widely held view that Paul is the greatest songwriter in history.

'There's something missing, for me. I'll say it again, he doesn't have what Lennon had. John had soul. There was a pleading in his vocal. Compare the two and Macca is Mr Cheese, smiling away, thumbs up, a bit kooky, a bit geeky, down to our level, being adored wherever he goes. Could he be just a balladeer, his many critics have wondered. If you go by "Hey Jude" or "Mull of Kintyre", you'd have to say, yes. But did he have soul? Did he suffer? I *know* he did, from the death of his mother onwards. Life is no picnic, not even for a superstar. But it seems he couldn't show that as well as John did. Which led me to question, even though I was a devoted, hundred-per-cent fan of his, was he a true, genuine, pained artist or just mildly cabaret?

'For the past fifty years, he hasn't produced an album that anybody cares about. *Because*, he misses John. The loss of his best friend since the age of fifteen made him slightly nuts. As my boss at EMI once said to me, "Get the nutters, Dave. Get the artists who are damaged. *They're* the ones who are going to be the stars."'

David teaches university undergraduates about the music industry these days. He continues to use the Fabs as the ultimate yardstick.

'The Beatles were the Beatles because they were first. They were the conjunction between post-war 1950s austerity and rock'n'roll. They were something different. They wrote their own songs and were quick-witted and mouthy. Will there come a time when the world gets over them, when they simply won't matter anymore? Possibly. Everybody since them has tried to be the next Beatles. I believe that I signed their successors: Duran Duran. I sat them down and taught them a lesson: "Don't leave the band. Do stick together, and you could well turn out to be the next Stones or Beatles. They listened to me, and did what I said. Look at them now. Still touring the world, selling millions, raking it in. They are mega. They are not the Beatles, granted. But for their own generation they were, and are.'

As David Ambrose identified, 1973 was the turning point. It might not have been, had things played out differently after they were apprehended in Sweden the previous August for drug abuse. Having realised they couldn't risk crossing a number of European borders with personal supplies of marijuana secreted in their luggage, they had made prior arrangements to have regular top-ups sent via Royal Mail to their accommodation in cities *en route*. But someone was onto them. When the roadshow reached Gothenberg, they were intercepted.

Denny Seiwell, Paul and Linda were arrested and interrogated, and somehow managed to escape with a fine. They laughed it off, refusing to learn their lesson, and would go on to commit the same offence again and again. Their cavalier attitude and arrogance would eventually catch them out. No way would they be allowed into the US or Japan with drug convictions under their belts. Scuppered for now, they retreated to lick their wounds.

Publicity can sometimes be the very thing you don't need. Back on the Kintyre peninsula, while the McCartneys were at home in Cavendish Avenue, the Campbeltown constabulary got wind of what had happened on the Continent. One in particular, Detective Constable Norman McPhee, who had attended a recent drug awareness course but who was more likely tipped off, went for a casual nose on the off-chance up at High Park Farm and was rewarded with a not entirely unexpected find: a clutch of cannabis plants sprouting away nicely in one of Paul's rickety greenhouses. Paul was surprised to receive a summons to appear at Campbeltown's sheriff's court in March 1973, where he would face charges of possession.

The cultivation of cannabis remains a criminal offence in the UK under the 1971 Misuse of Drugs Act (Section 6). The maximum sentence for possession of a class B drug is three months' imprisonment, a fine up to £2,500, or both. For the cultivation of cannabis plants, the maximum sentence on indictment is fourteen years' imprisonment, or a fine, or both. While it not an offence to supply or possess cannabis seeds, it is a crime to grow them.

Besuited Paul, accompanied by a bowler-hatted, obviously stoned Linda – who had apparently thumbed her nose at authority by smoking a joint on the flight up from London before nicking the titfer off the head of their barrister to sport in court – was saved by this technicality. The judge believed his story that a fan had sent him the seeds, and that he had planted them to find out what they were. He had expected to go to jail, he said. He wouldn't have minded, he added, as long as he would have been allowed a guitar. He would likely have minded very much indeed, had he been handed down the maximum penalty of fourteen years. It would have destroyed his family and have killed his career stone-dead. Lucky for him that he was let off lightly, with a fine of £100.

And 1973 *did* turn out to be the turning point. The metamorphosis from freaky folk group to worldwide rock sensation began to sizzle out of the blue, when the producers of the James Bond franchise, Harry Saltzman and Albert 'Cubby' Broccoli, invited Paul to create the title song for the eighth Bond picture starring Roger Moore as 007 and Jane Seymour as Solitaire. This happened during October the previous year, when Wings were back in the studio working on their second album, *Red Rose Speedway*. Despite the oft-peddled fable that the producers insisted on a female singer for the title piece, contracts have emerged recently to prove that Paul was always the primary choice.

The first-ever 'rock Bond theme', written by Paul and Linda and performed by Paul McCartney and Wings, was produced by 'the A&R man', George Martin. This marked the first time that the former Beatle had worked with their old producer in nearly five years. Their last studio time together had been in 1969, for *Abbey Road*. George wrote the parts and conducted the orchestra himself, at his own AIR Studios in London. So impressed were the film's producers by the orchestration that they asked George Martin to score the whole film. Thus concluded the Bond era of composer John Barry.

I have always adored the song, particularly when performed live. Paul has continued to feature it as a highlight of his shows for many years now. Its explosive pyrotechnic display is always amazing. Rarely more so than during his triumphant June 2022 eightieth-birthday Glastonbury return. Many younger rock fans assumed that Axl Rose wrote the song, being more familiar with the Guns N' Roses cover on their September 1991 album *Use Your Illusion I* than with the McCartney and Wings original.[2]

Red Rose Speedway persists as the album McCartney fans love to hate. I have never understood why. It was a defining LP during my earliest music-loving days, and it continues to thrill me.

The recording of it commenced at Olympic Studios, Barnes in March 1972, with Glyn Johns at the helm as engineer. The name of the British producer, engineer and guitarist, once signed to Decca Records as an artist in his own right, is synonymous with many artists and groups the likes of the Rolling Stones, the Who, the Kinks, the Eagles, Eric Clapton and Bob Dylan. He had worked as chief recording engineer on the Beatles' *Get Back/Let It Be* sessions. It was Glyn who came up with the idea of the Beatles performing on the roof of their Apple Savile Row HQ in January 1969, the gig that turned out to be their final live performance.

Born in February 1942 and just a few months older than Paul, perhaps the problems began right there. When Paul and the other Beatles worked with George Martin, there was natural deference and respect for the older man. George was sixteen years Paul's senior, and could at times seem even older, so 'middle-aged' and staid were his look and demeanour. The so-called 'bossy Beatle' could both collaborate with and take direction from him without issue. Post-Beatles, Paul produced himself on his first debut solo work, *McCartney*. He and his wife are credited as the producers of his second solo album, *Ram*, and then Paul took responsibility for production on the debut Wings album, *Wild Life*.

When it came to *Red Rose Speedway*, it was as though Paul recognised that it was in his own best interests to work with a highly experienced professional producer and engineer with a proven track record, hence the choice of Johns – with whom he had worked before. But when it came to it, Paul couldn't quite bring himself to cede control. It is said that Paul even spelled out to Johns that he was to treat him as 'just the bass player'. Taking him at his word, Johns managed to rile and offend McCartney, who had grown accustomed to being treated as both the 'boss' and the 'star'.

All too soon, the pair had fallen out. Paul was 'a genius in need of an editor,' as one wit commented. Glyn had emptied his locker before the month was out. He was irritated by Paul's attitude and superiority complex; infuriated by the amount of cannabis the band were consuming, and by their inability to quit jamming and get on with the job. All he wanted was for them to jump to it and focus like professionals.

He had arrived directly from working with the Eagles to sit around waiting for an ex-Beatle and his cronies to get a grip and stop wasting studio time. He stormed out and into the arms of Ronnie Lane and Ronnie Wood, to collaborate on the soundtrack for the film *Mahoney's Estate*. Glyn was the first to pick up on the 'Emperor's New Clothes' aspect of Wings, commenting that they were only masquerading as a band ... because what their set-up was really about was Paul McCartney, his wife and some not very well-paid musicians.

The 'band' downed tools to set off on their 1972 tour of Europe, and would resume recording that autumn, without Johns, in a string of studio facilities including Olympic, Abbey Road, Morgan Studios in Willesden, Trident in Soho and the Island studios in Notting Hill. Six engineers would be credited on the finished album, led by Alan Parsons and including Johns, but only in fifth place. The producer's credit went, of course, to McCartney. Denny Laine's songs didn't get a look-in: all the compositions featured were Paul's.

The album that had been proposed as a double was cut down, its single long-playing disc featuring songs written during the sessions for *Ram* as well as fresh compositions. Released on 4 May 1973, it disappointed almost everyone. The late music writer and producer John Pidgeon denounced it as 'lazy'. In his review for music monthly *Let It Rock*, he savaged it. He was on the same page as Johns regarding 'The Emperor's New Clothes': '*Red Rose Speedway* sounds as if it was written after a big tea in front of the fire with carpet-slippered feet up; listening to it takes about as much [effort] as going ten rounds with a marshmallow fairy.' Mon Dieu.

Even Macca himself was disappointed by the album. Just four years later, he was bleating that he couldn't stand listening to it.

Maybe it was weak and 'lazy' after all. Yet, to my childish, untrained ear back then, it was the aural equivalent of the Sistine Chapel ceiling. Paul was of course our Michelangelo. I was in awe of him and of it, 'if only' for 'My Love', its sole single release, and for 'Little Lamb Dragonfly', an exquisite, haunting masterpiece that deserves to be much more widely known. As for the wistful medley with which side two concludes, so reminiscent and yet so not of the sad withdrawing of the Beatles in the medley at the end of *Abbey Road*. Oh, lazy dynamite. I adored it. I wasn't alone. The album soared to Number Five in Britain. In the US, love carried it all the way.

It was inevitable that Paul would want to tour again as soon as possible, having regarded their initial two outings as warm-up expeditions. After rehearsing at High Park Farm, out they all dragged again, with pub rockers Brinsley Schwarz in tow as support, this time around the UK on the first full British Wings tour. They kicked off at the Bristol Hippodrome and concluded at Newcastle City Hall, taking in Oxford, Cardiff, Bournemouth, Manchester, Liverpool, Leeds, Preston, Edinburgh and Glasgow in-between. Eighteen shows in all during May that year, including three nights at London's Hammersmith Odeon, where the tour had been meant to end. But tickets were in such demand that additional dates were added, in Sheffield, Birmingham and Leicester.

As for the songs: 'Soily', a rock number Paul had penned in 1971. 'Big Barn Bed', the opener of *Red Rose Speedway*. 'When the Night', track two on side two of the new album. 'Wild Life', the title track of the debut Wings offering. 'Seaside Woman', Linda's reggae-infused number. 'Little Woman Love', the B-side of 'Mary Had a Little Lamb', and 'C Moon', from the double A-side with 'Hi Hi Hi'. Their new Bond theme 'Live and Let Die'. 'Maybe I'm Amazed', Paul's instant classic from his debut solo album. 'My Love', the only single from *Red Rose Speedway*. 'Go Now', performed by Denny for the first time on a Wings tour, and his own composition 'Say You Don't Mind', which he had aired on the European trek the year before. 'The Mess', released in March 1973 as the B-side of 'My Love'. 'Hi Hi Hi', put out as a single, and 'Long Tall Sally', Little Richard's screamer from 1956 and Macca's ever-popular encore. 'Gonna tell Aunt Mary 'bout Uncle John!' Their repertoire was growing ever stronger.

Robin Denselow attended one of the Hammersmith Odeon gigs, his heart in his mouth at the thought of having to draw inevitable comparisons with the Beatles' celebrated Christmas shows there. He needn't have fretted. The thunderous standing ovation put the doubters' minds at rest. Linda's unimpressive performances notwithstanding, Wings had made it over the line. Paul had won back his credibility. It was still a long way to Madison Square Garden.[3]

Of all the years in which to release a career-defining album, 1973 had the potential to be the most challenging. There were solo works by every former Beatle, all hell-bent on cash-piling while their Apple assets remained frozen in litigation. It was the year of George Harrison's fourth studio album *Living in the Material World*; of Lennon's fourth studio album *Mind Games*; and of Starr's third solo album *Ringo*. This last had the distinction of featuring contributions by all of his former bandmates for the first time since they had gone their separate ways.

The LP, released that November, spawned a pair of fat Number Ones: 'Photograph', featuring George on guitar, and 'You're Sixteen', on which Paul played kazoo. John not only wrote the opener 'I'm the Greatest', but played piano and sang backing vocals. And guess what, George played guitar. Making this the only time that three former Beatles ever recorded together between their dissolution in 1970 and John's murder ten years later.

John had written and composed the song after the band fell apart, and revised the lyrics for Ringo to sing. Its title was a nod to heavyweight boxer Muhammad Ali, borrowing his catchphrase.

The Beatles' old Hamburg mucker Klaus Voormann played bass, and another 'fifth Beatle', Billy Preston was on keys. The track couldn't have been more Fab had it tried.

Also in 1973 came Bowie's post-Ziggy ride *Aladdin Sane*, Pink Floyd's *Dark Side of the Moon*, *Tubular Bells* by nineteen-year-old Mike Oldfield – the album that launched Richard Branson's label Virgin – the Stones' *Exile* follow-up *Goats Head Soup* and the Who's *Quadrophenia*. Not to mention Stevie Wonder's *Innervisions*, Billy Joel's second scorcher *Piano Man*, Marvin Gaye's *Let's Get It On*, Elton's *Goodbye Yellow Brick Road*, Paul Simon's *There Goes Rhymin' Simon*, Bryan Ferry's *These Foolish Things*, and Lynyrd Skynyrd's *Pronounced 'Lĕh-'nérd 'skin-'nérd*, featuring its opus 'Freebird'.

As if that were not enough, Paul would find himself competing with his own work as well as with his own bandmates, when the soon-to-be outgoing manager of the other three, Allen Klein, curated and released a pair of double albums comprising fifty-four songs that would change music history.

Old songs? They did? *How?* Because they introduced the Beatles' back catalogue to new generations the world over, who had not been born or who were too young to have known and appreciate the band while they were still active. By which definition, they became the most important Greatest Hits albums ever released. The compilations, known as the 'Red' and 'Blue' albums, featured Klein's own selections, 1962–1966 and 1967–1970, and were released on 2 April 1973. The former Beatles themselves had no involvement. Yet it was they who reaped the rewards, and Klein who was sunk.

'I didn't take an awful lot of interest in them actually,' said Paul to *Rolling Stone* in 1974. 'I still haven't heard them . . . I haven't really taken much interest in Beatles stuff of late just because there has been this hangover of Apple and Klein. The whole scene has gone so bloody sick. The four ex-Beatles are totally up to here with it.'

On release day, a Monday, the Lennons flew to New York to give a press conference. Deftly avoiding questions about the albums, they made the announcement that John, Ringo and George were at long last sacking Klein. The old devil had got in first, however, having published his own press release ahead of their media gathering. John had the grace to acknowledge that Paul had been right from day one about Klein.

'It was something,' he said, 'we should have done a long time ago, but obviously "Que será, será", and now is the hour.' How were things between him and Paul at that point? 'Distant physically. And mentally, pretty OK,' John smiled.

Oh boy. Wasn't it 'a sign'. The world got itself in a panic and its boxers in a twist about a rumoured Beatles reunion. Down on my knees, I'm begging you, please, let it happen! Only two days after these albums appeared, all the former Beatles except Paul attended Barbra Streisand's Hollywood fundraiser for the Pentagon Papers Legal Defense Fund (related to the Vietnam War). A potential donor pledged $3,000 if The Three of The Four would croon 'With a Little Help from My Friends'.[4] They didn't. Their hostess sang it instead.

That same week, Paul released the Wings single 'My Love'. It would be shoved off the top by George's 'Give Me Love (Give Me Peace on Earth)' from his new album *Living in the Material World*. The 'Blue' album eclipsed its 'Red' counterpart. In the US, it was relieved of its Number One position by *Red Rose Speedway*. Twenty years later, both 'Red' and 'Blue' would be launched on CD at a press conference given by George Martin at Abbey Road. They kept on coming. The future of the most perfect pop songs in history was assured.

A good year for the Beatles, in all. A not so good year for the disgruntled hired hands and voices of Wings, who were still scraping by on meagre wages with the odd, modest bonus lobbed in to keep them sweet. They had expected a share of recording royalties once corners had been turned and Wings had established themselves. Ever the promise, never the goods. The Dennys and Henry were skint. Only Laine would ever see much of a share of anything, while the formerly frugal Maccas were splashing cash.

No one could compute the contradiction between their simple-to-the-point-of-spartan living conditions with the fortunes they were now shelling out on luxury cars, paintings and jewellery. Was Paul insensitive, blind or just mean? And if he were any or all of these things, where was Linda, his voice of reason? He listened to her. Why wasn't she jumping up and down in her manure-splattered wellies pointing out the blatant inequality and unfairness?

Wherever there were walls, there was writing. When Paul began to make noises about recording the next Wings album 'somewhere foreign', saying that he was keen to absorb fresh influences and alternative cultures, rodents were whiffed. Might the move not just be about tax concessions? The tentacles of EMI reached into some of the furthest corners of Earth's continents, including Africa and Asia. Paul considered Shanghai or Rio de Janeiro, but in the end decided that Lagos looked the business.

The multicultural financial capital of Nigeria boasted a rich musical history. From the ancient tribal Hausa music through Yoruba drumming and percussion to jùjú, fuji, African pop and more, rich seams were there for the mining. Artists such as Ayinde Barrister, Ebenezer Obey, King Sunny Adé and Afrobeat star Fela Kuti were already on Paul's radar. Mix it up a little, why shouldn't they? For drummer Denny Seiwell and guitarist Henry McCullough, it was the last straw. Henry and Paul hadn't seen eye to eye for some time. The competent and creative axeman was done with being bossed about. He walked one day without a word to his parsimonious paymaster, never to be seen again.

Denny Laine and Jo Jo were preparing to return to London for the birth of their first child when Jo Jo's waters broke. They'd never have made it as far as the capital. As things turned out their baby boy, whom they named Laine after Denny's assumed surname and Hines, Denny's actual surname, was one of the last to be born at Craigard Maternity Home on the banks of Campbeltown Loch, on 24 August.[5] The hospital was closed for good that year, and a new maternity unit delivered.

Henry gone. Denny Laine down. What would be the drummer's next move? No prizes. Denny Seiwell was in favour, and told Paul as much, of taking time to train McCullough's replacement, allow Denny to support Jo Jo through the early weeks of motherhood and only then regroup. In other words, take it easy and do things properly.

Paul wasn't having it. EMI had it all arranged in Lagos, he protested. The kids were primed, the family was good to go, they would fly out on 30 August and they would stick to the original plan. Last straw time. Furious words were traded down the phone. Paul hung up. Denny Seiwell was done. It would be years before they spoke again.

Paul and Linda must have rued the day. There was nothing exotic about Lagos. What a hellhole. It was the monsoon season, and there was a cholera epidemic. Their accommodation was infested. The streets were unsafe. The 'recording studio' was an ill-equipped shed about an hour away, with an inadequate set-up and negligible facilities. And a popular Afrobeat musician who also happened to be a political activist went on the radio to accuse McCartney of coming to Nigeria to 'exploit and steal' local music. If only for that reason, there is nothing remotely African-sounding about *Band on the Run*.

'I was imagining sunny skies, uplifting African visions, and encasing my songs in that atmosphere,' Paul reflected in *The Lyrics*. They got less than they bargained for. 'I hadn't imagined cholera or the mugging or the half-ready studios or my children being told they weren't allowed in the hotel swimming pool because they were naked,' he said.

His and Linda's cavalier attitude to safety almost cost Paul his life. Having braved Jamaica, they considered themselves fearless, as well as immune to the edgier side of life. They'd seen nothing yet. One night as they were walking back from Denny's place along an unlit road – Denny who had left his 21-year-old partner alone in

London with their six-day-old newborn – a car drew alongside and slowed to a standstill ahead of them. The male passengers shouted at the couple. Paul took it for banter, possibly assuming that they recognised him, and jested back. One got out and yelled at Paul. Who tried to shove his attacker back into the vehicle.

At which, things got life-threatening. Five intimidating males leapt from the car and held Paul and Linda at knifepoint while they stripped them of their possessions: wallets, watches, their tape recorder and their *Band on the Run* demo tapes. Only Linda's quick thinking caused them to let her husband go. 'Don't kill him!' she cried, 'he's a musician!' They later learned that muggers there tended to kill their victims to prevent them from identifying their attackers to the police.

That they survived was a miracle. Paul had to create the songs again, so what? Maybe his second attempts were superior to the first, given the tumultuous circumstances from which they'd withdrawn back home. Reduced to two career musicians and Linda, they had no choice but to improvise, with the help of trusty old Beatles engineer Geoff Emerick. All nine songs were written by Paul. On vocals, drums and guitar as well as bass, he was his own rhythm section. With Denny on guitars and backing vocals and Linda on keys, percussion and BVs too, they got away with it. But the heavy workload took its toll. Paul collapsed, and Linda was terrified that he was having a heart attack.

'It seemed stuffy in the studio,' recalled Paul, 'so I went outside for a breath of fresh air. If anything, the air was more foul outside than in. It was then that I began to feel really terrible and had a pain across the right side of my chest and I collapsed. I could not breathe and so I collapsed and fainted. Linda thought I had died . . . this was me in hell,' he said. The episode was later diagnosed as a bronchial spasm brought on by excess smoking. Which Paul was doing to try to reduce his stress levels.

When the team flew home to London after just over a month and a half, they must have asked themselves endlessly what it had all been about. Had decamping to African lands lent anything unique to the ensuing LP? Debatable. We'll never know whether Paul, Denny and Linda could have made just as good an album at High Park, at the EMI studios, at Trident, Olympic or anywhere else. Maybe *Band on the Run* was fuelled by dynamism of its own.

Howie Casey added the sax solos at George Martin's AIR Studios. Bolan and Bowie producer Tony Visconti handled the orchestral arrangements. An obvious departure from everything they'd made before, this album had an energy and edginess not previously evident on Wings recordings. It had cohesion, a theme – which is not to attempt to call it a 'concept' album (it isn't), but simply to pay homage to the mounting brilliance and flair that run through it like aural gold. It was as though Paul's commitment to and belief in his post-Beatles mission had finally paid off. Here was the zenith, the era-definer. The band's four further studio albums would never even touch its hem.

Its hooky, galloping title track; infectious 'Jet', the first of several hit singles; sublime 'Bluebird'; quirky 'Mrs Vandebilt'; the intriguing 'Picasso's Last Words' (allegedly written on the spot, during a dinner with Dustin Hoffman in Jamaica, when the actor enquired of the rock star whether he could really write a song about anything and proffered a magazine covering the death of Pablo Picasso as possible inspiration); and 'Nineteen Hundred and Eighty Five': the most Beatles-esque of the album's tracks with its blatant echoes of 'Lady Madonna', stark lyrics and crashing 'A Day in the Life'-alike conclusion. All superlative, unforgettable songs.

Could this be Paul's personal *Sgt. Pepper*? I'd wager that 'Nineteen Hundred and Eighty Five' comes closer than anything else. This was the only Wings or McCartney album with a Beatle-worthy ending. Even the dramatic prisoners-on-the-loose cover image featuring celebrities of the day – Liverpool boxer John Conteh, singer Kenny Lynch, actors Christopher Lee and James Coburn, television hosts Michael Parkinson and Clement Freud plus Paul, Linda and Denny – was reminiscent of the sleeve of you-know-what.

Paul had found his niche. He had found the 'Wings sound'. Even John Lennon, previously so critical of his old bandmate's post-Fabs output, was moved to shower this latest album with praise. '*Band on the Run* is a great album,' he enthused to *Rolling Stone*, soon after the record's release. 'Wings keep changing all the time [but] it doesn't matter who's playing. You can call them Wings, but it's Paul McCartney music – and it's good stuff.'

Paul no longer needed to be 'the Beatle'. He was not to know, and would not have wanted to, that this was as good as Wings would get.

CHAPTER 11

RETURNS

David Courtney first met his idol McCartney during the Flower Power years, at the Bag O'Nails. Sixteen years old and drumming in a band called the Urchins for waning pop idol Adam Faith, he grew up fast.[1]

'I remember seeing Paul in his Mini Cooper with its blacked-out windows, picking up girls, and thinking how nice of him it was to make sure they got home safely,' he says. 'Little did I know, but I soon learned.'

He had been a big Beatles fan ever since 'Love Me Do'. 'Seeing Paul in that club every night was like having died and gone to heaven. We were all wearing kaftans and little moustaches by then. The *Sgt. Pepper* influence was huge. I was there the night Paul met Linda. I remember it well. But I had no interaction with Paul at that stage. I would walk past his table and give him a look, he'd give me one back but that was it. There was no real interaction.'

Which was to change. David discovered Leo Sayer in 1971, fronting a band called Patches in Brighton. Leo was still Gerry in those days. It was David's Eureka moment: 'I'd started writing songs, I was looking for talent to record and perform them, and I signed the band.' The singer went solo, David teamed up with Adam Faith to manage, co-write with and produce him, and Leo scored many hits including 'Long Tall Glasses', 'One Man Band' and 'The Show Must Go On'.

Adam Faith starred in the popular TV series *Budgie* during the early seventies, but his new career was stalled by a serious car accident in August 1973 that left him with vertigo. This proved to be a turning point. When Courtney suggested that they make an album together, Faith was inspired. 'He said we should go away to write it. We went to Nassau and checked into a hotel. But because of the vertigo, he couldn't get out of bed for days. When at last he was able to get up, I spoke to the hotel manager and talked him into letting us use the piano in the ballroom. We'd go in there and write songs, and Terry [Adam's real name] was enthused.'

They returned home. Faith decided that he wanted big-name artists playing on his record. 'We decided to call it *I Survive*, a nod to the car accident,' says David. It was all, 'call Bowie, ask him to play sax. Who else can we get?' He pulled in a load of favours – even Lord Snowdon to do the cover image, which was shot in Kensington Palace and Gardens. I told him my biggest dream would be to get Paul McCartney. So of course, Terry rang him up. He could call anybody, everyone loved him. He was held in such high regard.'

Faith invited Paul and Linda to the stately RAC Club on London's Pall Mall. 'After dinner, the McCartneys, Terry and his wife Jacks [Jackie] went back to the mausoleum of a lounge with its huge stage, big piano and framed portrait of the Queen. "Will you do me a favour?" said Terry. "What?" asked Paul. "Will you play my favourite song for me?" "Yeah, sure, what is it?" "Let It Be." Paul played it. Halfway through the song, a concierge came rushing in. "Oi! You! Get off that piano!" Macca sat chuckling to himself. "Do you realise who he is?" asked Terry. "I don't care if he's Paul McCartney," growled the concierge, "I want him off that fuckin' piano."'

A couple of days later, Paul and Linda turned up at the studio. 'Oh my God, is this really going to happen?' said David. 'Am I really producing an album that McCartney is going to play on? My dream had come true. And let me tell you, they were such a delight to work with. The warmth between them was incredible. I've never seen two people more in love. He found his soul mate, no question. What I saw in Linda was genuine. She had a special light that shone out. She was everything to Paul: his mother, his lover, his friend. You could see it. It didn't surprise me, after I told him that "Maybe I'm Amazed" was my favourite song of his, when he said that he'd written it for her.'

Then came the tricky bit.

'I had to play him *my* song,' says David. 'It was called "Star Song". He was obviously going to hear that it was very Beatles-influenced. The string arrangement, the chunking cello. It's a very theatrical number. Paul and Linda loved it. They sang backing vocals on the chorus. He breaks into harmony, which he did off the top of his head. I didn't have to tell him any of it. On another track, "Never Say Goodbye", he played synthesiser. He asked us to get a Moog in.'

Were they paid for their contribution? 'No! What happened, Paul and Linda went off to Scotland and Terry and I sat down and talked about it. "We can't give him a session fee, can we?" said Terry. So he decided to have something planted at their garden in Cavendish Avenue. A sapling, as a thank-you. They were delighted. It must be a gigantic bloody tree by now. If it's still there.'

'Imagine what that does for a record, having Paul McCartney playing on it,' reflects Mike Batt. The composer, songwriter, musician and producer who wrote 'Bright Eyes' for Art Garfunkel and co-wrote, with Tim Rice, 'A Winter's Tale' for David Essex; created the music for television's *The Wombles* (eight hit singles, four gold albums); composed and produced classical violinist Vanessa-Mae's huge album *The Violin Player*; discovered, wrote for and produced Katie Melua, and has worked with a host of greats. Like David Courtney, Batt is not afraid to declare that Paul is his hero.

'His generosity to Adam Faith and David Courtney that you describe is so typical of him,' he says. 'That kind of thing seems to come naturally to him. He has this endearing habit of wanting to make you feel great by referencing something of yours. "That 'Bright Eyes' song is good," he'll say, "there's a few of yours I like." The first time he said that to me, it didn't make my day. It made my life.

'I don't believe he's perfect. No one is. I'm not a fan of his, exactly, but whatever you hear of his, you go, "Fuck me, that's good." He was a role model of mine when I was starting out. Even though I was deeply into symphonic stuff and wanted to do conducting and arranging, it was him I looked up to. People are always saying that McCartney doesn't write music. He *does* write it, he just doesn't write it *down*. As in, notate.

'I remember when Paul and his second wife Heather came to our home in the country. We had a nice lunch, then went into the studio. They'd asked if they could use my studio for a charity thing, and I was delighted. Heather was co-producing, as it was her charity. I went into the vocal booth, got on the same mic as him and we did some harmonies. I had a top line, and I showed him the sheet. He pushed it away. "Oh, I don't need that," he said.

'I realised afterwards that he wears his musical illiteracy as a badge of honour, because it draws attention to the brilliance of his ear. He hires people to do what I do. I just wish he'd hire me sometime, I'd do it for nothing.'

It's 'kind of quaint', Batt comments, that Paul felt he had to have another band after the Beatles. 'One of the things that always comes across is that he'd love to be ordinary – but he also loves being Paul McCartney,' he says. 'We all come from ordinary families and roots. But you can know you're special when you're really quite young, and I think Paul probably did know that. He wants to be perceived as normal, yet how can he ever *be* normal? He's Paul McCartney! The Queen loved a picnic in her raincoat and wellies, didn't she. Paul is similar.

'It might be why he formed Wings. He had a band, he loved being in that band, but then it broke up. He did some solo stuff, but then decided that he'd like to be in a band again, with a bunch of other normal musicians. That was "normal" to him. But he was a bit naïve to believe that his normal-ness was as normal as everyone else's in the band. He was always Paul McCartney, and that was the sticking point in Wings. The problem that they never got over. No one could ever not be aware of it. Especially not him.'

Mike and his wife Julianne attended Paul's and Heather's wedding in Ireland in 2002. 'There was a moment that day when Paul and I were talking,' he says, 'and I was having a moan. "You know what, Paul," I said, "I'm going to be a Womble for the rest of my life." "I know what you mean," he responded, nodding. "I'm always going to be a Beatle." He saw it as being the same problem! No matter what he went on to do, he was always going to be a Beatle. "I'll swap you if you want," I said. He did chuckle.'

No better Yuletide gift could Paul have received than news that he could finally visit the States again. It had been awkward not being able to, given that he had an American wife who wanted to see her family. Banned from entering for the previous two years on account of his marijuana conviction back home, his visa was unexpectedly granted. As soon as the news reached them in Jamaica, where they had gone with their children for 'the holidays' (Thanksgiving and Christmas), they made straight for New York, to visit Linda's clan.

'I hope to tour this country in the coming spring,' he told a reporter from the *New York Times*. 'We've got to put a band together first, do a few other things and then we can come on tour. We hope to do a benefit concert for Phoenix House [an addiction treatment centre with branches across Manhattan and on Long Island] when we're in New York.' He then discussed the triumph of *Band on the Run,* and the surprise Oscar nomination for Best Original Song for 'Live and Let Die'. It was the first time that a track from a Bond film had ever been nominated.

After 'Chrissy', he told his interrogator, explaining his slang for Christmas as Liverpoolese, he revealed that he was about to work on an album with his brother Mike in January, and then on some solo tracks of Linda's. 'It's called Suzy and the Redstripes, so that people don't buy it because it's Linda McCartney, wife of . . . you know who. It's supposed to be a gentle, kind of anonymous thing, but then here I am talking all about it.' He also hinted at the likelihood of the former Beatles playing together again in the not too distant, once exhausting business matters had been put to bed.

He made no bones. All he wanted was to see John again. By then, Lennon was living with May Pang in Santa Monica, and working with singer Harry Nilsson at Burbank Studios on Nilsson's new album *Pussy Cats*. You could have floored him with a plume when on 28 March 1974, Paul and Linda walked in.

It was the first time in four years that the two ex-Beatles had seen each other. The bitter years of attack and recrimination evaporated. None of it seemed to matter anymore. They had obviously missed each other. They had grown up a little, and had gained perspective. There were now growing children, complicated personal lives and other things to worry about. 'There was magic in the room,' May Pang told me. 'John looked at Paul and Paul looked at John, and they were them again.'

In a 1975 interview conducted by broadcaster Bob Harris and recorded on BBC TV's *The Old Grey Whistle Test*, John 'shocked the world' when he revealed that he and Paul had recorded together that night. 'I jammed with Paul,' he said. 'I did actually play with Paul. We did a lot of stuff in LA. But there were fifty other people playing too, and they were all just watching me and Paul.'

It was the first time they had played together since 1969, on *Abbey Road*. Unbeknown to them then, it would turn out to be the last.

For years, no one was the wiser. Nobody elaborated. No recording found its way into the public domain, as might have been expected. Neither John nor Paul commented publicly. Not until May Pang published her first memoir, *Loving John*, three years after his murder was it confirmed that the 1974 session had taken place. But May did not reveal what exactly had been recorded, what had become of the tapes nor the identity of the other musicians.

'Fifty'? There were perhaps no more than half a dozen others present. Typical John, the occasion had been so loaded that he exaggerated it to fifty in his mind. At least now we knew that the childhood friends had made their peace. It would not be until the long, lost tape emerged as the bootleg recording *A Toot and a Snore in '74* that we learned the names of the personnel.

As well as John, Paul and Linda, saxophonist Bobby Keys, Stevie Wonder, Harry Nilsson, record producer and bassist Ed Freeman (who just happened to be working with Don McLean in the adjacent studio), guitarist Jesse Ed Davis and 'Fung Yee' (as John called his girlfriend, her full name being May Fung Yee Pang; her Chinese name means 'Phoenix bird') all featured, the latter on tambourine. Keith Moon and Ringo missed it, as they had left the studio at around midnight before the McCartneys turned up.

They may have done themselves a favour. The session was no more than a smacked-up, boozed-out jam. But when the recordings emerged unofficially in 1992, those nine sloppy 'tracks', including several attempts at 'Stand By Me', 'Lucille' and a Beatles-style medley at the end, could have competed for spiritual and historical status with the Holy Grail. Never again would Lennon and McCartney get to play together. Mal Evans, the Beatles' faithful old roadie and PA, who as it turned out had only twenty-one months left to live, is credited on the bootleg for 'tea'. Was he there?

Paul discussed the slapdash session in passing during a 1997 interview with Australian writer Sean Sennett, describing proceedings as 'hazy'. Sales of the bootleg were later blocked. Could that have been Macca, wielding his influence and cheque book again?

The family celebrated Paul's thirty-second birthday with a barbecue on a rented ranch in Tennessee. Old pal Roy Orbison was the special guest, along with the newly appointed members of Wings.

Drummer Geoff Britton was from Lewisham, south-east London. The karate and judo expert was great company and loved by most, but he would linger less than a year. Henry McCullough's replacement was a loose cannon. Jittery Jimmy McCulloch, a tiny Glaswegian, looked wet behind the ears and was only just out of his teens. Long-haired, rodent-faced and lightning-fingered, the girls adored him. His guitar-playing with Thunderclap Newman, his work with the Who's John Entwistle the previous year and his great friendship with the Ox and other members of that band, had given him a sip of the big time. He was ripe for more.

'Some of us were still wondering, even post-*Band on the Run*, what this whole Wings caper was about,' says John Altman. He knows. The prolific composer, arranger, orchestrator, conductor and saxophonist has worked with Little Richard, Van Morrison, Phil Collins, Bob Marley, Jimi Hendrix, Eric Clapton and Amy Winehouse; has produced many hit records including Aled Jones's 'Walking in the Air' from *The Snowman* and George Michael's 'Kissing a Fool'; and has scored, written and arranged for many films, among them *Little Voice*, the period music in *Titanic*, and 'Always Look on the Bright Side of Life' for Monty Python's *Life of Brian*.

'People don't realise how quickly things moved in the sixties,' he says. 'The Beatles were very quickly old hat. Paul was seen as an anachronism. Careers back then tended to last months rather than years – like now, except that the creative talent was far greater. I hate to say that Paul was once seen as old-fashioned. But compared to Hendrix, Blind Faith, Cream and so on, he was. Pop music in those days occupied a far greater place in people's lives than it does now. It really mattered who you liked. Many of the Liverpool bands had faded. We had to wait for the revival tours years later to see them again. Once Bowie, Bolan and Slade came along and the whole glam rock thing had kicked in, Paul had become a bit of an irrelevance. The other thing was that he was not nineteen or twenty anymore.'

Despite the huge success of *Band on the Run*, John reports, the industry was still questioning Paul's decision to put Linda in his band.

'The jury was out, for me. Paul has enough natural taste and musicianship not to shove someone totally inept into a band with highly competent musicians. So she couldn't have been as bad as everyone said. The original musicians didn't think she was in the band on merit, but I never got that from Denny Laine, Henry McCullough or Jimmy McCulloch.

'It's a shame,' John muses, 'when you think of all the great musicians who went through Wings. All wonderful players. Paul had singled them out. They were incredibly keen to work with him. But some of these guys didn't want to tour, which seemed to be Paul's obsession. A lot of session musicians don't want to go on the road. They can make more money getting hired to do sessions in the studio, plus touring is so disruptive.

'Not only to one's family and home life, but you lose your first-call status: when you are a producer's first choice as a player of a particular instrument. They never say, "Ok, we'll wait for you." They need you there and then, this morning, last night, so they simply move on down the list. You daren't turn something down because then your replacement gets offered all the work going forward that you would otherwise have got.'

It was significant, Altman points out, that Lennon was living in America. 'That seemed to give the Beatles greater status there than at home. Paul and Wings were more popular in the States because of that. And all the other Beatles were jealous of George, who had become bigger than all of them,' he says. His opinion. 'Jimmy McCulloch told me that Paul resented his reputation as a family entertainer while John was regarded as the cool, edgy one. For me, the two things that defined Paul throughout the seventies, throughout the Wings years, were self-sabotage and defiance. There has always been a superiority about him that he can never quite get past, because he doesn't know that he's like it. Whenever I bumped

177

into him, I realise now, we were not having a conversation. I was being interviewed.'

Of Wings music, John insists that it does stand the test of time. 'Real musicians making real music was never really in fashion,' he observes. 'So it can never be out of fashion. It becomes timeless, and that's important. Maybe musicians haven't covered Wings tracks the way they have endlessly covered Beatles tracks. This means that you have to go back to the magic of the originals to hear what they were about. In my view, that's no bad thing.'

On what would have been John Lennon's seventieth birthday, 9 October 2010, Yoko Ono gave an interview crediting Paul for having brought her and John back together. 'I want the world to know that it was a very touching thing that he did for John,' she told *The Times*. 'He was genuinely concerned about his old partner. Even though John was not asking for help – John, Paul, all of them were too proud to ask for anything – he helped. John often said he didn't understand why Paul did that for us, but he did.'

Yoko claimed that Paul and Linda had gone to see her in New York in early 1974, during her separation from John, and that Paul asked her what it would take for her to take John back. She said she told Paul that John would have to court her. Flowers, date nights, romance. Paul allegedly conveyed this to John when they met up in LA. Yoko said that John acted upon it, and returned to New York 'immediately'.

He didn't. She was rewriting history. May and John got together in mid-1973, in the arrangement enforced by Yoko, and moved west that September. For her birthday the following month, John bought her an orange Plymouth Barracuda convertible, and drew pictures of her driving it. They returned to New York briefly in February 1974 for John to attend meetings with his lawyers regarding his immigration status; and in June 1974 when, May said, 'Yoko told John she wanted a divorce and ordered him to her attorney's office to sign the papers.'

If there were divorce proceedings, these stalled along the line. John did not reunite with his wife at that point, nor did he start taking her to galleries and cinemas as Yoko has claimed. He was with May, and they were joined at the hip. They lodged at the smart Pierre Hotel on the Upper East Side, a mere ten-minute walk via West 59th Street, Central Park South and Central Park West to the Dakota on the Upper West Side. Then they moved to a penthouse, 'The Tower', in the Southgate apartment building at 434 East 52nd Street. They got a couple of cats, Major and Minor, fixed up a bedroom for Julian, and settled into sweet domestic bliss.

It was from the roof of that building that they both saw a UFO, they said, on 23 August 1974. 'I wish it had taken us both away,' John whispered to May in bed that night. He wrote about the experience in his song 'Nobody Told Me', recorded during the *Walls and Bridges* sessions and included on his posthumous album *Milk and Honey*.

His fifth album *Walls and Bridges* topped the US Billboard chart and reached Number Six in the UK. John also scored his only American chart-topper during his lifetime, 'Whatever Gets You Through the Night' with Elton John. That's May saying John's name on the track '#9 Dream'. And 'Surprise, Surprise (Sweet Bird of Paradox)' is about his young lover. Would he be writing and recording songs with and about another woman had he made up his mind to go home to Mother?

CHAPTER 12

VELOCITY

The Beatles' divorce was made absolute at the turn of 1975. The last legal ties between them were cut in a private hearing before a High Court judge on 9 January. It came almost exactly four years after Paul had issued his writ appealing for dissolution. In a 2020 interview to mark the fiftieth anniversary of their separation, Paul reflected on the widely held assumption that the four hated each other's guts.

'What I realise now is that because it was a family, because it was a gang, families argue and families have disputes,' he shared with *GQ*. 'Some people want to do this and some people want to do that . . . I was thought to be the guy who broke the Beatles up and the bastard who sued his mates. And, believe me, I bought into that. It was so prevalent that for years I almost blamed myself.'

The only way that he could save the Beatles and Apple, and establish the means by which future projects such as Peter Jackson's *Get Back*, *Anthology* and the Beatles remasters could be realised, Paul explained, was to sue the band. 'If I hadn't done that, it would have all belonged to Allen Klein. The only way I was given to get us out of that was to do what I did.' Paul had taken the risk, and he had pulled it off. Apple was liberated, and would go forward under the guidance of old pal Neil Aspinall.

The McCartneys celebrated in New Orleans, where they found Mardis Gras in full swing. They hurled themselves into the mayhem, attending boogie-woogie pianist and singer Dr John the Night Tripper's Lundi Gras concert at the St Bernard Civic Center on 10 February dressed as clowns with painted faces, and sported the same get-up at Carnival the next day. Their daughters dressed as fairies. Jimmy went as Napoleon, and Denny as the Wolfman.

Not that their trip to Louisiana was purely holiday. Paul had long been fascinated by the music and history of the Mississippi bluesmen. He had longed for years to return and immerse himself in the birthplace of modern music, whose roots stretched back further than he knew. The city's musical history had its roots in the ancient traditions of the region's original inhabitants: the indigenous Chitimacha, Atakapa, Caddo, Choctaw, Houma, Natchez and Tunica tribes. The French colonial era of the early 1700s introduced European instruments and styles.

Congo Square, located today in Louis Armstrong Park north of the French Quarter, was the city's original musical hub. Enslaved Africans, granted Sundays off, would gather there to hold their markets, play their own traditional and local songs and dance tunes, to shake a leg and carouse. After Louisiana became part of the United States in 1803 following the Louisiana Purchase, such gatherings grew. By the early nineteenth century, a period of intense immigration especially from Spain, Portugal, Germany and Haiti, they had swelled even more.

Music in the square became infused with multiple influences. By the mid-1800s, brass bands and later marching bands were mushrooming all over the city. Jazz music crystallised and diversified. Latin American tresillo and habanera rhythms and the back-beat – a fundamental of R&B but in fact a feature that had arisen significantly earlier, in gospel music – the syncopated rhythms of ragtime, and Sicilian and Cuban music further enriched the mix.

Rock'n'roll reared its head after the Second World War, out of rhythm and blues. The earliest rockers loved to record in New Orleans using bands made up of local musicians, because they were the best to be had. Rich in racial and ethnic diversity, modern

New Orleans surely rivals Toronto, Miami, London and Sydney as one of the world's most multicultural cities. Got to get it into his life: Paul wanted a sprinkling of the 'Noo Orlins' magic on his own recordings.

It was as though his connection to this place would somehow validate him as a 'real' musician. Because those old McCartney doubts, that bewildering lack of confidence, were, as Linda knew, never far away. He was here to experience this place full-on, in all its thrilling uniqueness. John was not there. Paul wanted him to be. He called him up, and asked him to bring May down to join him and Linda and the kids. The flight time from New York, he said, was only three and-a-half hours.

Paul and John had been there once before, but only briefly. The Beatles had given their debut performance there eleven years earlier, on 15 September 1964: a thirty-five-minute stint at the City Park (later the Tad Gormley) Stadium. Clarence 'Frogman' Henry, a popular local singer and pianist, was one of the warm-up acts.[1] The gig was a blast, but the boys were deprived of their promised sightseeing day off.

We can only imagine how the foursome would have gone around earwigging the dialects, tasting Cajun gumbo and crawfish, squinting up at the piggledy French and Spanish Creole architecture and hanging on historic Bourbon Street. The latter may well have resonated with them. Its delights echoed those of Hamburg's Reeperbahn. But Brian Epstein accepted a lucrative last-minute booking, and it was off to Kansas City in the morning. More than a decade elapsed before Paul got round to returning. He was at long last able to get to know the place.

The Beatles hadn't left New Orleans disgruntled. A special guest happened to pop his head around the door of their trailer before they took to the stage that day in 1964: Fats Domino, one of their greatest musical heroes. It would be impossible to overestimate the effect of the 36-year-old boogie-woogie legend's presence on the callow, starstruck twenty-somethings. His 1955 hit

'Ain't That a Shame' had been the very first song that John learned to play. His 1956 number 'I'm in Love Again' was the first rock'n'roll record George Harrison heard.

'He was wearing a huge star-spangled, diamond-encrusted watch, which was our first encounter with bling!' commented Paul in October 2017, after Domino died. 'His voice, piano-playing and musical style was a huge influence on us, and his appearance in the film *The Girl Can't Help It* was truly magnificent. As one of my favourite rock'n'roll singers, I will remember him fondly and always think of him with that twinkle in his eye.'

Fats Domino was the creator, according to some historians, of the first rock'n'roll single: 1949's 'The Fat Man'. They can argue that one until the herd is back in the shed. The hit transformed him from band pianist into overnight sensation. He was the first artist to sell a million copies; the man Elvis Presley would later call 'the real king of rock'n'roll'.

His greatest hit, 'Blueberry Hill', a cover of a jazz standard from the 1940s recorded by big band leader Glenn Miller, became his signature. It shifted more than five million worldwide between 1956 and 1957, and would later be reworked by Elvis, Little Richard and Led Zeppelin. Fats is reckoned to have sold more than 110 million records. Compare that to the Beatles' more than 291 million certified units; making them, you guessed, the best-selling artists of all time.[2]

Fats co-starred in the fifties musical pictures *Shake, Rattle and Rock!*, *Disc Jockey Jamboree* and *The Big Beat*, as well as the Jayne Mansfield vehicle *The Girl Can't Help It*: films that proved hugely popular among music-mad teenagers like Paul and John. He appeared on *The Ed Sullivan Show* nearly seven years ahead of them. By the time the Beatles and other artists of the so-called British Invasion of America were swerving public taste, Fats and others like him were on a downslide. His chart career was as good as over by the end of 1964, not helped by unfavourable changes of record label.

There would be comebacks. He performed in London in 1967, in one of Brian Epstein's concerts at London's Savile Theatre; and in 1973 he headlined at the Hammersmith Odeon, a show described by Richard Williams in the *Melody Maker* as 'magnificent': 'Unlike Chuck [Berry], he wasn't cynical or saddled with a poor backing band; unlike Jerry Lee [Lewis], he didn't want to sing country ballads; unlike Little Richard, he wasn't carried away with his own divinity. He was, quite simply, Fats Domino. He sang almost nothing that wasn't a million-seller, or close to it, and he sang them exactly as he'd laid them down on the original recordings.'

Paul has said he may have told American record producer Richard Perry (the Pointer Sisters, Rod Stewart, Carly Simon, Diana Ross and a thousand others, notably Ringo, whose 1973 eponymous album featuring all the other Beatles he steered) that 'Lady Madonna' was 'based on' the big guy. What he meant was that, inspired by Fats's number 'Blue Monday', he sat down to attempt to write a song in the same vein. This worked in reverse. It led to Fats covering 'Lady Madonna' on his 1968 album *Fats Is Back*.[3] A year later, he also took on John's banger 'Everybody's Got Something to Hide Except Me and My Monkey' (which Paul suspected was a song about heroin) from the 'White Album'. John adored his hero's rendition.

The McCartneys remained in town for around six weeks, until late February 1975. They recorded at Allen Toussaint's Sea-Saint Studios in Gentilly, on the Bayou St John, on whose banks the downtown Mardis Gras Indian tribes congregate for their Super Sunday parade following Carnival. Much of the fourth Wings album *Venus and Mars* was taped there.

Toussaint, a master of New Orleans soul and R&B and one of America's most successful songwriters and producers, contributed to the recording and played on the track 'Rock Show'.[4] A seemingly endless stream of Toussaint's legendary local 'music royalty' friends graced the studio while McCartney was in residence, not least 'Mr Personality'/'true king of the fifties' Lloyd Price, Earl 'Let the Good Times Roll' King, Dr John and Professor Longhair.

Mobbed daily outside the studio by a couple of hundred fans and onlookers, Paul and Linda would always stop to pose for photos and sign autographs. They were living at the Le Richelieu Hotel, a charming colonial establishment on Chartres Street in the French quarter, just a ten-minute walk from Bourbon Street and Jackson Square. Paul drove them around in either a VW or an old Chrysler Valiant.

When work on *Venus and Mars* was done, Paul and Linda invited their New Orleans pals to Long Beach, California, where, on 24 March, they entertained them and a gaggle of A-listers on the ocean liner *Queen Mary*. Professor Longhair, New Orleans funk band the Meters, Lee 'Working in the Coal Mine' Dorsey, Ernie 'Mother-in-Law' K-Doe, and funk and soul group Chocolate Milk all performed. The Meters and Longhair both released live albums of recordings made that night.[5] The occasion also marked the first time that Paul met his future collaborator, Michael Jackson.[6]

The recording of *Venus and Mars*, three tracks for which had been worked up at Abbey Road the previous November prior to departure, and on which work later continued at Wally Heider Studios in Los Angeles, was not without problems. The relationship between the two new boys Jimmy and Geoff, for a start. They couldn't stand each other. It had been the elephant in the room for some time, but things came to a head six months in. Britton downed sticks and departed. Paul found himself in the sorry position of having to audition yet another new drummer. Lucky for him American thumper Joe English was available. He was hired to complete the album.

Another possible contributor had been expected. His presence and collaboration might have changed the course of history. May Pang and John Lennon did accept Paul's invitation to join the McCartneys in New Orleans. Then Lennon went and spoiled it all, by leaving May and returning home to Yoko.

What if they'd come? What if John, like Paul, had been seduced by the sights, sounds, aromas and music of New Orleans, and the old spark between them had flared, just as it had in California the previous year? What else might have come of it? John strumming a bit of guitar and singing backing vocals on a track or two destined for *Venus and Mars* could have led to anything. Such as Paul and John regrouping to make a Lennon/McCartney album? Followed by a tour to promote it? Not so far-fetched. John certainly discussed the idea with May. When he asked her what she thought about him writing again with Paul, she squealed with excitement. 'Are you kidding?!'

The single 'Listen to What the Man Said' heralded the fourth Wings long-player in May 1975. That's Joe English on drums. There's also Dave Mason (ex-Traffic) on guitar, and Tom Scott (the Blues Brothers, L.A. Express) on soprano sax. Number One in the US, Number Six in the UK, result. It's a breezy canter with an infectious beat and riff, great backing vocals, an audible kiss by Linda, a receding tempo towards the end and a poignant, satisfying orchestral fade. The wonder of it all, baby. Post-Fabs Macca at his finest. Gorgeous song, terrific record, what's not to like.

There would be two further single releases: 'Letting Go' and 'Venus and Mars/Rock Show'. The second of which just missed the American Top Ten and did zilch back home. 'Medicine Jar' would have made a fabulous single, too, but for the fact that Jimmy McCulloch wrote and sang it, not Paul. Can't have that.

The album? Well. Released May 1975. Number One wherever it mattered. Four million or so sales. Which would do for most. It's just that it wasn't *Band on the Run*: in excess of six million sales worldwide, and EMI UK's biggest-selling album of the 1970s. Two months earlier, it had bagged a pair of awards at the seventeenth annual Grammys – for Best Pop Vocal Performance by a Group, and for the work of engineer Geoff Emerick.

More notable, the night of 1 March at New York's Uris Theater, was the appearance of John and Yoko together, looking like extras out of *The Addams Family*. Her long, white marabou-trimmed dress and his Bob Cratchit-esque Dickensian-clerk garb rendered them curiosities in the glamorous crowd. They had eyes only for each other. Didn't they? Or could that have been a blatant bit of flirting captured by an on-ball lensman, of John and his erstwhile lover? Not May, David Bowie. Days later, John and Yoko are said to have renewed their marriage vows and enjoyed a honeymoon in their front room. Their son Sean was born on 9 October, John's thirty-fifth birthday, that year.

Having rekindled his marriage, John withdrew from the world for the next five years. Ostensibly to be a house husband, bake bread and bring up the baby, but during which he became a demented, stricken recluse, secretly sinking further and further into depression and drug dependency. He suddenly became unavailable to Paul and Linda when they dropped by to see them, fobbing them off with 'go away and grow up' rants – even though he had welcomed them with open arms and enjoyed nights of fun with them when they'd visited previously – whilst also reaching out to Paul in simple, plaintive songs on home-recorded cassettes that would not get through to his boyhood best friend until it was too late.

John doted on their little boy. He parented Sean wholeheartedly in a way that had not been his elder son's experience. Maybe he did that because he had not been there for Julian. The boy had barely seen or known his father, after John left him and his mother Cynthia for Yoko when Julian was five. It was only while John was with May

Pang that relations between father and son were restored, and they were able to get to know each other again.

Had John never gone back to Yoko, he and May would likely have bought the cottage they'd spotted during a trip to Long Island to see Mick Jagger, and have moved to Montauk. They would have had their babies, and have grown old together. It seems highly likely, too, that John and Paul would have resumed their songwriting partnership and have gone again.

Not as a Mark II Beatles, but as a Simon and Garfunkel-style duo, perhaps. Imagine *that* come-back concert in Central Park. –

On the *LennonNYC* episode of the American Masters podcast, *Double Fantasy* producer Jack Douglas, who was so close to John that he worked regularly with him on songs while lying beside him at home in bed, talks about a Beatles reunion for another Ringo album in 1981.[7] John wrote 'Stepping Out' and 'Nobody Told Me' for that. Both songs came posthumously to our ears via his and Yoko's *Milk and Honey*. Paul wrote 'Attention', which was recorded in 1980 in the South of France. Ringo sang it, Paul played bass on it and produced it, and Linda sang backing vocals. Another *Double Fantasy* collaborator, guitarist and former Bowie sidekick Earl Slick, told me that John had asked him to clear his diary for 1981, as he was planning a world tour.

Who else was he thinking of asking along?

CHAPTER 13
OVER AMERICA

Back to the records. In March 1975, Paul was lapping up recognition for *Band on the Run,* and mixing and mastering *Venus and Mars* at Wally Heider Studios in LA. Paul and Linda were riding high.

Perhaps too high. While driving from the studio to their rented Coldwater Canyon place one night, Linda in the passenger seat and the three girls in the back, Paul ran a red light on Santa Monica Boulevard. The hard-to-miss 1974 silver Lincoln Continental rental was pulled over. As the cop stood writing out the ticket, he caught a whiff of something familiar. Everybody out. A swift search yielded the inevitable: marijuana, about sixteen grams of it, or just over half an ounce. No more than what would be classed as 'for personal use', but enough to get nicked for.

The police officer hadn't had to get forensic. It was right there in Linda's handbag, which was careless of her, as was smoking the stuff in a moving vehicle. California reclassified cannabis possession from felony to misdemeanour that year. It was still illegal, however, under federal law. Had non-US citizen Paul taken the rap for their modest stash, it could have led to deportation and permanent exclusion. There would have been no *Wings Over America,* no 'Wings as biggest band in the world', no future.

Linda was arrested and carted off to the local precinct. Paul got the kids home and was then faced with the embarrassing dilemma of having to phone a friend or several to borrow the $500 in notes required to meet the wife's bail and get her out of clink. Which was all a ridiculous inconvenience. Why did it have to be so difficult? *Yes*, there were ATM machines in Hollywood by then, so Paul wouldn't have had to wait until the next morning to make a trip to a bank during office hours. But there were then, as now, restrictions on daily withdrawal amounts. Consider that $500 back then is the equivalent of about $2,800 or £2,200 now.

Linda was permitted to return to the UK on 2 April 1975. She then faced a six-month 'drug diversion' programme. In addition, the court was informed in her absence, she committed to counselling with 'a psychiatrist' (more likely to have been a psychotherapist) in London. The matter was resolved by the end of the year, with one newspaper reporting in November: 'Wings' Linda McCartney has had charges for the possession of marijuana dismissed by a west Lost [*sic*] Angeles court.' A member of Wings in the City of Fallen Angels. As they say, you couldn't make it up.

The Maccas should have taken a long, hard look at themselves at that point. If only for the sake of their three children. After close shaves in Sweden and Scotland, their flippant stance regarding their drug habit and their flagrant disregard for law and authority was always bound to catch up with them.

The peripatetic existence of the McCartney daughters could never, to date, have been mistaken for a secure routine. In and out of school whenever their superstar parents felt the urge to hike across the globe, resented and bullied misfits in the classroom one minute (Stella has said that she did her fair share in return), helicoptered by nannies and micro-managed by private tutors on the road the next, they can't have known what time zone they were in or which way was up.

Paul admitted that the schools didn't like their arrangements, and that he and Linda had needed to plead their position. They were musicians. They had a family. They made records that required promotion. To achieve that, they needed to tour and play live. When it was put to them that they should leave their kids at home to be cared for by someone else in their absence, so that they could continue to attend school, their response was succinct.

What would happen, Paul said, if they were on tour in, say, Australia and someone called to say that one of the children had a raging temperature? They would want to be there for their sick child. How could they possibly get back in time from so far away? He and Linda had made a decision that they should keep their close family together, and the teachers were forced to back down. Paul regarded their endless globetrotting as the finest education to be had. All of their children, he said, did better academically than he and their mother had.

Enamoured of the rural existence, the family attempted to replicate it wherever possible. Even in London, at their smart, prime-location villa on Cavendish Avenue, with their chickens, dogs, ducks, bunny rabbits and horses, flourishing vegetable patches and wholesome mess and stench. It was akin to a city zoo, and it infuriated their well-heeled neighbours. Not least the crowing cockerel that Linda laughed so hard at when we revisited those years. 'I don't think we were the favourite family on the block!' she said.

They still had High Park to retreat to, but its remote location rendered it impractical as their primary home. They had to be within easy reach of London, and that left Blossom Wood Farm, the 160-acre country estate that Paul had bought in 1973 at Peasmarsh, near Rye, in East Sussex. Stella and Mary attended the Thomas Peacock Community College (now Rye College). Linda tended and rode her horses without getting up the noses of her neighbours. They lived a secluded, mostly private existence when they were not in the studio or on the road.

As for getting back out there, Paul's feet were never still. He had laboured to pull the perfect latest line-up together, and was excited to show them off. *Melody Maker* duly reported the upcoming 'mammoth worldwide trek'. The band rehearsed for it, quaintly, at Rye's old Regent Cinema.[1]

On 6 September 1975, Wings performed a 'dress rehearsal' on a sound stage at Elstree Studios in Borehamwood, Hertfordshire just north of London, for more than a thousand EMI employees, their own tour staff and families, and a hundred members of their fan club, along with special guests Elton John, Ringo Starr, and Freddie Mercury, Roger Taylor, Brian May and John Deacon of Queen.

Three nights later, on Tuesday 9 September, they let rip on opening night at the Southampton Gaumont. They then stalked the length of England and visited Wales (Cardiff) and Scotland (Edinburgh, Glasgow, Aberdeen and Dundee). Liverpool on the 15th was a highlight, as was Hammersmith Odeon on the 17th and 19th. Then it was on to Australia. They had also been scheduled to perform in Japan. That excursion had to be cancelled after news reached Tokyo that they had been busted in Sweden four years earlier. Next stop America.

In addition to the ever-expanding Wings repertoire, Paul performed, for the first time since he had left his old band, songs that he and John had written for the Beatles: 'Lady Madonna', 'The Long and Winding Road', 'I've Just Seen a Face', 'Blackbird' and 'Yesterday'.

Press reviews were unanimously positive. Was the fact they had come on leaps and bounds down to lead guitarist Jimmy McCulloch having raised the band's game? It was hard to argue with that. Linda had improved beyond measure? Not wrong, but then again so had everyone. How do you get to Carnegie Hall? You know. The sound, lighting and special effects – including the volcanic fireworks display during 'Bond' theme 'Live and Let Die' that Paul would go on to feature in almost all of his live shows – had gone space-age.

Everything was big and grand, even the piano. The darned, organic, home-made vibe had been consigned to the compost heap. This was slick, superlative, electrified rock for the premium-paying masses. McCartney had found his groove. Wings had found their feet as a world-class act. Now let's see what they make of it in the land of Vegemite.

Their roadshow proceeded to Perth on 28 October . . . once the Maccas had managed to scrape themselves out of bed and race against time to make their scheduled but held Qantas flight. Nine gigs in five cities over eighteen days was the itinerary, performing in stadia so that they could get the hang of bigger venues and polish the act.

This was Paul's first time back since June 1964, when the Beatles toured Australia and New Zealand for the only time. When they came and went to scenes of mass hysteria. When the crowds that turned out were bigger than for Her Majesty the Queen, and four of Sydney's best hotels refused them lodgings. They played twenty shows, two a night, commencing in Adelaide where an unprecedented 350,000 fans stormed the city just to catch a glimpse. They looped to Melbourne, then Sydney, and spent eight days in New Zealand before spinning on back to Brisbane.

Down Under was more down-to-earth for Wings than it had been for the Beatles.

The Maccas took a breather in Hawaii, where they scored superior hash; then spent Christmas 1975 in New York, where they shared it. Not with Linda's family but with the Lennons, on whom they called at the Dakota to meet the baby Sean. Paul and John were getting on better than ever.

The New Year brought unsettling news. Old faithful Mal Evans was dead. The burly Beatle roadie and aide who had started grafting for them in August 1963, who had been at their side, beck and call wherever they went in the world and had even been involved in their recordings, had lost his way, his wife and his high-flying life after they crumbled. He fled to LA and attempted, with the help of a co-writer, to commit his extraordinary experiences to paper. This estranged him from them. As his January publishing deadline loomed, he was floored by depression. His drug use spiralled out of control and his live-in girlfriend couldn't reason with him.

She called his co-writer, who arrived to try and calm him down. Big Mal reached for what was reported to be a shotgun, but which was 'only' an air rifle. Still capable of killing a human. He waved it at the police officers who responded to the emergency call. They killed him. No Beatle attended his funeral. George Martin, Neil Aspinall and Harry Nilsson went instead. Mal's urn was despatched back to his family in England but got lost in the post. Although it is recorded that it was never seen again, that's just another Beatles myth. It surfaced eventually.

As did a trunk containing his paperwork and personal effects, discovered in the basement of a New York publisher's offices. This, too, was returned to his family. His former wife seized her chance. She sold some of the contents of the trunk at auction for drop-dead sums. Handwritten original lyrics by John and Paul for their songs 'A Day In the Life' and 'With a Little Help from My Friends' were sold, along with a notebook of Paul's in which he had jotted lyrics for 'Hey Jude', 'Sgt. Pepper's Lonely Hearts Club Band' and 'All You Need Is Love'.

Paul was enraged. His lawyers argued successfully through the London High Court that the lyrics were the personal property of the Beatles. They had never been Mal's or his beneficiaries' to sell. Other items such as his personal diaries remained with the family. Beatles historian Kenneth Womack was given access to them, and was appointed to write Mal's memoir, *Living the Beatles' Legend*.

Recording for the band's fifth album, *Wings at the Speed of Sound*, continued at Abbey Road soon after the winter break. Having worked up two songs there, 'Beware My Love' and 'The Note You Never Wrote', between August and October ahead of the Australia tour, they were in front and keen to capitalise on their growing popularity. Paul, Linda, Denny, Jimmy and Joe worked swiftly and efficiently, fuelled and enthused by their live work and the positive reaction to it. The album was signed off by the end of February, and on the shelves by 26 March.

If it differed from its predecessors in any significant way, it was in its cohesion as a Wings album; as opposed to the work of a revered former Beatle careering around the world with his missis, a chum from way back when and a couple of guns for hire. Every member of the line-up was afforded lead-vocal status on at least one song; notably Linda, who sang a ditty, 'Cook of the House', that she and Paul had written together. He also contributed double bass. Denny Laine took the main mic on 'The Note You Never Wrote' and 'Time to Hide'. Jimmy did the honours on his own, doubtless autobiographical song 'Wino Junko', and Joe English did 'Must Do Something About It'. But the album's stand-outs, 'Silly Love Songs', 'She's My Baby' and 'Let 'em In' are all led by Macca.

Call me sentimental but the gem, if you're asking, is the penultimate B-side track, 'San Ferry Anne'. Ça ne fait rien: 'It doesn't matter'. Perhaps Paul picked up the French phrase in Paris or New Orleans.[2] Its nativised spelling makes the words sound like a woman's name. French-infused and brass-heavy, its accompaniment is trumpety and cacophonous. But the vocal is pure Paul, clear as a bell, and the sentiment is uplifting. 'Let your feelings leap away into the laughter,' he coaxes. Nothing to get hung about.

The critics weren't bothered by At the Speed of Sound. Some gave the impression that they were waiting for Paul to fail. He could look them in the eye, though. Off to Number One in America it zapped, just like the previous three. Number Two back home. Its pair of singles both made the Top Five in both territories. 'Silly Love Songs', a blatant dig at everyone (including John) who had ever accused Paul of writing nothing but silly love songs was another American chart-topper. The album notched three and a half million around the globe.

That March, just as Wings were due to begin a brief European tour – two shows in Copenhagen and one each in Berlin, Rotterdam and Paris, to sharpen them ahead of the American crusade – Paul's father Jim died. He passed at home in Heswall on the Wirral, at the age of only seventy-three. Having long suffered from crippling arthritis and bronchitis, he had contracted pneumonia, had developed heart problems, and was cared for to the last by his second wife Angie.

This opposed the wishes of the family, who wanted him in a home. They had demanded that he be transferred to an establishment where he could be looked after by professional nurses, and with doctors on hand. Although it has long been claimed that John Lennon was the one to call Paul to impart the sad news of McCartney senior's death, there is no evidence. That rumour must have arisen after John's own estranged father Alfred died a fortnight after Jim McCartney. John phoned Paul to tell him about it because . . . who else was he going to call? Once again, as they had been because of their mothers right at the start, the boys were united in grief by the death of parents.

Paul missed his father's funeral. His brother Mike made excuses for him, that Wings were on the road and couldn't get back for it. Paul gave a press conference about the tour in London the next day, but neglected to mention his bereavement. The band departed for Denmark, without Paul informing them, either. He and Linda could easily have popped back from Europe for Jim's cremation, as they didn't have a gig that night. They failed to appear, nor did they show their faces for the scattering of the ashes the day after.

It could be that Paul feared the inevitable circus and press frenzy if he pitched up, which would have robbed both solemn occasions of their dignity and might have upset the rest of the family. Maybe his fury towards his stepmother for what he must have perceived as neglect held him back, for fear that he might lose control and give her a piece of his mind in front of the mourning throng.

Or was it simply a case, as his sympathetic brother insisted, of Paul being not only intensely private and fiercely protective of his personal life, but also being emotionally unequipped to deal with such things? He was just getting on with work and keeping his mind on the job, to prevent himself from going under. Knowing too well, as did Linda, that if he let grief get the better of him as it had done in the past, it stood a very good chance of wrecking him.

Because he harboured guilt. Paul had grown quite close to his father after his mother's death. He had shared with his dad the spoils of success, lavishing him with houses and even a racehorse. When Jim remarried, Paul made an effort with his stepmother and stepsister. But those relationships soured, resulting in estrangement between father and son.

The show must go on. So it would have, on 8 April 1976 in Fort Worth, Texas, had not feisty little Jimmy got himself into a steaming brawl with American teen idol David Cassidy in the bar of the Paris Georges V hotel. With a fractured little finger, he wouldn't be playing anything for a while. Down tools, chill out, let it heal.

Healing was clearly what Paul had in mind as he persisted with John. He and Linda went to the Dakota on 24 April to find Lennon watching NBC's *Saturday Night Live* on television. They squished themselves down beside him, and couldn't believe their eyes when a friend popped up on screen, talking to camera and addressing them directly. It was the show's stylish, good-looking young executive producer, Lorne Michaels, a friend of the McCartneys on Long Island.

The newspapers had been going overboard of late, flying unsubstantiated page leads about a Beatles reunion concert and the incredible sums they could command, if only they would agree to it. John and Paul were gobsmacked. The studio audience and the show's 22 million viewers must have been too.

Michaels focused his puppy-dog eyes down the lens. 'The Beatles are the best thing that ever happened to music,' he said. 'It goes even deeper than that. You're not just a musical group, you're a part of us. We grew up with you. It's for this reason that I'm inviting you to come on our show. [*Studio laughter.*]

'Now, we've heard and read a lot about personality and legal conflicts that might prevent you guys from reuniting. That's something which is none of my business. You guys will have to handle all that. But it's also been said that no one as yet has come up with *enough* money to satisfy you. Well, if it's money you want, there's no problem here. The National Broadcasting Company has authorised me to offer you a certified cheque for three thousand dollars . . .'

The studio audience cracked up. Michaels reminded the boys that after all, they knew the words to their own songs. It would be easy. 'If it helps you to reach a decision to reunite,' he deadpanned, 'well then, it's a worthwhile investment.' Nailing succinctly the issue that a possible Beatles reunion had never been and would never be about money – just as Oklahoman impresario and promoter Bill Sargent had found when he offered them $10m to reform in 1974. After seeing the new appeal on *Saturday Night Live*, Sargent trebled it. The press went berserk, but to no avail.

Yet John and Paul did consider it. Fleetingly. They asked each other in all seriousness whether they should just get in the lift, hop a yellow cab and tear across town to the studio. No frills. No prep. Wearing what they were standing up in. 'For ye cracke.'[3] Whatever it was that made them hesitate, the moment passed. But, imagine.

Paul and Linda returned to see the Lennons the following night. All change. Some reports say that John came to the intercom, was short with them and didn't let them up to the apartment. John implied as much himself, in his 1980 interview with *Playboy*. But across his interviews, he commonly gets things wrong and contradicts dates and facts, more than likely because he simply couldn't remember.

Linda said that they did go up. But they were not welcomed warmly as they had been the night before. John seemed less accessible, more agitated. He was irritable. Their easy exchanges, their resumed ability to communicate via their eyes without speaking, 'it just wasn't there,' said Linda. What had happened, did she think? She had no idea. It was as though a light had gone out, she told me. John had seemed fine the night before.

The change echoed what May Pang had experienced the previous year, when John went back to the Dakota to see Yoko, vanished for three days and then returned to her in an altered state of mind . . .

before stunning her with the news that he was dumping her. Paul was shocked by the unanticipated volte-face. It has been suggested that John was miffed by the monumental success of Wings, and couldn't contain his envy.

Paul and Linda were enjoying a massive profile in the US that by rights should have been his and Yoko's. *They* were the ones who had made America their home. Paul had this huge new group, while John was nowhere. Paul's records were flourishing in the charts, while John had stopped writing and recording, apart from demos he made at home that the world didn't know about. Paul's personal fortune had soared to over $25m. That's nearly $134m today or around £105m.

John had no idea how much money he and Yoko had, but he knew it wasn't anything like that much. He left business, investments and other financial concerns to his wife. So it was staring John in the face. Proof that Paul no longer needed him. 'The size of it?' I asked Linda. 'The size of it,' she said.

Off went Paul with a flea in his ear and a splinter in his soul. He took to the skies for the band's *Wings Over America* stadium tour that began on 3 May 1976. If he dared to pause and ponder matters between himself and John, he would have known that they were still inside each other, deeply embedded in one another's hearts. Had he counted back to that fateful Saturday, 6 July 1957, when he and John first met in the church hall in Woolton, he might have been surprised to realise that they had known each other for a lifetime of nineteen years.

The Liverpool lads had come of age to the same records. They had written songs that would reconfigure history from the same humble realms of reference. They had honed themselves in Hamburg, taken on America, and had proceeded to conquer the world as unintentional instruments of cultural revolution, to the point that the world would never be the same again. Yet they were still exactly who they had always been. Those nippers, those lads shared so much that no one but them could have understood. They were conjoined as if by an umbilical cord that could never be cut.

This was what Linda understood, but Yoko didn't. Linda got the fundamental importance of John in Paul's life. She was mature enough as a woman and secure enough as a wife to stand back and make room for their renewed relationship. She encouraged it, nurtured it and applauded it. May Pang, likewise. It was one of the many reasons why she and Linda got on so well. Yoko, on the other hand, was threatened by it. She put her own needs first. She seethed and schemed. She wanted John away from Paul, and at times, it seemed, from the world. She wanted him, it appeared, all to herself.

So much common ground they could have retrodden. So much unfinished business could they have resolved. Neither one of them was ever truly happy without the other. Neither, it could be argued, ever made music to outdo what they had conjured together. Could they do it again? They would never know. After that fateful night, 25 April 1976, they never saw each other again.

The Maccas did not do things by halves. With typical extravagance, they rented not one but four houses in strategic locations across America for the duration of the tour. Comfortable domestic set-ups were deemed preferable to lavish hotel suites. It meant that they could 'go home' every night. The houses they selected were in New York, Chicago, Dallas and LA. They also took on a British Aircraft Corporation 'one-eleven' jet airliner, slapped a distinctive band logo on its side, and modified the cabin to resemble that of a private jet.

Out went the confining rows of seats. In came the sofas and the beanbags, rendering the craft an airborne version of the touring double-decker bus. They threw in a disco down one end to amuse the children. Their entourage included a road manager, a security guard, Rose the housekeeper and their upbeat horn section.

A frustrating amount of downtime is par for the course on a rock tour. It's when recklessness tends to take hold. Linda and Paul laid down the law. As on every other Wings tour, they would be keeping things child-friendly. Hard drug-taking, excessive boozing and the entertaining of groupies would not be tolerated, either on the plane or backstage. Having their daughters around was conducive to good band behaviour. Paul was in his element. He had his woman, his children and his work in one place. It was almost a case of back to where he once belonged.

From Houston and Detroit they nipped over the border to Toronto, where Ringo and George attended their concert at the Maple Leaf Gardens sports and concert venue. Back to Cleveland, Philadelphia, Landover, Atlanta and Uniondale, Boston; and two nights at New York's Madison Square Garden – finally! – where everyone was hoping, not least Paul, that John would scrape himself into some street clothes and come down to support his pal. The press were excited. Paul was reserved. It was as though he knew that it would never happen. Back to the newsroom, boys.

There were compensations. Britain's *Daily Mirror* flew in a planeload of fans to experience the thrilling spectacle. Former first lady Jackie Kennedy Onassis graced the stand. It was taking a lot to impress McCartney by then. You might have thought that her presence would have had some effect. Nah. Paul was much more taken with his own achievements.

'This is what I have been working towards,' he enthused to journalist Bob Hart. 'This is what I wanted the band to do when it was good enough. Now, it is good enough. I am not even nervous, because I have spent five years making sure that this would be great.'

On to Cincinnati, Kansas City and Chicago, where they took a short break. Paul and Linda relaxed on horseback. In Minneapolis on 4 June, the band and crew celebrated little Jimmy's twenty-third birthday. At the after-show, the cake ended up in his face. That was as badly behaved as proceedings got. Three days later they were in Denver.

Then it was north-west over Wyoming, Idaho, Oregon and Washington State to the city of Seattle, where the gigantic Kingdome stadium had only just been built. Wings were the first rock band to raise the world's largest concrete roof, over the heads of 67,000 fans. After which, if it was Sunday 13 June, it had to be San Francisco. San Diego, Tucson and LA brought up the oddly planned zigzag rear. They finished over three nights at the Inglewood Forum, then the home of the Los Angeles Lakers. Ringo was with them for the opener and partied with them afterwards. Cher and Elton John were in the audience. The tour wrapped there on Wednesday 23 June.

End-of-tour bash? With knobs on. The venue was the old Hollywood abode of silent movie star Harold Lloyd. The dress code was blistering hat-to-sock white. The guest list heaved with legends: George and Ringo, Bob Dylan, the Jacksons, Cher, the Eagles, Warren Beatty, Dustin Hoffman, Elton John and on and on. Entertainment came courtesy of a string quartet and synchronised swimming, or was it water ballet? When the valets returned cars to their owners at bedtime, each had a white rose tucked under the wiper blade and a note from the hosts: 'Thank you for coming, Paul and Linda.' White gardenias, after all, were Yoko's thing.

As if all that were not enough. Home they flocked, to deliver seven concluding shows in Europe that September. From Vienna to Zagreb and on to Venice, where they took part in the UNESCO-backed 'World Week for Venice'. The idea was to raise funds to save the sinking city. They mounted their show in St Mark's Square . . . where their heavy tour trucks must have caused the endangered site to sink a little further. The 30,000-strong crowd who turned up to rock out didn't help matters either. They fled north into West Germany, and then channel-wards, in time to deliver three shows that October at Wembley's Empire Pool.

Wings Over America, the triple live album of the Stateside tour, appeared in December 1976 and exceeded expectations. Number One in America early the following year, it was their fifth and final consecutive long-playing chart-topper in 'Lennon territory'. Back home, it achieved a respectable Number Eight. The bizarre thing about it was that Paul took a Biro to the classic Lennon–McCartney credit for the five Beatles songs included on it – 'Lady Madonna', 'The Long and Winding Road', 'I've Just Seen a Face', 'Blackbird' and 'Yesterday' – transposing it as McCartney–Lennon.

Why do that? Was he still insecure or could it have been petty retaliation for that snub back in April at the Dakota? Maybe he felt that at last that he had outclassed his old friend and foe, and he had now earned and was giving himself deserved top billing. Was he trying to force a reaction out of John? Again, disappointed. Not a murmur. Not even Yoko jibbed, nor was there a whiff of legal action. He'd got away with it.

Paul would pull the same stunt nearly three decades later, twenty-two years after John's murder, on his double live album *Back in the US*. This was a completely live capture of his first concerts there for almost ten years, billed as the 'Driving US' tour and mounted to promote his studio album *Driving Rain*. This time, the widow Ono Lennon threw her toys out of the pram, and objected bitterly.

Nineteen Lennon–McCartney compositions were featured on that album: one for each year the two had known each other. They were credited to 'Paul McCartney and John Lennon'. This was primarily a hit-back against George and Ringo for refusing to allow Paul the use of that credit order on the 1995 *Beatles Anthology*. Yoko threatened to sue. Paul argued that the selected songs had been his own work, not equal collaborations, and that there had been negligible participation from John on those songs.

This was Paul getting even for Yoko's axing of his co-writing credit from her and John's 'Give Peace a Chance' on the 1997 compilation *Lennon Legend: The Very Best of John Lennon*. Tit, tat. Tat, tit. It is so painfully often the case that artists of the greatest global stature and mind-boggling wealth are the ones who engage in the pettiest so-what disputes. At ease, everyone. Life, short.

February 1977 saw the band back at Abbey Road, where work was due to begin on their sixth studio album *London Town*. Heavy snow had fallen throughout December. By January the country was battling six-foot snow drifts. The freeze persisted into the following month, rendering London cold, wet and soggy. It was challenging just getting around.

By the end of March, Paul was tired and frustrated by it all. He hauled his family off to Jamaica for a holiday, no doubt picking up 'supplies' while they were there. He informed his musicians that they would resume recording on a boat in the US Virgin Islands. Actually, three boats, to accommodate family, musicians, captain and crew, engineers Geoff Emerick and Mark Vigars, and their portable recording studio.

This new caper was a swerve for Linda, who was about four months' pregnant at the time. Just through the dodgy period, past the morning sickness and the extreme fatigue, glowing from hormonal surges but minding how she went. She was then thirty-six years old. Heather was fourteen, Mary eight and Stella six. Their new baby was due in September. Those were big gaps, between first and fourth and second and fourth. They hadn't intended to get pregnant, she later told me. Nor had they not intended it. 'Nature takes its course,' she added. 'I've never not had reason to trust it.'

Paradise is often half as nice as you imagined it. Tropical weather proved just as burdensome as doom and gloom back home. Folk were not yet routinely taking care over sun exposure. They burned. The novelty of the location wore off. There were inconveniences, accidents and mishaps. And they were lucky not to get done for dope again. Interrogated by local rangers, they were slapped with stern warnings about drug abuse and threatened with arrest and serious consequences if they ignored the regulations. Had Paul assumed he would be able to do whatever he liked out there on the open ocean under the stars, he was mistaken.

What the hell. It was summer back home. There was a new baby to look forward to, and he and the girls were excited. High Park beckoned.

CHAPTER 14

SONS OF KINTYRE

'Teaching the pipes is a massively important thing in Scotland,' says Ian McKerral, pouring tea in his large sitting room looking down over Campbeltown harbour, loch and marina: a scene of postcard perfection contradicted by the storm that blew us in.

'Campbeltown is really rich in piping history,' he tells me. 'At one point we had four bands, and we've won the world championships three times. My father got me into it. He was an accordion player and singer. He bought me my own accordion when I was four or five. He then got me a chanter, which is an instrument similar to a recorder. You start on that, I was about ten when I did. Then you move on to the pipes.'

Ian's chanter teacher was the janitor at his school. 'Four of us came on leaps and bounds,' he remembers. 'We had the aptitude, flair and technique. It came easy to us. So we joined the local pipe band. We may never have progressed beyond that, had not Pipe Major Tony Wilson – who was born in Campbeltown, moved away, joined the Scottish Guards, then the police, then came back – taken over the Campbeltown Pipe Band. My friend to this day John Brown and I joined when we were twelve. Tony had us playing in competitions, he took us to the world championships in Corby when we were in Grade Two, all sorts. We really enjoyed it. He was a great character and a real mentor. We owe him everything.'

Ian is famous throughout the realm, and internationally in the world of the bagpipes. The 61-year-old recently retired piping instructor was not yet sixteen when Paul chose the Campbeltown Pipe Band, of which Ian was part, to swell the sound of the Wings single 'Mull of Kintyre' and to perform in its promotional video. Its echoes have never faded. Not only did the hit record put the Kintyre peninsula on the map. It also remains the biggest thing that has ever happened to the pipers and drummers who performed on it. On the back of its global success and enduring popularity, they have dined out and basked in its glory for the best part of half a century.

The pipers and drummers selected by Tony Wilson, all Campbeltonians, joined the McCartneys and crew on 9 August 1977 at the bothy on High Park Farm that Paul had converted to a fully functioning recording studio. The band donned their full regalia to record, as is tradition. Paul wanted to record them in the open air, the better to enrich the skirl of the pipes with the swirl of the elements and the farmyard. They nailed it, Ian recalls with a grin, in just one take. The young musicians later reconvened with 'the Beatle' and Co. to film the track's video at Saddell Bay, a twenty-minute ride north of Campbeltown. Its backdrop would be the view across the Kilbrannan Sound to the majestic Isle of Arran.

Saddell Castle, standing virtually on the beach is, thanks to its starring role in the film, now a world-famous, much-visited landmark. It had risen during the sixteenth century from the ruins of an earlier fortress in which medieval Scottish king Robert the Bruce, from whom our monarch is directly descended, had sought refuge during the First War of Scottish Independence. Construction was augmented with remnants from the destroyed Saddell Abbey. The castle is also the ancestral home of the MacDonald clan. Everything here is steeped in history.

There are futuristic touches too, not least in the shape of Antony Gormley's cast iron sculpture *GRIP*: a large, exaggerated male figure that appears to ascend at low tide from the rocks below the castle. Installed in 2015 as part of Gormley's *LAND* installation to mark the

Landmark Trust's fiftieth anniversary, the intended temporary fixture was afforded permanence by way of a secret donation from an individual with longstanding connections to the place. Someone renowned in these parts for private acts of investment and generosity. Someone who may or may not once have been a Beatle.

'There is an excitement about making a sculpture that can live out here amongst the waves and the wind, the rain and snow, in night and day,' stated the artist when his work was unveiled. 'The sculpture is like a standing stone, a marker in space and time, linking with a specific place and its history but also looking out towards the horizon, having a conversation with a future that hasn't yet happened.' Note the reference to 'a standing stone'. Had Gormley visited High Park Farm, and been inspired by Paul's personal megalith there?

That summer of 1977, Ian was 'coming up sixteen. We'd left Campbeltown Grammar and had gone to work at the local shipyard. I got an apprenticeship as an engineer. One day, out of the blue, Tony came down to see us and said that he'd been approached by Paul McCartney.

'We knew who he was, of course. We'd seen them around the town for the past few years. Paul told Tony he had this wee song, and he wanted to see if it worked with the backing of a pipe band. We burst out laughing.

'"No! Honest!' Tony protested. "I'm going up there," he insisted. "I'll let you know how I get on." We dismissed the idea as a huge laugh, and never thought any more of it. But sure enough, Tony did have a meeting with Paul and Linda McCartney up at High Park Farm, and he brought back a tape. It was just Linda on the keyboards, playing the melody. Tony told us he was going to write it out in bagpipe music. After that, he picked us. Seven pipers and seven drummers. His best players. We practised for six weeks. It's quite a simple tune, not at all difficult to play, which of course is its magic. Sometimes simple is best. They say McCartney is the master at that.'

Recording day arrived.

'"Get your kilts on!" said Tony, and we went away up to High Park. We went into this recording studio built on the side of their house [the lower farmhouse], and there were Geoff Emerick the Beatles engineer and assistant engineer Mark Vigars. Paul had on a waistcoat and welly boots. It was the first time I'd ever met him and Linda. They were very laid-back, incredibly humble. They never came across as superstars. The times we met them afterwards, they were just the same. We all shook hands. Then we tuned the pipes up, we set up in the studio, played the thing once and McCartney said, "That's it! Done! You's done it in one take!" They played it back to us, and it did sound really good.'

Out came the sandwiches, the beers and the whisky.

'We had a wee party,' says Ian. 'Half and half in the recording studio and outside. One of the pipers got a bit drunk and fell into a horse trough. Och aye, it was amazing. Paul and Linda's daughters Mary, Stella and Heather were all there. Mary and Stella were just wee girls. Heather was about our age. I can remember that she was quite an attractive girl. We boys were all lusting after her, only joking. Linda was heavily pregnant with their son James, who was born the following month. When you see her in the video carrying a baby down from the bothy, that's not the baby boy she'd just had, but a wee doll. She carried it like a real one, of course. It all looked very realistic. We made the video a couple of months later, on the beach at Saddell Bay.'

Saddell was actually the second choice for video location. The first, Ian reveals, was Carskiey Bay: the broad, mile-long, silver-sandy expanse down at Southend. That is where the Irish Christian Saint who evangelised Scotland is said to have first set foot in Argyll in AD 563, before sailing on north towards Iona. St Columba's Chapel and 'footprints' can still be found there, at Keil, just below the huge, derelict Keil Hotel where the lesser members of Wings were once billeted.

But the gleaming beach is haunted by darker history. Four hundred years ago it was awash with the blood of the 300 men, women and children, all MacDonalds and their supporters, who were massacred during the 1647 Battle of Dunaverty. Which is hard to imagine, when you walk there now. It's such a peaceful place. Its pink, rocky outcrops and seaweedy pools would have lent bright colour to director Michael Lindsay-Hogg's 'Mull of Kintyre' footage.[1] Its magnificent views of Sanda Island, Northern Ireland and Ailsa Craig[2] would have made a dramatic backdrop.

'But the weather was bad,' explains Ian. 'We were all set to go there, but it was decided at the last minute that we would go up the east side after all. To Saddell, which is more sheltered. That was a long day, let me tell you, marching up and down that beach. No one-take pipe band this time. There were a *lot* of takes. It may have been November, but we were sweltering in our feather bonnets, kilts and tunics, the plaid [length of tartan cloth thrown over the shoulder], the crossbelt, the waist belt, the horsehair sporran, the hose tops, the white spats and the black brogues. It all weighs a ton. We also had these big heavy black capes on, to protect our gear from the rain.

'Despite which, the filming day, like the recording day, was unforgettable.'

McCartney himself feared ridicule and even disaster if he dared to release such a twee, nostalgic song during the gritty, aggressive punk rock era.

'I mean, it was madness,' Paul said. 'But I just thought, "Well, sod it." But even though I was a Sassenach, it became a big Scottish song ... And the strange thing was, even punks liked it. One day, Linda and I were in traffic in London in the West End somewhere, and there was a big gang of punks who looked very aggressive, and we were kind of crouching a little bit, trying not to get noticed and thinking, Jesus, what are they gonna do? And then they noticed us, and one of them comes to the car, so I wound down the window a little bit, and he goes, "Oh, Paul, that 'Mull of Kintyre': it's fucking great!"'[3]

The track was released that November with 'Girls' School', an upbeat rock number in stark contrast to the haunting, mellow ballad it accompanied. Because the single was a double A-side, those two tracks counted jointly as the band's only UK Number One, topping the charts for nine weeks in December 1977 and January 1978 and breaking the record previously held by the Beatles' 'She Loves You'. 'Mull of Kintyre' became that year's Christmas Number One.[4] It was the first single to sell over two million copies in the UK, and was Britain's best-selling single of all time until Band Aid's 'Do They Know It's Christmas' in 1984, seven years later.

It remains one of the biggest-selling singles in chart history, is the highest-selling single of Paul's entire career, and has sold more copies than any track released by the Beatles. It also appears on the 1978 compilations *Wings Greatest*; the 1987 McCartney compilation *All the Best!*; the 2001 compilation *Wingspan: Hits and History*; and the 2016 compilation *Pure McCartney*. It has been earning its keep, in other words, for almost half a century.

'At the time we didn't really realise how big it was going to be. I don't think anybody did,' remembers Ian. On the back of it all, life for the young pipers and drummers ran away with them for a while.

'I wish I had been a wee bit older when it all happened,' he grins. 'I could have gone for a pint, to celebrate. When the record went to Number One, we were whisked down to London in a bus that waited for us there the whole time. It was my first-ever time in London. Jim Miller, a junior reporter from the local paper, the *Campbeltown Courier*, came with us. He was allowed to be with the band on the condition that he never sold any photos from his day with us. They put us up at the Holiday Inn, Swiss Cottage, all expenses paid. We were very well taken-care-of.

'They had us make another video, this time in a studio setting, to show on *Top of the Pops*. Paul, Linda and Denny Laine sitting on a rock, with the band marching through them. We also did a recording at BBC Television Centre for *The Mike Yarwood Christmas Show*. I remember afterwards, I watched it at home with my parents.

'We became superstars in the town here. A lot of newspaper people, journalists and photographers, came looking for us. Many of them printed stuff we'd never even said!'

He who pays the piper calls the tune. But did he? Controversy exploded shortly after the record became a hit, and rumours have persisted ever since, that the pipers were treated unfairly and even exploited. Although the McCartneys earned enormous royalties from global sales of the recording, the pipers were paid only the standard Musicians' Union rate. Critics were outraged that the boys were offered no bonus or royalty share for their contribution, which undoubtedly gave the song a special dimension. He must have been irked by the criticism, for Paul allegedly sent each performer a cheque for £200 for his trouble. As it happens, this wasn't true.

'I'd like to set the record straight once and for all,' states McKerral. 'We were sixteen and seventeen years old, and not very interested in money. The deal they offered us was this: you can have the royalties or you can have a one-off payment. It was decided – not by me – that we would take the money. Which was *not* two hundred pounds each, but seven hundred and fifty pounds each' – the equivalent today of around £6,000 per musician; a veritable fortune to part-time pipers working in the local shipyard.

'So we were *not* "done by McCartney". I need to make this clear, and you are hearing it here for the very first time. We made the decision ourselves, as a band. We should have had the royalties instead, but it was *not* his fault. Someone later worked out how much we would have earned from a record that became such a big global hit. It was about three quarters of a million pounds each! But I have no regrets. None at all. The band *was* offered royalties. *We* turned that offer down. We each had to join the Musicians' Union in order to be paid our money. Everything was done above board.'

Even so. Given McCartney's immense wealth – estimated at the end of 2022 to be in the region of £865m, making him by far the richest musician in the UK;[5] and given the fortune that 'Mull of Kintyre' reaps in royalties each year since its original release – a rough guestimate puts this at in excess of half a million pounds a year, based on Performing Rights Society records – could he not have been a little more generous?

That single recording has likely made a staggering £23m over the forty-six years that it has existed. Paul is reckoned to earn about £56m annually via royalties from various sources including his Beatles songs (he now owns a share of the publishing rights to 251 songs recorded by the Beatles, worth £800m), and the catalogues of Buddy Holly, Carl Perkins and others – couldn't he have spared the pipers who piped and the drummers who drummed, fourteen of them in total, a modest million apiece for their trouble?

'No grudges are held,' insists Ian. 'After "Mull of Kintyre", Geoff Emerick and Mark Vigars were really keen for the band to do our own LP. Back down to London to record it at AIR Studios we went. McCartney paid for absolutely everything. We were allowed to call it *Mull of Kintyre* by the Campbeltown Pipe Band. It featured our own instrumental version of the title track, 'Lara's Theme' from *Dr Zhivago*, and traditional songs such as 'Floral Dance', 'Highland Mary', 'Soldier's Return' and 'Flower of Scotland'. We loved doing it. Unfortunately, it wasn't a success.

'Yes, people have said that if McCartney were anything, he would have given us all a chunk of money. He being a billionaire. He probably never thought if it, and we weren't going to ask him. There has never been any animosity about it. Money's not everything.'

What comes across loudly and clearly is that those pipers and drummers would have done it for nothing. Forget wages. It was an honour. It was the outside world that made a fuss about it all, not them.

Forty years later, in April 2018, a McCartney came knocking again.

'I was working up at the school, teaching the pipes as usual,' says Ian, 'when this girl called. Out of the blue. She said she was looking to get twelve pipers down to Cuskiey beach for a photo shoot. "I can't say who," she said. "Ok," I said. "I take it you'll pay for transport down and the band will be given a small fee?" At the time we were charging only two hundred and fifty pounds per engagement. For the whole band. She readily agreed to it.

'This was on the Friday. On the Monday, I got told that we had to go down to the beach at half past nine, and that it was for a shoot for Stella McCartney. There's a magnificent big house down there, the Carskiey House Estate and Shore Cottage. It gets hired out for private use. Weddings, house parties, film shoots. People go wood-cock-shooting and sea-fishing there. There's a great golf course. That's where they all were.

'We went away down with the young pipers. It was like a film set on the beach. Three models modelling handbags and sunglasses for Stella. I was just standing there, taking it all in when Stella herself appeared out of the blue. She came over to where I was standing with the pipers and she said, "Who's Ian?" "That's me," I told her.

'She flung herself at me and gave me a massive hug. She knew. "You played on 'The Mull' (she kept calling the song 'The Mull') with my mum and dad, didn't you! Can you do me a favour? Can you get the pipers to play 'The Mull'?"

'As they were starting up, she went up onto a rock with her phone. "What you doing?" I called out to her. She said, "I'm Facetiming my dad!"

'"Did you get him?" I said, after the pipers had finished.

'"He's not answering," she replied. "But I've recorded it. I'll get it to him later!"

'So Paul missed his daughter's big Guess Where I Am moment. More a case of Guess Where I Was.'

Did Paul know where Stella had gone that day and was he aware of what she was doing there? Knowing how sentimental he has always been, and how he struggles with emotion, was it simply that he couldn't bear to see, via a tiny mobile phone screen, that concen-trated, poignant scene with a band of plaid-clad pipers no older than the lads who had accompanied him and Linda misty moons ago, at High Park and on Saddell beach. When Stella and his other daughters were still children, and his only son was in his wife's womb, about to be born; when he was still a young man with everything going for him, everything to play for, and when the love of his life was still alive . . .? It is hard not to speculate.

'Who knows,' says Ian. He rubs his eyes. His hand reaches up to cover his mouth. Maybe he's back there.

'Anyway,' he says. 'Stella gave me another massive hug, then she turned to go back to the house. She was away up the beach when suddenly she turned again and came running back. "Ian! Ian!" she was yelling, and I could see she was on her phone. "Come and speak to Mary!" She'd managed to get hold of someone significant after all. She put them on. And suddenly there was her big sister on the line, thanking me profusely. "Ian," Mary said to me, "you have made Stella's day. Thank you." She was thinking of her mum, she said. They both were.'

It occurred to me that Linda would have been gone almost twenty years to the day, that day. Could that have been the reason why Stella chose to stage her shoot on Carskiey beach, where Paul, Linda, Denny and the Campbeltown Pipe Band so nearly shot the video for 'The Mull'?

Stella gave Ian £1,200 for his pipers' trouble. Almost a grand more than Ian had quoted. His teenaged troupe were more than happy with that.

'She later came back for her husband's birthday, and asked me if she could get the *full* band this time,' adds Ian. 'We delivered, of course, and she was so happy. This time, she asked for my email address. "If I ever come back, and if I need pipes for anything again," she promised, "I will definitely be in touch." I've never heard from her since, but who knows? I waited forty years the last time.

'That day, and the way Stella spoke so fondly about the song, made me realise how much "Mull of Kintyre" means to the McCartneys. It was not just another song by an ex-Beatle which by some fluke became hugely popular all over the world, a sort of all-things-to-all-people tune. It is much, much more than that. It's the soundtrack of a family's life. It's about a remote but welcoming place that was and remains very dear to them. They were people so famous that wherever they went, they could never get away. Not really. But they were able to get away from it all here.

'It's such a simple song, when you boil it down, but it says so much. It taps into something deeply personal and unreachable. Not only for them, but for all of us. There's something in it that takes you back, to the places and the people you loved then. If that's all it is, it's more than enough.'

Nostalgia . . . the indefinable, unquantifiable, at times unbearable force that folds us back on ourselves, ripping at the heart. The pain it provokes can cause suffering. Because it depends on death and endings, of people, places and times that we have loved.

Fellow piper John Brown, Ian's lifelong friend, tells, as you might expect, an almost identical story. We meet for copious Black Velvets, the champagne and Guinness cocktail, at the bar of Campbeltown's Royal Hotel.

'It's etched on my heart, that lovely summer's evening at High Park Farm,' John reminisces. 'I don't mind telling you, it was the highlight of my life. A minibus picked us up and off we went. We got the plaids on, helping each other. A wee quick tune-up outside, because the pitch of the pipes changes in the open air. We had to acclimatise. We were all waiting patiently in the studio when some-one said, "Here's Paul coming!". This wee door opened and McCartney walked in. I was stunned. A living god. I'd never seen him before. There was a superstar in our midst, and it felt surreal. My jaw must have hit the floor, I think.

'He had his waistcoat on, the one he always wore, plus a pair of cords and cowboy boots. He must have known how nervous we all were. He came over and shook all our hands. "I'm glad you could make it," he said. "Let's have a wee take. We'll do the pipes first, then the drummers."

'It was all so quick, I wanted it to last longer. They played it back to us and we were all amazed. We'd never heard a recording like that, in that kind of situation. "Right, boys," announced Paul, "I think that deserves a wee refreshment."

'Linda turns to Denny Laine and a couple of roadies and says, "Go get the refreshments," and they came back with a wheelbarrow full of McEwan's Export.[6] Then she looked at us and said sternly, "Coca Cola for you boys. You're under-age!"

'She was quite the mother figure, very homely and kind. I protested, cheekily. I pointed to the lad beside me and said, "I'm the same age as him!"

'"Okay," she said, "you can have *one* beer. But that's it!"

'You could tell how excited Paul was by it all,' John remembers. 'I have never forgotten it. You could feel it in the room. It was all quite magical.'

When his copy of the single arrived in the post, John tore the package open and ran to the record player to play it.

'"Turn it up!" said my mum. "Louder! Come on!" She sat down with my fisherman dad in the living room. They never said a thing. My dad sat there shaking his head. Oh no, I thought, he doesn't like it. But then when it got to the end, he looked across at me and went, "That's absolutely brilliant. Play it again." Over and over again. He could not have been more proud of me.'

He is glad that the pipers' album was not successful, John insists.

'It wasn't very good! A lot happened . . . Tony Wilson changing the reeds the night before, other things going wrong. You have to remember that it's not about dreams here. It's about reality. I always find myself measuring everything against the landscape. We're surrounded by breathtaking natural beauty here, but nobody's exploiting it. It would not be right. You've got to have some parts of the world that remain completely unspoilt. A place like this reaffirms your faith in humanity.

'I believe that's what Paul discovered when he came here. At least, it's what Linda helped him to realise when he brought her here. A global superstar drops down in the middle of all this and goes, "Yeah. This is where I belong." It tells you everything.'

Unlike Ian McKerral, John Brown did get to see Paul in Campbeltown again. Although he can't remember the year, he recalls that Paul returned with second wife Heather Mills during the period between January 2003 (they had married in June 2002) and their separation in 2006. Linda's statue in its memorial garden had been unveiled in November 2002. Paul, who was on tour in America at the time, was unable to attend. Eventually – imagine how challenging it must have been for him – he got round to returning to Kintyre to see it.

'I was just jumping out of my van in the square, and there they were,' says John. 'I'd not seen him for more than twenty years. Not since Christmas 1979, when Wings brought us up from under the stage at the Glasgow Apollo on the Saturday night of their shows there to surprise the audience. It was unannounced. What a moment that was. Another one! I remember looking up and seeing Paul through a crack in the floorboards, singing "Yesterday". The next number was "Mull of Kintyre", so up we came, dressed in our full regalia. It was thunderous.

'We weren't mic'd up, we didn't have ear plugs, the crowd was deafening, we couldn't hear ourselves playing, and suddenly I knew what it must have felt like to be a Beatle. There's a recording of it, and you can barely hear the pipe band. There we were, lined up behind Wings, and the audience was going crazy. Playing live with Paul McCartney and Wings: that was the big one. Playing that song with them on stage. Can you imagine? I wish we could go back and do it again. Because I don't think we really took it in at the time. The age we were, maybe it was a bit young. Ian's the same, I know he is. We talk about it. The more you think about "Mull of Kintyre", the more meaningful it gets.'

And that was it. Until one afternoon in the square in Campbeltown, almost a quarter of a century later.

'I looked up,' says John, 'and there they were. Paul and Heather, standing right in front of me, a few feet away. "How you doing?" I blurted. "You all right?!" he beamed back. "Aye, no' bad." He was friendly enough, as he always is to everyone, but I couldn't tell whether he recognised me or not. I decided not. Why would he, really. I was only a bairn at the time of the recording. It had been decades. He must have met a million people since. More! So I plucked up the courage. "Paul," I said, stepping towards him, "I hope you don't mind. It's a long time since I've seen you. I was one of the pipers who played on 'Mull of Kintyre'."

'He stared at me. Then he stepped towards me. "John," he said. Nodding. Smiling. "Can I just shake your hand? I'm glad you stopped. Absolutely delighted. How are you boys doing? How's the band?"

'"It isn't going anymore," I told him. "It's a schools' band now." His face fell. Then I mentioned a bit about the championships, which he seemed very interested in.

"Do you remember that night up at the farm?" I asked him.

"Of course I remember!"

"And d'you remember all the McEwan's beer in the wheelbarrow?"

"I remember that, too! Happy, happy times, John."

"Happy, happy times."

"You'd'a had plenty of hair the last time I saw you," he said.

"Aye," I said, "I did."

"What happened to it?"

"I suppose it's like the 'Mull of Kintyre'," I told him. "My hair is history now."

'I had to get away, I had a pipe practice in Glasgow – for the band I was playing in at the time, the David Urquart Pipe Band. I made my excuses. "Just a minute," he said, and he beckoned Heather to join us. "I want you to come and meet one of my pipers." She said hello, nice enough, but I had the feeling that she wanted to get away. Well, I had to as well, so no bother. Paul and I shook hands again.

'That moment when we looked into each other's eyes is almost too much to recall. A crowd was beginning to gather around him now. He's like the Pied Piper, isn't he. Wherever he goes, that happens. "Tell all the lads I was asking for them," he said, as he turned to leave. He had his head down as he walked away. Then he glanced back over his shoulder. And I did. We both smiled. I thought for a minute, I might cry, here. That's the last time I've seen him.

'I couldn't contain my excitement. I drove straight up to my mum and dad's, my heart pounding. I ran in and said, "You'll never guess."

'"You're joking!"

'"I'm *not* joking! I had to cut him short, I had to get away, I'm going to be late . . ."

'"Is he still there? Can you take us down?"

'It was too late, of course. Always too late. But I still think about that evening. "One of my pipers." What a line. One of my proudest moments. Paul McCartney said that to me. If I hadn't realised it before, I knew it then. "Mull of Kintyre" was a love letter to the place that meant the world to him. The place that saved his life.'

What about John? Does he still like living there?

'Och aye,' he gruffed. 'There's no better place. And I've seen a fair bit of the world, I don't mind telling you, through piping. America. Europe, especially Switzerland and Germany. I loved Holland. Lovely people, lovely country, but flat. Boring landscape. I've taught piping all over, I had a lot of success as a solo piper in many countries. But nothing compares to these times. The "Mull of Kintyre" times. Twenty-five miles north of Campbeltown, go and sit with a tin on a lovely summer's night. Look across to the isle of Islay and all the way to Ireland. There's no finer view anywhere. Paul knows.'

The one feisty Scot in Wings, Jimmy McCulloch, did not get to play on 'Mull of Kintyre'. It was a terrible irony. An alleged drunken night at High Park Farm, so the story went, had ended in tears. Different people tell different versions of what went down. There had been dissent for some time. McCulloch walked, and didn't look back. He joined drunken, snarling pseudo-punk Steve Marriott and drummer Kenney Jones in the re-formed Small Faces, in time for their second comeback, a nine-date tour of England.

'It should, could have been good,' reflects Jones. 'P.P. Arnold had joined us as a backing singer . . . and Jimmy McCulloch . . . was added to the line-up, giving us a much bigger sound. But Marriott blew it. It was such a shame. I don't like to think of him in those days. He was so much better than that.'[7] As was McCulloch.

Kenney and Jimmy shook their heads, and went off to launch rock band Wild Horses. They were the last band that Jimmy ever played with. After just three years with Wings, and within less than two years of leaving them, which he regretted bitterly, one of the most proficient, promising young guitarists of his generation was dead. The 26-year-old's body was found by his brother in his Maida Vale flat, in September 1979. He had died from heart failure caused by morphine and alcohol poisoning.

'Jimmy left Wings over money,' insisted his older brother, drummer Jack, who had played alongside him in psychedelic rock band One in a Million. 'He was getting session fees, he was getting paid for being on the road,' Jack says. 'But he wasn't getting any royalties for the records, and he wanted more money to stay in the band or he wanted some sort of royalty. That's basically why that argument started. That was the case of like, "I'm the star and I can get anybody else in because everybody wants to play with me, and if you don't like it you can leave." So he did. It was basically, "I think I'm worth a little bit more than you're giving me."'

Sweet baby James Louis McCartney arrived on 12 September 1977. The family had returned to London for the birth. He was born at the Avenue Clinic, St John's Wood, a short walk from their Cavendish Avenue home. He was named for his father (Paul's first name being James) and his late grandfather Jim McCartney. His middle name was given in honour of Linda's late mother Louise.

CHAPTER 15

SAYONARA

London Town was released in March 1978. It heralded a down-turn. Although it still went to Two in the US, Four in the UK and sold a million, it lacked the oomph and originality of their previous albums' killer run. Any stand-outs at all? Let's go for 'Girlfriend'. Or maybe it amuses me because it was written for Michael Jackson, who included it on his *Off the Wall* album – effectively meaning that Paul covered his own composition before the artist for whom he had written it got round to it. Nice one. I like Paul's falsetto, anyway. I enjoy the lilt of it, plus the rocking-out bit in the middle.

The valiant 'With a Little Luck' scored them another American chart-topping single. That was about it. Wait. I am forgetting 'I'm Carrying': the most memorable cut on the whole thing. Does it echo Paul's greatest Beatles composition, 'Yesterday', or am I hearing things? 'By dawn's first light I'll come back to your room again' . . . what an opener that is. What a promise. No, Paul said, he didn't write it for Linda. He is supposed to have composed it about a lover from a different life. Jane Asher? Did he still think about her? Were there still thoughts and regrets unresolved?

'He writes about what he writes about,' shrugged Linda when I asked her. 'He's got to have levels inside him where I don't fit, just as I have where he doesn't. None of us can deny our past. That would be stupid. We certainly never set out to.'

Brief. Succinct. What a wise owl she was. Accompanying himself on an acoustic guitar, Paul's wistful vocal wavers to a backdrop of agonising strings. Jane, you say? Listen again. I'm not there with them on that. That's not his once-upon-a-fiancée fading behind the plaintive chords. I'd say that's John.

Drummer Joe English had quit Wings after 'Mull of Kintyre'. His moaning about money was falling on deaf ears. His heroin addiction was ruining him. He wanted out and he was missing home. He returned to Macon, Georgia, started playing with Chuck Leavell's band Sea Level, found God, and became a born-again Christian. By 1978, 'the band' were back to the core trio of Paul, Linda and Denny. They were the root. But there was one more album to make, which would need a promotional tour, and for that they needed a replacement guitarist and drummer.

A crucial pointer to the likelihood that Paul's obsession with Wings was waning was the fact that he delegated responsibility. It was unlike him. He couldn't be bothered to audition musicians, and flung the task at Denny Laine. Who opted for a pair of young bucks, guitarist Laurence Juber and drummer Steve Holley. Lessons had been learned. For these guys, there was more favourable remuneration and a substantial share of tour profits. Laine, by this time effectively Head Boy, had worked his way up to a cut of recording royalties too. That summer saw the new, improved line-up back in Kintyre, where they began work on the seventh studio album, *Back to the Egg*.

Did Paul know that first day when he rolled up his sleeves in the Spirit of Ranachan studio and turned the pegs on the headstock that it would be the last? Everything that occurred immediately afterwards points to the possibility. Still, he cracked on with the task, setting up to co-produce with George Martin protégé Chris Thomas. But nothing clicked. Paul made a late decision to take the project back to London, where they cracked on for a while at Abbey

Road. But the vibes were out. Paul was restless. He retained studio time at Abbey Road but took the work home to Peasmarsh.

He didn't yet have a studio down there, so he rented part of nearby Lympne Castle overlooking Kent's Romney Marsh. The Grade I listed, fortified medieval manor had once been home to the Archdeacons of Canterbury. The location is glorious, the property mystical, but it hardly made up for lost time. Paul was distracted by other projects, including an ill-advised film, and scores for others. He was signing new record deals; chasing and being gifted heritage catalogue rights. He made his musicians take time out from work on 'the Egg' to record hasty singles that didn't do anything. It was as if he was throwing a ton of mud at the walls in the hope that some would stick.

Back in London, he ordered the construction of a studio in the basement of his Soho Square MPL offices, and gave it a control room that mirrored Studio Two's at Abbey Road. He called the new facility Replica Studio. He might as well have called it 'Home from Home'. Was all of this the best use of his money and time? To which the retort would have been, 'It's my money, it's my time, and I can do what I like with both. You don't like it, there's the door, let me open it for you.' And all the while, there was a new baby in the house. A dear little boy who could have done with a bit more of Dad.

Pause . . . to consider that little boy. Who seemed never to smile, at least not in photos. Who was practically born on the road – reminding me of Linda Creed's and Thom Bell's sensational 1973 song 'Rockin' Roll Baby', recorded by the Stylistics: '. . . his ma and I were travellin' on the road . . .'[1] Little Joe in the song and baby James seemed one and the same.

Wings were at the tail end of their heyday. The rock'n'roll childhood his sisters had enjoyed was drawing to a close.

James received his first guitar at the age of nine: a Fender Stratocaster that had once belonged to American rockabilly star Carl 'Blue Suede Shoes' Perkins. He was a fish out of water at the local school. In 1993, at the age of sixteen, he was swept out to sea on the south coast while out surfing with friends, and was missing for several hours. It seemed symbolic.

Like his father, James would lose his mother during his formative years. He was only nineteen when Linda was diagnosed with cancer. Mother and son made music together. He played guitar on a song of hers the month before she died. 'The Light Comes from Within' would be released both on her album *Wide Prairie* and as a single. 'It was her answer to all the people who had ever put her down and that whole dumb male chauvinist attitude that to her had caused so much harm in our society,' said Paul in the album's liner notes. 'God bless her . . . my little baby literally had the last word. She also loved the idea of our son James playing guitar on it.'

At twenty, James was weeping in bed beside Paul every night in the immediate aftermath of his mother's passing. The devastated pair grew very close. It didn't last. They were to become estranged soon after Heather Mills arrived on the scene, only a year and a month after Linda left them. James didn't get on with his father's new love. He found himself cut adrift. He had only just graduated from Bexhill College with A levels in Sculpture and Art, and didn't seem to know what to do next.

Two years after Paul and Heather married, he was living near the beach in a rented flat, studying music and working local part-time jobs to make ends meet. When Beatrice, the youngest McCartney daughter, was born in October 2003, James's estrangement must have felt complete.

He spent the next few years honing his skills as a guitarist and songwriter. After his father's divorce, he and Paul found each other again. James had worked with his dad before, on albums such as 1997's *Flaming Pie*. Now, they would collaborate more.

He comes across in some ways as an extreme version of Paul. Where Macca is a committed vegetarian, for example, James is vegan to the point that he won't touch milk or honey. Other aspects of life in which Paul is interested become obsessions for his son. As for the spiritual dimension, James is passionate about Transcendental Meditation.

'TM plays a big role in my life as it has done for my father and the other Beatles,' he told his friend, the best-selling self-help coach and author Arvind Devalia. 'I meditate regularly – twice a day – and I have learnt four advanced TM techniques. I find that just thirty minutes of TM refreshes me as if I had slept for a few hours!'

James undertook an extensive tour of America of his own in 2013, playing forty-seven small-venue gigs over a couple of months. He performed for a number of years under a pseudonym, learning his craft, growing his confidence and distancing himself from his hugely famous parentage. In the flesh he seems reserved and wary, as though weary of people always wanting something from him. He is unlike his father. There is no hint in his personality of McCartney Senior's goofy gregariousness. He gives little away. He seems to resist the urge to reveal any sense of humour.

His debut full-length album *Me* was released in May 2013. His most recent, *The Blackberry Train*, followed three years later. Both were co-produced by Paul. And you know, it's nice music. There's raw power in his voice. His writing is intelligent and compelling. Check out his songs 'Waterfall', 'Too Hard' and 'Angel'.

There was talk, in 2012, of him getting together with other Fab sons, to launch a band he mused about calling 'The Beatles: The Next Generation'. The line-up would be himself, drummer Zak Starkey, now fifty-seven, son of Ringo; the now 47-year-old Sean Lennon, and George Harrison's now 44-year-old son Dhani.

But why, why would they even consider such a risky move? Zak has built a successful career over many years drumming for the Who, Oasis, Johnny Marr, the Lightning Seeds, Paul Weller and everyone else. Sean has released many albums, both solo and as part of The Ghost of a Saber Tooth Tiger, the duo he formed in 2008 with his girlfriend Charlotte Kemp Muhl. Though their music has not set the world alight, both are accomplished multi-instrumentalists. Dhani has been in and out of bands, toured with Eric

Clapton and has composed extensively for the film industry. Of the four sons, it seems that only one really needed such a band to happen. Nothing came of it. At least the motivation was never money.

James is now forty-six. Every note he has ever composed, every lyric line he has ever penned have been compared to his father's and found wanting. His official website has not been updated for a decade. Recent photographs depict a sagging, overweight, middle-aged man with a sad baby's face; as though he froze in time and became stunted the day he lost his mother . . . at exactly the same age as Linda had lost hers.

Why on earth didn't he choose to do something else for a living?

The problem, explains psychotherapist Richard Hughes, is that the children of rock stars are confronted with their parent's image and the sound of their voice on a daily basis. 'We do not let the likes of David Bowie or John Lennon die. They live on forever. We resurrect them as technology develops, or when the record company needs to make a quick buck. Linda McCartney was not immune to this. A household name during her lifetime, her vegetarian sausages are still in every supermarket freezer. Imagine popping into Tesco and being reminded of your mother every single time.'

Paul's grief for Linda was the subject of intense scrutiny and speculation. 'From a psychological perspective, when we talk about grief, we try to avoid using terms such as "moving on" or "getting over it",' says Hughes. 'But this is almost expected of celebrities. Fans want the next chapter, and quickly! People desperately wanted Paul to find happiness again. To move on. To get back to being Paul McCartney the music legend. I wonder if he felt that pressure. The psychological cost must have been high.'

So why would any child of a music legend even think about trying to follow in their parent's footsteps?

'Because "I want to be just like my father,"' the psychotherapist explains. Suggesting that it can be endearing, especially when expressed by a nicely brought-up child.

'We indulge them, nod sagely, and secretly hope they rebel and find their own path! Every age has its own narcissistic characteristics. For infants, that involves modelling and mirroring their parents. When there's good enough parenting, infants learn to socialise and become functioning human beings. As that happens, they begin to make their own informed, autonomous choices. I believe this is what Sigmund Freud meant when he wrote, "A hero is a man who stands up manfully against his father and in the end victoriously overcomes him."[2] Doing our own thing, making our own decisions, and being "healthily" competitive with our father could be seen as an outcome of working through childhood narcissism.'

The assumption is made, unfairly or otherwise, that when a young adult follows the same career path as their father, developmental narcissism, mirroring and modelling get stuck, he says.

'It certainly poses the question, why would a child put themselves through the intense scrutiny and forensic comparison that goes with that? Perhaps the decision to make a career in a parent's world feels familiar. There is safety in that. There is always a "child part" within us that that wants to delight our parents. By inhabiting their world, the hope is that they see and validate us through what they understand and relate to.

'Borrowing a key idea from Carl Jung, the shadows are dark with fathers who shine brightly. Highly successful fathers can be generous and supportive. It is a wonderful thing to be cocooned and encouraged in that creative, financially stable orbit. The shadow side is a little more complicated. Successful fathers can be patriarchal, domineering and competitive. The largesse may be firmly on their terms. They can be jealous or vindictive if the support is rejected or taken for granted. Even with well-meaning fathers, it can be hard for them to accept that their child is forging their own path, and in doing so may surpass them and "fly higher".

'With so much at stake, it is curious that the child of a successful father would decide to make their father's world their own world. It feels like an existential high-stakes gamble. Deep down, they may believe they have what it takes to succeed. To prove the critics wrong. To be the one who shines more brightly.'

Or maybe they have convinced themselves that music is in their blood, and that creativity is not about fame and fortune?

'Perhaps. But while their relationship with their father might not be the first question a journalist asks at the album promotion junket, it will come up eventually. Usually about five minutes into the interview. I'm always intrigued by how frustrated and annoyed progeny get about this.'

November 1978 saw the release of a 'holding' compilation, *Wings Greatest*, so that fans would know that the band had not gone away. *Back to the Egg* was scrambled, in some ways, before it even came out. Which it did to some fanfare in June 1979. Comparatives are always pointless and misleading. On its own merits, you'd have to call it successful. Set against the tidal wave generated by *Band on the Run*, it was but a ripple. Yes, it featured 'Rockestra Theme', an initiative of Paul's into which he had drawn the exuberant talents of various superstar friends: members of Pink Floyd, the Who, Led Zeppelin and others. That recording would bag the Grammy for Best Rock Instrumental Performance the following year.

Other than that, there is not much here to amaze the discerning music lover. Pin me to the wall and I'd admit that I'm partial to 'Baby's Request'. It's an old-fashioned spin with a 1920s vibe, a jazz-dive tone and elegant harmonies. That's Laurence on a Gibson 335, Paul on bass, Denny on piano and Steve on drums. It was recorded at Abbey Road, where Paul later overdubbed a 'trombone' solo on a Moog synthesiser.

Paul wrote the song after he and Linda happened to catch the legendary American jazz and pop vocal quartet the Mills Brothers while on holiday in the South of France. The guys, who had been the first black artists with their own show on national network radio back in the 1930s, were now in their seventies. They were performing there in cabaret. 'I went to see them backstage,' Paul recalled. 'One of them said, "Hey Paul, how about writing the Mills Brothers a song?"'

So he did. A fall-out with management over money ensued. The brothers had got the wrong end of the stick, and thought that Paul had agreed to pay them to record it. So Wings did it instead. Given that those poor old men were in the last hurrah of their careers and lives while Paul was a mega-rich superstar with half a century or more of recording and performing ahead of him, couldn't he have done them a special favour? What a sweet, generous gesture on his part that would have been; to agree graciously, bung them a few quid and help them put out a record. Banking favours is never a bad idea. We are accustomed, are we not, to Paul's hesitance in the arena of munificence.

That aside, I'm into the song. It puts me in mind of Linda, who confided that 'Baby' was one of her husband's names for her: 'He always calls me "Lin" or "Baby", that's it.'

Paul spent a leisurely summer 1979 with his family – big sister Heather now seventeen, Mary ten, Stella eight and little James coming up two – in Peasmarsh and at High Park, experimenting with songs and synthesisers. One of the tracks he worked up, playing every instrument himself, became the Yuletide classic 'Wonderful Christmastime'. It would be released as a Paul McCartney (not Wings) single that November, with a video shot at a Sussex pub featuring the members of the band, even though they were not on the track.

He also started planning a UK tour for the coming winter, for which they would rehearse at the Hippodrome Theatre in Eastbourne. On 24 October, he and Linda attended a ceremony at Les Ambassadeurs Club in London, where he received a *Guinness Book of Records* presentation disc honouring his status as the most successful composer of popular music of all time. A month later, the band were back in the bus on a twelve-date British tour. It was the only Wings tour on which Laurence Juber and Steve Holley ever played.

The support act was unexpectedly eccentric: an accomplished bossa nova throwback artist by the name of Earl Okin. The quirky, talented teacher turned musician was recently down from the Cambridge Folk Festival.

'On what turned out to be the very last Wings tour, they thought they would do something different for support,' remembers Okin. 'A stilt walker? A juggler? Steve Holley suggested me. I was offered fifty quid a gig plus hotels and per diems. They call McCartney mean, but that was not my experience of him. In those days, a lot of artists *paid* to be the support on such tours, especially for a star of his calibre. I was rich!'

Earl cherishes the memories. Of Rod Stewart turning up skunk-drunk backstage at Wembley, and Paul and Linda having him thrown out because they didn't want their kids exposed to the lunacy. Of film star Omar Sharif knocking on his dressing room door, just to let him know how much he'd enjoyed his performance.

'And of Denny Laine, who let us not forget was now married to Jo Jo, but she was not on the tour. Not only did Denny and Jo Jo have two small children by then, but Jo Jo and Linda did not get on.

'It's the middle of December. We get to Newcastle, where we have a gig at the City Hall. We're staying in a nice, modern hotel there. We all go to bed. The next morning, after breakfast, we get ready to go to Scotland, for our show there that night at the Edinburgh Odeon.

'Denny hadn't come down for breakfast. I called his room. No answer. I'd noticed the night before that he rather liked the hotel's blonde barmaid. It turned out that he'd chatted her up, gone off with her back to her parents' house and spent the night with her, in her room. Her mum and dad made him breakfast the next morning.

'Back at the hotel, the tour manager is having a conniption. Paul is standing at the door of the tour bus with baby James in his arms. "Where's Denny?" he says. "We don't know, Paul." "Has he scored?" "Well, yes." Paul is calm. "Well, look," he says, "we'll go on ahead, he can join us later." I wasn't travelling on the tour bus, I had my car with me. I stayed behind so that I could drive him up to Scotland. We managed to trace the taxi firm, found out where he'd been taken the previous night, and I went round there to get him. The poor barmaid's mother and father carried him out, threw him in the back seat and he slept all the way north.'

The swansong took place back at Hammersmith Odeon on 29 December 1979, in support of the stricken people of Kampuchea.[3] The last of those four nights was not designed to be, but would turn out to be the last-ever Wings gig. It was a fitting showcase for Paul's 'Rockestra': some thirty British musicians on stage including Gary Brooker, John Bonham, Pete Townshend, Kenney Jones and more, around thirty musicians in all. Audience reaction was so wild, they had to perform it again. What do you do for an encore, Paul? 'Lucille'? You can do better! With the help of Mother Mary, as always, he did.

Rock stars always have unfinished business. Places off the beaten track to which they have forever meant to go but never got round to it. Destinations they have visited and performed in before, and have longed to go back. Greater than Paul's fixation on New Orleans was his 'thing about Japan'. His determination to mount a Wings tour to rival what he had achieved there with the Beatles almost proved his undoing.

Towards the end of June 1966, the Beatles touched down in Tokyo to deliver five shows at the Budokan, home of Japanese martial arts and a place of almost religious significance. There was widespread objection to what was perceived as disrespectful misuse of a site so redolent of traditional Japanese values. The country was changing rapidly, to growing approval, but also to the dismay of many still rooted in its ancient ways. These hedonistic British upstarts who dared to drop in with their devilish music and all-consuming western habits to corrupt Japan's rising youth were feared as harbingers of doom.

The media was awash with criticism. There were assassination threats. Holed up for safety in the Tokyo Hilton – although John did manage to nip out at one point, to go shopping – they were heavily guarded. They took up painting together to alleviate their boredom, when art paraphernalia was delivered to them. At the gigs, which did go ahead, 3,000 police officers watched over audiences of 10,000, most of them feverish girls. Revered Japanese author Shūsaku Endō compared the reaction the boys provoked to the religious hysteria he had witnessed in churches around the American Deep South.

John had, through Yoko, maintained his connection to the land of the rising sun. They trekked back to her homeland several times together during the fourteen years that were left to him. The only time that George Harrison toured after his disastrous excursion across the US and Canada with Ravi Shankar in 1974 was in Japan; but not until 1991, a decade before he died. Ringo has performed there multiple times, and augmented his popularity by appearing in television commercials.

Paul has since become akin to a god there, attracting the coveted three-generation audience. Ten years after the visit that could have killed his career, he returned for six shows in 1990. He donated all of his concert proceeds to charity. He would be pulled back, again and again, in 1993, 2002, 2013, 2015, 2017 and 2018. He played the Budokan again in 2015 on his *Out There* tour and in 2018 he went there to promote his album *Egypt Station*. He has honed, over the years, a great love of Japanese culture, attending sumo wrestling matches and cycling through beautiful city parks. The nightmare of forty-three years ago is but a puffball spore on a gasp of forgotten time.[4]

But what was he thinking back then? He must have realised what to expect when Wings arrived in January 1980 to deliver eleven concerts in Nagoya, Osaka and Tokyo, including seven at the

Budokan. There was much at stake. In excess of 100,000 tickets had been snapped up, and the eyes of Japan were upon him. He knew better than anyone that the planned Japanese leg of their *Wings Over the World* tour in 1975 had to be scrapped because of his previous drug-related misdemeanours – his 1972 marijuana arrest in Sweden, and the 1973 fine in Scotland – had scuppered his chances of being granted a visa.

He was by no means unaware of the country's draconian stance on drug-taking, where no distinction was made between marijuana and heroin. He had assured the Japanese authorities that he was no longer using drugs. But when he and Linda landed at Narita International Airport from New York during the afternoon of 16 January 1980, Paul with baby James in his arms, customs officials discovered half a pound of weed in his luggage that could not have got there on its own.

He did not deny having packed the suitcase himself. He admitted immediately to bringing the drug into the country, but protested that it was only for personal use. Dragged away in handcuffs, he was flung into the Tokyo Narcotic Detention Centre where he was registered as Inmate No. 22. Nine days of harsh interrogation followed. A representative from the British Council in Tokyo came to his aid that first night, and warned him starkly that he could be facing seven or eight years' hard labour. Almost amusingly, a blanket ban was issued on all Wings music being played on radio and television.

Linda and Paul were separated for most of that time. She wrote him letters and delivered science fiction books to him, but at first was prevented from seeing him. It was the longest time since their wedding day eleven years earlier that they had ever spent apart. When eventually Linda was permitted to visit her husband, they had to sit separated by a grille, and could not touch. She had been urged to take the children home to England, but no way was she going to leave him there, going through all that. She waited for him: they would make their way home together. He was glad.

Other visits were allowed after that. Linda would take him sandwiches to supplement his meagre meals. She hid love letters inside his food.

Paul kept his head down. He exercised. He bathed with other prisoners without complaint, possibly fearing that acceptance of privileges would invite bullying and persecution. George and Olivia Harrison sent him a 'keep-your-spirits-up' telegram.

Startling rumours later did the rounds, that John and Yoko had been involved in both the arrest and Paul's eventual release.

On the one hand, they had allegedly been infuriated by Paul's casual announcement that he and Linda would be staying in the Presidential Suite at Tokyo's luxurious Hotel Okura. The Lennons were said to regard it as 'theirs', and feared that the Maccas would destroy their 'karma' there. It was claimed that Yoko pulled strings to tip off customs officials about their 'stash'. Though how could she have known about it? John and Paul hadn't seen each other for more than three years. Other 'insiders' insisted that Yoko wielded her influence to get Paul out of jail. Any way the wind blows. There is no proof.

Negotiations were held. In the end, the Japanese government appeared all too willing to offload their superstar detainee. Global press attention and reflected shame cannot have thrilled them. The prevailing supposition is that Paul's legal team purchased his passage out. As in, bribed? To the tune of at least a million, they say, plus the £186,000 (100m yen) he had to pay in compensation to his Japanese concert promoter. The world's press converged on Tokyo to witness and report his release. He walked free on 25 January, landing in Amsterdam the following day. The family, all together again after the most terrifying experience of their lives, were tucked up back in Peasmarsh by the end of the month.

Of the band, Denny Laine was the most furious. One minute Wings had stood to reap unprecedented rewards from this tour. He had looked forward to solving his money problems and to being relatively rich again. The next, it was over the side. Of the

Wings musicians, he had been there the longest and had invested the most: not only in terms of time and talent but in what he gave of himself, to the detriment of every other relationship in his life. He expressed his frustration in a song, 'Japanese Tears', the lead single of a new solo album with the same title that was released that December.

There is what happened, and there is what people say happened. Would any sane individual sabotage their own massively expensive tour and deliberately risk long-term imprisonment in a distant land whose language they didn't speak, for the sake of winding up a band he was no longer interested in? Yet Paul stood accused of exactly that. In years to come, he even suggested as much himself.

What? He would have thrown it all away for a smoke? To prove ... *what*, exactly? He would have dumped his beloved wife and children, his livelihood, his career, his reputation and his future all over the side in one careless move, *why*? Bizarrely, it looks as though he did just that. Could he have suffered a cataclysmic midlife crisis? When asked in an interview whether he might have contrived subconsciously for it to happen so that he could call time on Wings, he said this:

'I *think* that it might, psychologically, it might have been that. There might have been something to do with that, because I think I was ready to get out of Wings. I think also, more importantly, we hadn't really rehearsed much for that tour, and I felt very under-rehearsed. I cannot believe that I would have myself busted and put in jail nine days just to get out of a group. I mean, let's face it, there are easier ways to do it than that – and also having to pay a million [British] pounds [*sic*] to the promoters in default. I think the only thing ... it might have just been some deep, psychological thing. It's a weird period for me.'[5]

And just like that, it was all over. Album, tour, album, tour. The relentless grind of studio rehearsing, recording, tour rehearsing, airports, planes, immigration, hotel rooms, sound checks, dodgy food, the freakery of ever-changing time zones, contradictory climates, endless road ailments and the psychological damage sustained by being far away from home more often than you were there.

What was it all about? Adulation. Affirmation. Validation. Meaning something in the world. Never feeling able to take your foot off the gas because they might have forgotten you by next year, and some young upstart will have wafted in and taken your place. But look now. All for nothing. Not that this was stated at the time. Wings limped on, convening for rehearsal sessions at Finchden Manor, another stately property not far from Peasmarsh. There was talk of another album. Always talk of another album.

Denny took himself out on a solo tour that summer, inviting bandmate Steve Holley along to drum. Paul spoke during a local television interview of going to France to record with Ringo. Those sessions did indeed take place, in Berre-les-Alpes: a picturesque little place in the mountains above Nice, not far from the Italian border. Wings guitarist Laurence Juber was also part of that project. While they were there, they recorded Linda singing her song 'Love's Full Glory'. It, too, was released eighteen years later, six months after her death, on her album *Wild Prairie*.

Back the McCartney family trekked to Kintyre, for the annual summer re-charge. Life there was the same as it had always been. They drew comfort as ever from its space and pace. Paul recorded several demos there that Denny, Laurence and Steve took to be signs of life. Wings would soon be underway again, they felt sure, once the fallow period was over and Paul had taken as much stock as he could gulp. Those songs included 'Take It Away', 'Ballroom Dancing', 'Ebony and Ivory', 'Dress Me Up as a Robber' and various others, recordings that would later make it into the public domain as the bootleg album *Tug of War Demos*.

Paul summoned his band to Pugin's Hall, a mid-nineteenth-century rectory in Tenterden near Ashford, Kent, to rehearse them. But a lot had happened since the last time they had played together.

The glue had gone dry. The chemistry was unstable. It must have felt, to Paul, like the last days of *Let It Be* revisited. He would later admit that he had lost all interest in Wings.

Then a wild card. Frustrated and directionless but niggled by a hunch, Paul got on the phone to George Martin. They were at Martin's AIR Studios working on Paul's compositions 'Ode to a Koala Bear' and 'Rainclouds' when the news about what had happened to John arrived.

It took time for Denny Laine's dream to die. Paul had got his hopes up, after all. He invited Denny out to the Caribbean to George's Montserrat studio in February 1981 – without Steve, without Laurence – to work on a number of songs for an album entitled *Tug of War*. Why wouldn't he have expected that to be the comeback Wings album? Only after he returned home did word reach him that Paul was now working with former 10CC star Eric Stewart. Denny, it dawned, had been replaced.

Laurence said later that he had seen what was happening for himself. He upped sticks and relocated to New York. Steve Holley read about his own demise in London's local newspaper the *Evening Standard*, under the headline 'Paul's Wings are clipped'. He got straight on the blower to Paul, who said sorry about that. 'It's all understandable,' said Juber in an interview with music writer Glenn Williams. 'And his reason for the band being dispersed, by the way, was that he wanted to work with George Martin again, and George Martin wanted to work with Paul. But not within the constraints of Wings, which is very plausible.'

Tug of War was released in April 1982. McCartney, solo superstar, took flight. Once he knew for sure that it was all over between them, Denny Laine turned on Paul and Linda. Their relationship was never the same again. His efforts going forward never amounted to much. There were solo concert tours that had to be cancelled due to poor ticket sales; and in 1986, a bankruptcy. At seventy-nine, he still runs from gig to gig across America, strumming his guitar, singing his own and McCartney's songs and telling his rock'n'roll war stories. In July 2023, he married his long-term girlfriend Lizzie.

Paul, on the other hand, has walked on water. In hindsight, it's hard to see Wings as anything more than an elaborate, self-indulgent, ten-year experiment that facilitated his transition from Beatle to solo artist. He was no Icarus. He didn't fly too high on flimsy feather-and-wax wings, risking meltdown from the heat of the sun that would plunge him. He ascended carefully and methodically, a step at a time, finding his levels until he reached optimum altitude. When he no longer needed the wings, he threw them away.

'Wings was a halfway house for Paul,' agrees clinical psychotherapist Richard Hughes. 'A safety blanket. Being in another band, not having to put himself fully out there, was exactly what he needed at that time. Macca was the pin-up. There was universal love for him. People cared about him.'

We should not, he says, underestimate the symbolism of a pair of wings: 'Not only can they extend behind you, they can also fold in front of you and conceal you. Like the wings of the Archangel Gabriel, messenger of God in the Christian faith. We have this image of wings closing across us and protecting us. During that early post-Beatles period, Paul also grew a massive beard, and incredibly glossy, leonine, Samson-like hair. There was such strength in that image, but it was also concealing who he was. There is a fine line between something being your strength and being the thing you hide behind. The paradoxical element is always fascinating.'

Paul probably was, observes Richard, deeply depressed just before he formed the band. 'He was self-medicating with a lot of weed and booze. Anyone who's been through the legal process, the break-up of a marriage or a business or creative partnership, knows too well how devastating that is. It's a form of bereavement. In Paul's case, it took him all the way back to that developmental early place: the loss of his mother.

'Even if he wasn't aware of it, if he wasn't feeling that exactly, it was what was going on. He struggled ever after with loss and endings. Not attending his father's funeral is an obvious indication of that. Linda's role as mother and lover was absolutely crucial to his survival. We must never underestimate her importance in the Paul McCartney story – both on a personal level and in terms of his musical evolution.'

'I was at home and I got a phone call,' Paul told Jonathan Ross during an interview in 2014. 'It was early in the morning. I was in the country and I just got a phone call.' He didn't say who from, but one assumes it was Yoko. 'I think it was like that for everyone, just so horrific, you couldn't take it in. And I couldn't take it in. Just for days, you couldn't think he was gone. Yeah, it was just a huge shock and I had to tell Linda and the kids. It was very difficult . . . for me, it was just so sad that I wasn't going to see him again.'

Devastated by John's death, Paul was at long last excused the question that had dogged him daily for the past decade, wherever in the world he went, whoever interviewed him, whoever interacted with him for whatever reason: in a shop, say, or simply passing him in the street. 'Hey Paul! When are the Beatles getting back together?'

Not anymore. Not that the vast majority of fans really needed the boys to reunite and give the magic another spin. The Beatles could never be again what they had been before. Not as men in their late thirties and forties, as they were in 1980. No, the sixties were over. That decade was never coming back. The longing was a fantasy, one that represented the impossible turning back of time, so that they, the fans, could be as they had once been: youthful, vigorous and carefree with a glow in their hearts, hope on the horizon and everything to live for. The boys had seized their chance. They had taken on the world on their behalf. The fans had felt part of it, proud, and gloriously alive. Once there was a way.

Paul never found a replacement songwriting partner. There was no one as perfect for him as John had been. What he'd had with John was far more than melodic and lyrical compatibility. Their creative chemistry arose out of Liverpool, lost mothers, shared youth, and common culture, ground and experiences. Of course no one else could have stepped into Lennon's shoes; just as no other musicians could have been the Beatles. All kinds of accomplished instrumentalists could be, and were, in Wings. But that band had only ever been about Paul and Linda.

He has since worked with the same backing band far longer than he ever worked with Wings or the Beatles. Abraham 'Abe' Laboriel Jr has been drumming for Paul's recording and touring band since 2001. Officially, he also sings backing vocals. Unofficially, he also hits Paul's high notes where the boss no longer can. The line-up also features guitarist Rusty Anderson, keyboardist Paul 'Wix' Wickens, and bass, rhythm and lead guitarist Brian Ray. Having a band is not the same as being in a band. He knows that now.

CHAPTER 16

DEAR FRIEND

To this day, Andy Peebles feels played for a fool. Something 'didn't feel right at the time' when he was charged with helping John and Yoko to promote their 1980 comeback album *Double Fantasy*, in what was to be an extended interview broadcast by the BBC. 'It seemed fake,' he tells me today. 'I have good antennae,' explained the former DJ and music and sport expert, to whom millions tuned in to hear his daily and weekly shows on Radio 1. 'I had a very unsettling feeling about it all. If you set out to make idiots of the world by presenting a completely loved-up front for the sake of selling a record that may not have done brilliantly had not the tragedy occurred, what does that make you?'

It is clear from our frequent conversations about it over the years that he has never healed. To have had the dream opportunity of interviewing his childhood idol only for John's life to have been extinguished just two days after they met, hung out and even dined together in New York, still feels to him like a nightmare.

Andy's memories are startlingly clear. He recalls seeing the 'pudgy-faced twenty-something' that would turn out to be John's assassin Mark Chapman hovering on the sidewalk outside the Dakota building when he and the production team arrived, to discuss logistics with Yoko and hoping to meet John ahead of the interview. He had never met the Lennons, and was filled with anticipation.

As it happened, Yoko refused to allow them to say hello to her husband ahead of the appointed interview day, even though he was right there in the apartment. She even attempted to renegotiate the deal, suggesting that London station Capital Radio or Radio Luxembourg would have been a better fit; and perhaps, having dragged them all the way from London to New York, they should change it. Executive producer Doreen Davies explained patiently that Capital was a local station, while Luxembourg frequently suffered signal fade. She managed to convince Yoko they were better off with the BBC.

The interview took place the next evening at the Hit Factory, where ghosts reverberated: of the Rolling Stones, Paul Simon, Bruce Springsteen, Stevie Wonder and the countless who had cut albums there. John and Yoko arrived late, at around six that evening.

John 'fell on me like a long, lost friend,' says Andy. 'He was clearly dreadfully homesick, having not been back to England for almost a decade. Once the tape was rolling, we talked candidly for hours. No subject was taboo. Yoko said afterwards that she was amazed by much of it; that she'd learned things she'd never known before.'

It remains the interview that Andy cherishes most. It concluded, at the Lennons' invitation, in a dinner at Mr Chow, an upmarket Chinese establishment and one of their favourite New York restaurants. John and Andy rabbited on into the night, and left each other promising to meet again soon and to continue the conversation. Which was never to be.

On the evening of Monday 8 December 1980, Texan-born itinerant Chapman, who had lain in wait outside their apartment building for the Lennons to return from the recording studio, fired five shots from a Charter Arms .38-calibre pistol. Four of them hit John. He was rushed by police officers in the back of a patrol car to the Roosevelt Hospital, minutes away, where the wrong surgeon took the credit for having tried to save John's life.[1]

★   ★   ★

'I never saw the Beatles live,' laments Andy. 'That was a matter of great regret to me. But I did get to meet Paul at the Hard Rock in Manchester in May 1973. I remember there being lots of scream-ing girls. They hadn't come to see Wings, they were there for their heart-throb Paul McCartney. Wings were still establishing them-selves at that point, but they were extremely good. I was introduced to Paul in the dressing room afterwards. That was the first time that I'd met any of the Beatles.

'What struck me was that Paul was trying to recreate what he had just thrown away. Because he needed it. Beatlemania and everything that went with it was a drug to them. The buzz of walk-ing on stage and adulation being poured upon you is pretty special. You heard all sorts of things about McCartney, as we do to this day – one of which was that he is a total control freak. I didn't get that impression. But I did get that he was in charge of his destiny, and wanted the right people around him.'

Andy joined BBC Radio 1 in 1978: which was through the Wings heyday and out the other side, when they had recorded and were promoting *London Town*. 'By December 1980 I had done at least one interview with Paul, and I did five or six more fairly major interviews with him after that. He was tremendous: lively and witty, with a terrific sense of humour. By that time his brother Mike had become my friend. Mike said to me one day, "My brother's very fond of you. He just likes you. You ask good questions. He enjoys being in your company." I took it with a pinch of salt, as one does, though I was secretly flattered.

'From the off, Paul and I got on. I remember when we were talk-ing before we began recording that first interview, and he remarked, "Presumably at some stage you came to see us" – meaning the Beatles. "I didn't," I said. "I wouldn't have been able to stand the noise!" "Yeah, it was awful," he nodded wryly. "It was one of the things that John just couldn't stand."'

News of Lennon's murder was broken to Andy only after his plane home from New York landed at Heathrow. He was met from the aircraft and escorted to the BBC's airport studio, where he had to summon the professionalism to talk about what had happened live on Radio 4's *Today* programme without even a minute to prepare himself. Two hours later he was at BBC Broadcasting House, north of London's Oxford Street, co-hosting a live tribute to the late Beatle with fellow DJ John Peel. He was then driven to Television Centre in west London to appear live on BBC2's *The Old Grey Whistle Test*, alongside DJs Anne Nightingale and Paul Gambaccini and *Melody Maker* music journalist Michael Watts.

'Long faces, few words,' he told me. 'I sat there in shock. It hadn't sunk in yet. The greatest rock star who ever lived was dead – and I had been one of the last people on earth to talk to him. Annie cued the video of "Imagine", the one with John at the white piano. The next thing, the red light on the desk started flashing with an incoming call. It was Paul. "Linda and I are watching," he said. "Tell the gang they're doing a great job."'

Hearing the voice of John's childhood pal and primary collaborator forced Andy to take on board the magnitude of what had happened. Yet he didn't cry. Forty-three years later, he still struggles. 'I know I should have wept it all out and tried to get over it,' he can now admit. 'But I didn't. I bottled it all up. I have only recently come to terms with the fact that I am profoundly damaged by it.'

A couple of days after *Whistle Test*, Andy was in his office at Broadcasting House when the phone rang. '"Andy Peebles?" said a voice I recognised. "Yes, sir, it is." "I'm ever so sorry because this is not going to be easy," said Beatles producer George Martin. "I'm sure you are not feeling anything but absolutely shattered. None of us wanted to do "The Old Grey Whistle Test" when they asked us. We didn't feel up to it. But I want to ask a favour. Could you come to the studio tomorrow at about three in the afternoon? Somebody would like to talk to you."

'I guessed who.

'The next day, I walked from Portland Place down to Oxford Circus and checked in at AIR. George greeted me and led me into the studio. There was Paul, sitting on a stool in the middle of the room. He was holding a guitar. When he saw me come in, he got down, put the guitar on its stand and came towards me. Silently, we put our arms around each other. We just stood there, for what felt like hours. Neither of us was capable of saying a word.

'After a while, I blurted, "Last Saturday, I spent six and a half hours with your best friend." "That's lovely," he said. "That's why I asked you to come down, *our Andrew*." "Our". It was what John had called me when we went for dinner in New York. A typical Northern thing. A term of endearment they use to a child, a sibling, a close friend. Then he came straight out with it.

"It's a simple question, really," he said. "Do you think John still loved me?"

"Why are you asking me that?" I said.

"Because you were with him more recently than anyone else I know."

'I told him I was convinced he truly did,' says Andy. '"He talks about you in the interview," I said. "He is sarcastic, funny and irreverent, as only John can be. But there is no doubting his fondness for you. It was as if he couldn't help wishing you were right there in the room with us." I have never forgotten the encounter. It cut me to the bone. Paul, more than anyone, now had to face a bitter reality: that the greatest songwriting partnership in the history of pop music was finished for good.'

Andy says that at that point he replayed in his mind the reluctant, disastrous interview that Paul had given to reporters waiting for him outside the studio, after John's death was announced.

'What was your reaction to the death of John Lennon?' said one. 'Very shocked, you know,' said Paul, 'it's terrible news.' 'How did you find out about it?' 'I got a phone call this morning.' 'From whom?' 'From a friend of mine.' When asked whether he had discussed the tragedy with George or Ringo, Paul replied, 'No'. 'Do you plan to?' 'Probably, yeah.'

The monosyllabic responses and obvious impatience to get away should have given his interrogator a clue. Paul was clearly in shock, extremely distressed, and trying desperately not to show it. He gnashed the gum in his mouth and scratched his face, indicating confusion, frustration and stress. Still, the guy kept on at him. Viewing the footage back, it's a wonder that Paul didn't lose his temper.

'What were you recording today?' the reporter asks. 'I was just listening to some stuff,' responds Paul. 'I just didn't want to sit at home.' '*Why?*' 'Well, 'cos I just didn't feel like it,' Paul replies flippantly. 'What time did you hear the news?' the guy persists. 'This morning sometime.' 'Very early?' 'Yeah.' More inane questions, further monosyllabic answers.

Then comes the killer comment that the reporter has been pushing for. Broadcast gold. The moment when Paul trips himself up. 'A drag, isn't it,' he says. 'Okay. Cheers. Bye bye. Thank you.' Perhaps realising his error, he jumps into a waiting red estate car and is driven away . . . damned by four little words that have shamed him ever since, because they misled the world into believing that he didn't care.

'He severely blotted his copy book, didn't he,' comments Andy sadly. 'He should never have said it. He knew it the moment he blurted it, and it must haunt him to this day. He was obviously grief-stricken. Also, the genie was out of the bottle now. He must have been terrified that someone would come for him next. As evident from the fact that he went to ground soon afterwards, and massively stepped up his security. We saw nothing of him for the next five years.'

Paul and Andy next came face to face at Wembley Stadium on 13 July 1985, at the Live Aid Feed the World extravaganza.

'I was one of the hosts, there to present various acts live on stage. When Paul and Linda arrived, they made a beeline for me. "How are you, our Andrew?" he said. Linda gave me a kiss.' Paul later performed 'Let It Be' with David Bowie, Bob Geldof, Pete Townshend and Alison Moyet.

All those years ago. Does Andy dare to think about it now? What goes through his mind when he allows himself?

'All sorts. I think how lucky I was to have known and worked with both Paul and John; and to a modest extent, that I could count two of the greatest songwriters in the history of popular music as friends. I feel incredibly fortunate that they were the group that I idolised when I was a teenager. There are emblems of the Beatles that are embedded in my mind. John's Rickenbacker guitar. Paul's Hofner bass. Ringo's absolutely classic silver Ludwig drumkit. They are images that I will take with me to the grave.'

There was little hope for Wings in the early aftermath of the aborted Japanese tour. Banned from Japan for at least twelve months, Paul's crime would have repercussions in many parts of the world. There was not much point in attempting anything. He naturally withdrew, to lick his wounds and figure out a future. Back home, he wrote a diary of his journey to hell, entitled *Japanese Jailbird*, that ran to some 20,000 words. He did it for the kids, he said. He wanted to commit it to paper while he could still remember the details.

At first, he said that he had only the original, and that he had lodged it in a bank vault. He showed it to Laurence Juber before he locked it away. It later emerged that he had made copies for all his children, but had no idea whether any of them had read it. In 2017, his fashion designer daughter Stella told Kirsty Young about it when she was interviewed for BBC Radio 4's *Desert Island Discs*. She selected it as the book she would take to read if marooned.

The band still had their *Cold Cuts* collection of outtakes to finish. Dating back to 1975, it was revisited several times before being abandoned altogether. Paul did what he always does in times of trouble. He threw himself into writing and recording songs for yet another new album. This was the one that would become *McCartney II*.

Synth-heavy, with all the instruments played by Paul as on the original *McCartney* album ten years earlier, it features three memorable songs: the soothing 'One of These Days' with its receding echo; 'Waterfalls', a loaded and solemn dirge; and the song credited with having made John decide to start recording again after his extended break, when he heard it played on the radio. Two versions were recorded, Paul's solo studio original and a live variation performed by Wings. The song is 'Coming Up'.

The album was poorly reviewed, but who cares about that. Number One in the UK, Number Three in the US. There would be sixteen solo rock albums and five classical albums to come. And counting?

Some months after John's death, Paul asked one of his greatest idols, American rock'n'roll legend Carl 'Blue Suede Shoes' Perkins, if he would play on 'Get It' – a song that would make it onto his first post-Wings album *Tug of War*. Perkins obliged. He penned a song of his own post-session that night, which he took to the studio to play for Paul the next day. On hearing the lyric line, 'Think about me every now and then, old friend', Paul choked. He left the studio. At which point Linda turned to Carl and explained why. Those had been John's last words to Paul, she said, the very last time they met.

John's murder had changed everything. In 1981, Paul and Linda withdrew to their Peasmarsh farmhouse and battened the hatches. As Linda would later reveal, they wanted to bed down and 'lie low' for a while. She mentioned that there had been a few threatening incidents, and said that they'd had to increase their security. It looked as though life would never be the same again.

CHAPTER 17

ALL YOU NEED

In the cluttered, flag-stoned old kitchen at their home in Peasmarsh, East Sussex, the once boar-infested estate beyond the glare of fame that Paul has owned since the 1970s, Linda and I sat nursing mugs of tea. I forget now which kind. Maybe green. The McCartneys lived a bohemian life there, carting their old stuff to jumble sales, showing their faces at village fêtes, conveying their children to and from their local schools, and bombing about in old Land Rovers and Volvo estates. They tended to their menagerie of mutts, moggies and chickens, and to their conservation pond that teemed with life.

While Linda exercised their ponies in a paddock with underground heating, Paul would go to work in his recording studio in a converted windmill, Hogg Hill Mill, Icklesham, on the Rye to Hastings road about twenty miles south of home. He had bought the former working mill in 1981, and spent about four years converting it, installing a desk and setting it up as a fully working studio. He would eventually record his eighteenth solo album *McCartney III* there in 2020, during the COVID-19 pandemic lockdown. Released on 18 December 2020, it gave him his first British Number One solo album, since 1989's *Flowers in the Dirt*, for thirty-one years.

The house was a muddle of falling-apart furniture and bric-a-brac. Guitars were piled like firewood. Mud everywhere you looked. In one small, cosy side room with a smoking wood fire, I spied a

Van Gogh. Clearing a space among the heaps of baskets, bottles, pottery and home-made loaves on the kitchen table, Linda gestured to me to sit. It was there that we discussed her autobiography. She was interested in me ghostwriting it. I had suggested a title that she adored: *Mac the Wife*.

She talked, I scribbled. We mapped out a rough outline. About thirty chapters would trawl her childhood and teenage years, wade through the Beatles and Wings eras, and would review her roles as a devoted wife and mother while also exploring her vegetarianism, her animal activism, her photography, her own recording and songwriting, and her philosophy on feeding a family as an act of love.

Giles Gordon, my literary agent at the time, had three possible publishers up his sleeve. He was looking forward, he said, to pitching them against one another and earning Linda a record-breaking advance for which she clearly had no need and that she would probably have donated to charity, as well as a healthy 15 per cent for himself. As a writer for hire, I would be paid a non-negotiable flat fee for my time and trouble. I did not stand to receive a percentage of royalties from sales after the book had earned out. That's how it works. Every time we spoke on the phone during that brief period, Giles would breeze, in his soft Scottish brogue, 'Let battle commence!' I miss him. He's dead now.

But Linda had made clear from the outset that her husband would have the last word. Have it he did. She sounded tearful sometime later when she called to impart the bad news, that Paul 'wasn't going to let her do the book' after all. She never told me why, exactly. We never got round to discussing it. We vanished back into our respective frantic schedules, and that, regrettably, was that.

On 11 March 1997, when 54-year-old Paul was knighted by Her Majesty Queen Elizabeth II for services to music, Linda became Lady McCartney. She was by then two years into her diagnosis of breast cancer. It metastasised to her liver.

'The doctors had told me privately that we caught it too late, that she'll have about eighteen months,' Paul told broadcaster Sir David

Frost fourteen years after her death, in an October 2012 sixty-minute interview show on television channel Al Jazeera English. 'And that was what she had.'

As everybody who knew her would have expected, Linda did not take the news lying down. She put up a fight. She travelled relentlessly to and from New York for the latest treatment then available. They threw money at the best, to no avail. She was fifty-six when she died at the family ranch near Tucson, Arizona on 17 April 1998, surrounded by her children, and in the arms of her husband of almost thirty years.

Just four years later, a potential new Lady McCartney shimmered over the horizon. Heather Mills, aged thirty-one, a former model with an apparently racy past, met 57-year-old Paul at the Dorchester Hotel on 20 May 1999, during the *Daily Mirror* Pride of Britain Awards. He was there to present an honour in his late wife's name. Heather was doing the same, as well as promoting her Heather Mills Campaign for people who had lost limbs in war zones.

Paul, still bereaved and immensely lonely, was so impressed by the young woman that he donated £150,000 to her cause. He couldn't believe it when he discovered that she wore a prosthetic lower leg, having lost her own in an accident with a police motorcycle. The paper's then editor and future TV star Piers Morgan, my former boss, took credit for having introduced them, but would come to rue the day. The newspapers said, 'She's gone to his head.'[1]

It is said that a widowed husband who remarries in relative haste is paying the ultimate compliment to his late wife. That it's a mark of how remarkable the previous marriage had been, that he cannot live without it; and all he can think of doing to relieve his pain is to try to replicate it. An alternative school of thought holds that, if a bereaved husband adored his wife that much, she would be irreplaceable and he wouldn't dream of it. The psychological adjustment to loss can, for some, be overwhelming.

'The gender gap in late life remarriage, where widowers are more likely than widows to remarry, has been explained by the adage "Women mourn, men replace",' says Professor of Sociology Deborah Carr. 'The implication of this characterisation is that heartbroken widows mourn the loss of their irreplaceable late husbands, whereas widowed men quickly find a helpmate and confidante to take the place of their late wives.'[2]

What would Linda have thought about it? We cannot guess. All we know is what she said herself, that she couldn't imagine him ever doing so.

When Heather Mills was born, on 12 January 1968 in Aldershot, Hampshire, the Beatles were already winding down. More than a quarter of a century Paul's junior, she had lived an early life of neglect and petty crime, but had turned herself around. Paul 'did all the chasing,' insisted Heather's ghost Pamela Cockerill, who wrote her 1995 memoir *Out on a Limb.* The book recounted her exploits collecting prosthetic limbs and transporting them to Croatia during that country's 1991–1995 war of independence. All proceeds from the sales were donated to charity.

As Heather's friend, Pamela witnessed the McCartney courtship first-hand. Enchanted by the beautiful force of nature, Paul wasn't taking no for an answer. He wooed Heather with a £15,000 sapphire and diamond engagement ring, and married her on 11 June 2002 in a lavish celebration at Castle Leslie, Glaslough, in Ireland's County Monaghan. It was a second marriage for both of them.

The wedding was in stark contrast to the day he had married Linda. This shiny new bride wore a £10,000 gown that, tellingly, was not designed or made by Paul's daughter Stella. The wedding breakfast was served on gold-rimmed plates, and the nuptials were sealed with a £100,000 firework display. Paul obviously sanctioned the expenditure willingly at the time. He seemed dangerously cavalier about his vast fortune, a mistake that would return to bite him. The marriage didn't make half a decade.

Although it ended in bitter and bloody divorce, it did yield Paul a beloved fifth child, whom the couple named Beatrice after Heather's mother. Paul would cut a crushed figure as he collected his youngest from home and later delivered her back. His heart nearly broke, his right-hand man Geoff Baker confided. I bumped into my old Fleet Street mucker long after Paul and Linda had sacked him. We went to the Groucho Club for lunch. I discovered at long last the reason why *Mac the Wife: The Autobiography of Linda McCartney* had been cancelled.

'It was Paul, bless him, being a control freak,' said Geoff. 'You know what he's like. There's too much going on in his head. He gets a bit confused sometimes, and loses sight of what matters. When Linda told him that she wanted to do it, he lost his rag.' It was along the lines of, Geoff added as an aside, 'There's only one fucking star in this family.'

When I heard that Paul and Heather were divorcing, at an eventual cost to him of nearly £25m (about one tenth of what she had demanded – newspaper headlines blared 'Gold Digger!') my thoughts turned inevitably to Linda. I wondered with heaving sadness what she might have made of her replacement, and of the mess her lovely family was now in. Her son James in particular had lost his way. Into my mind flooded her awkward smiles, her tideless warmth, the squiggly hearts she drew over everything. I thought about what Baker had said to me: that when he returned to London, Paul had cried in Geoff's arms every day for a year.

Paul worshipped his baby Lin to the end of her days, with every shred of himself. After she died, I wrote to him to express my sorrow and condolences. Weeks later he wrote back, which I had not expected, saying that it had given him great comfort to be reminded that I had been Linda's friend. He must have written many thousands of such letters. More than likely, the same letter to us all.

I was annoyed with myself for not having written what I really wanted to say. I have been kicking myself over it ever since. 'You should have let us do that bloody book, you know,' I should have said to him. Because the story that Linda had to tell, as wife of a member of the world's greatest-ever group, who would be forever at odds with legions of fans around the world, would have been moving, enthralling and real. 'Write it anyway,' I was urged by friends and colleagues, 'it'll be dynamite.' How could I? We could have gained from her so much fascinating insight into Paul and the inner workings of the Beatles.

Perhaps that was what Paul feared: Linda's frankness, her fearlessness, her dogged insistence on calling a spade a spade; that she would tell the truth *too* much. Newspaper journalists had been mean to her for years. No matter now hard she tried, she could never do right. Some criticised her even beyond her death. Their heartlessness knew no bounds. He 'should have married that nice Jane Asher'? You're not still banging on about that! He didn't. She wasn't The One. Linda was. As time proved. Get over it.

Don't it always seem to go. Because no one but Linda could tell her true story, it can never be told. Maybe that's exactly what Paul wanted. We are all the poorer for it. As for there being just one star in their family, he was wrong.

Paul had known his third wife-to-be for many years. They met in the Hamptons, Long Island, where they both had homes, and socialised together as family friends. The McCartney children nicknamed Nancy Shevell 'Jackie O' after former US first lady Jacqueline Kennedy Onassis, on account of her gigantic sunspecs and rich glamour. Maybe they were also familiar with one of her famous quotes: 'The first time, you marry for love, the second for money, and the third for companionship.' Not that Nancy needed McCartney's dough. She was sitting on a fortune of around $200m of her own.

Their friendship changed at some point during 2007. A switch flicked. Both were, effectively, singletons. Paul, at that point sixty-five, had separated from Heather the year before. Slender brunette

Nancy, forty-eight, seventeen years her suitor's junior, was separated from her first husband Bruce Blakeman, the father of her son Arlen.[3]

The following year, Paul was devastated by the death of Neil Aspinall, his lifelong Liverpool friend and former head of the Beatles' company Apple Corps, while Nancy was grieving for her brother Jon, a former professional basketball player turned partner in the family firm. On 3 March 2008, Jon was found dead in his bungalow at the Beverly Hills Hotel in LA, where he had been staying for nearly three weeks. The cause of death was established as multiple drug intoxication. He had ingested cocaine along with a cocktail of tranquillisers and painkillers.

Paul had dabbled in heroin and cocaine and had long smoked marijuana. How did they meet in the middle on that one? They must have had the conversation, because Paul has admitted that Nancy made him give up dope. In 2015, he told the *Daily Mirror* that he no longer used the drug to which he was allegedly introduced by Bob Dylan four decades earlier, because 'I don't really want to set an example to my kids and grandkids. It's now a parent thing.' He professed a preference for a glass of wine, 'or a nice Margarita'.

The world, or at least the media, was flabbergasted by the speed with which Macca immersed himself in yet another new relationship so soon after the demise of his second marriage. His daughters were said to be angry and upset, especially Stella, who apparently reminded him in bald terms that he didn't have to marry 'every single girlfriend'. When the media began their inevitable dig into Nancy's past, they got more than they bargained for. Investigators found themselves with not only her brother's sinister death to unravel, but the shady past of her father, the suicide of his brother, her Uncle Daniel, and even dealings with some of New York's most dangerous Mafia godfathers.

Nancy was born the only daughter of wealthy American trucking magnate Myron P. Shevell, known as 'Mike', whose family had worked in trucking since the 1920s when they began transporting seafood up the coast from New Jersey to New York. Mike started out as a driver with Apex Express during the 1950s and progressed to Associated Transport with brother Daniel in 1974. Their company had at least one notorious mobster on the payroll.

In 1975, federal government officials filed charges of fraud against the brothers. Though they never faced trial, they were forced out of business and went bankrupt in 1976. Daniel, thirty-nine, took a gun to his skull. In 1977, Mike relaunched himself in the industry, assuming control of troubled company NEMF, New England Motor Freight. That firm became part of the Shevell Group, of which he was chairman. Within a decade, Nancy's father had created one of the biggest haulage firms on the US East Coast. He also funded the political ambitions of his son-in-law, Nancy's first husband Bruce, a lawyer who once aspired to become mayor of New York.

In 1988, after an investigation by the government's Organised Crime Strike Force, Shevell was accused of making Mafia pay-offs and of maintaining a corrupt eleven-year relationship with mobster and former union leader Tony Provenzano, which allowed him to operate outside union rules. Barred for nine years from engaging in union negotiations, Shevell somehow went from strength to strength.

By 2011, the year when the former Beatle proposed to his daughter, Mike's Shevell Group owned six trucking companies, employed 5,000 staff and was turning over $400m a year. Eight years later in 2019, NEMF and ten other Shevell Group companies filed Chapter Eleven bankruptcy papers. All operations closed down in 2020. Mike died in 2022.

In one of the very few interviews she has ever granted, Nancy revealed that she played with toy trucks from an early age.

'I used to line them up in my room, right next to my Barbies,' the former football-playing tomboy told New Jersey newspaper the *Star-Ledger*. 'While other kids would go feed ducks at the park, we would go to my father's truck terminals, to places like Pennsauken [a township in New Jersey] every single weekend.'

Now sixty-four, Nancy was born in New York on 20 November 1959. Like Linda, she was raised in a Jewish family, in Edison, New Jersey. She obtained a degree in Transportation from Arizona State University, where she met her first husband, and where she was the only female in her graduating class. The couple's son Arlen was named for Nancy's mother Arlene, whom she lost to breast cancer in 1991.

She joined the Shevell Group of Companies in 1983, when she was twenty-four, rising through the ranks to become Vice President. She also served on the board of New York's Metropolitan Transportation Authority for ten years until 2011. She founded the Arlene Walters Shevell Endowment Scholarship Fund in her late mother's name, offering access to self-help groups for parents with drug-addicted children, and financial help to people going through rehab.

Her head turned by Paul, Nancy relinquished most of her busy social life, surrendered her Republican political allegiance, quit feasting on steak, turned vegetarian and became a dab hand at the avocado-and-tomato sandwich lunches and pumpkin ravioli suppers to which Paul is partial. She may have been anything but a sleeves-up, scrubbing-brush-out, Liverpool wife, but she was making her desire for him clear.

You could only admire them for keeping their relationship cool until Nancy's divorce was finalised. From then on, open season. In March 2008 they took their first holiday together in Antigua, residing chastely in a two-bedroom suite at private resort Jumby Bay. Five months later, during August, they hit the road, taking a trip down 'Route 66' through the mid-western states in a 1989 Ford Bronco. A month on, Paul's new love was by his side when he performed in Tel Aviv, Israel, dedicating his song 'My Love' to his lovely Linda in front of Nancy. No threat from a dead wife.

That October, he took her to Stella's fashion show in Paris. While Paul sat in the front row with son James and Stella's husband

Alasdhair Willis, Nancy took a discreet seat elsewhere. A further snatched holiday saw them pitch up in Morocco, in 'a quiet little hotel I knew', Paul told *The Times*.

'But we didn't stay together in the same room . . . it rained the whole bloody time, and we had paid all this money to come away to this paradise, and we might as well have stayed in Manchester!

'It was Valentine's Day. I was thinking all sorts of loving thoughts towards Nancy, and while I was at the piano, I could see that the waiters who were clearing up were listening. You can tell when someone's got half an ear on you, even when they're pretending just to do their work. But it was nice and romantic, it was a perfect moment, and I thought to myself, we're not going to stay in separate rooms tonight.'

The song Paul penned that rainy day, he tucked away for posterity. He didn't breathe a word to Nancy. But he had an idea.

Come November, they were seen wandering down Abbey Road together. Tout Londres was agog. Would the boy never learn? When quizzed about Nancy in an interview with the *Sunday Times*, he would say only, heartbreakingly, 'I just like being in love.'

In May 2011, the couple announced their engagement and Nancy flashed her rock-and-a-half: a $650,000, five-plus-carat solitaire diamond with strips of onyx on the band. It would be matched by a diamond and platinum Art Deco-style eternity/ wedding ring designed by the same jeweller, Neil Lane. They were married just over four months later on 9 October in a simple afternoon ceremony at Marylebone Register Office, where Paul had taken Linda as his wife in 1969. The date was obviously chosen deliberately. It would have been John Lennon's seventy-first birthday.

The couple's registrar was Alison Cathcart – who, by coincidence, also married my former husband and me. Same venue, fifteen years earlier. This time, the bride was attired by the groom's designer daughter in a simple, white silk, knee-length button-down dress. A single white bloom adorned her loose, glossy hair. Stella also designed and made her dad's wedding suit. Sister Mary took the wedding photos, Paul's brother Mike was Best Man, little Beatrice was the bridesmaid and son James proposed the toast. Among the guests were Ringo and his wife Barbara Bach, George's widow Olivia Harrison and Nancy's second cousin Barbara Walters, the famous American television talk show host.

Then it was back to Cavendish Avenue for a party and two wedding cakes: one for the veggies, the other for muggles. After which, late in the evening when the typical McCartney clan rabble-rousing had dampened down and proceedings were mellowing, Paul sprang an unexpected wedding present. To the amazement of all who witnessed it, he performed a brand-new song and dedicated it to the bride. He had cooked up the little tune, he explained, on a rainy day in Morocco one time. The night he'd made up his mind that Nancy wasn't going to bed alone. The moving song, which he has often performed during concerts since, is 'My Valentine'.[4]

They raised jugs to John on his birthday before the happy couple wafted away, to spend a low-key honeymoon at the small, modest Firefly Hotel, near Cotton House Beach on Mustique.

When Paul was declared a Companion of Honour by the Queen for his contribution to music in 2018, elegant, navy-clad Nancy was at Buckingham Palace beside him.[5] She has been beside him since she won him, just as Linda was. Appearances excepted, the two Jewish American women had much in common. Both were educated in Arizona. Both were diagnosed with breast cancer, at around the same time. One was taken. The other survived, and went on to found a cancer resource centre in the Hamptons, a place they both loved. Both were passionate about the causes they had elected to support, and both gave of their time and their resources, endlessly and selflessly, in the pursuit of helping others.

One shared enthusiastically in his music-making. The other has kept her distance from stage and studio. Older, wiser and with nothing left to prove, octogenarian Paul is content to leave his wife in the wings, singing and clapping along with the backstage throng. Inspired since childhood by strong, determined women, time had taught him his limits with this one. About Nancy, there is a sense that Linda would approve.

In October 2020, Sir Paul and Lady McCartney celebrated their ninth wedding anniversary. Paul paid tribute on Instagram to his still fantastic-looking wife. 'Congratulations, Nancy,' he posted. '. . . thanks for nine beautiful years of marriage. You are my rock and roll, you are my A side and B side, you are my verse and chorus. I love you. Paul.'

'I try to be helpful as a husband,' he said in *The Lyrics*. '. . . if there's a problem, I like to be the guy that will lend some strength to it. I'm always really happy to be the person Nancy relies on, and to be her strength when she goes through tough times.'

As Linda had been to Paul, so Paul became to Nancy. His extraordinary odyssey, like every human voyage, has seen its share of despair and unbearable tragedy. Many have been the hazards on the long and winding road. He got good at those. He is not done yet. Long may the Beatle dwell among us.

P.S. I LOVE YOU

It was the year before lockdown. 2019. The last year when the world was still normal, before COVID-19 stripped us of liberty and dignity and deprived millions of their loved-ones and lives.[1]

David Stark, owner and publisher of the Songlink International music business resource and drummer with tribute band the Trembling Wilburys, is a Companion of LIPA: the Liverpool Institute of Performing Arts, housed in Macca's old school and of which Paul is patron. He invited me to accompany him to that summer's graduation ceremony, at which a string of entertainment luminaries would also receive Companionships, including our mutual friend Mike Batt, Rowan Atkinson and Stephen Fry.

We had been warned in advance, with written instructions issued by email, that we were not to approach Sir Paul. We must resist the urge to engage him in conversation. No selfie may be sought. I was surprised, therefore, when he wandered into the Green Room ahead of proceedings, made straight for Mike and Julianne Batt and me, and engaged *us* in conversation. He obviously knew the Batts from before. They'd attended his second wedding.

Paul and I had crossed paths a number of times over the years, but mine was just another forgettable face. He would never remember me. Except that he did. In a heartbeat we were back at Linda's kitchen table in Peasmarsh. I stood recounting to him what had happened when she and I walked the wards at Great Ormond

Street children's hospital. 'Lin,' he said, his eyes glazing for a second. 'She really was a lovely girl.' He leaned in more closely, to read my ID badge. He mumbled my name, as though making a mental note. Then, 'I'd better move on,' he said. Gotta mingle!' He shrugged and turned on his heel, to work his magic around the room. My mind buzzed as we took our seats in the auditorium.

It was buzzing more loudly several hours later when we all reconvened in the Green Room, gagging for a drink. After a few minutes, in walked the star of what had been a spirited and enchanting presentation. I was on the other side of the room with my back to the door. No announcement was made. No one said anything. I knew he was there.

It's one of the weird things about superstars. I had experienced the phenomenon before. My mind was cast back to occasions when I had been in the company of Freddie Mercury, Michael Jackson, Frank Sinatra and Madonna. Whatever folk think they mean by 'star quality' or the 'X factor', we do sense an 'aura', a 'glow', a corona of vibrancy that seems to elevate them and make them superhuman. A frisson rippled across the room. Brows lifted. Chatter froze. Where do you look? None of us turned to acknowledge him.

Suddenly I felt a hand. His right hand. It swept lightly across my back and gripped my right shoulder. 'Come on, Lesley-Ann, let's have a picture,' he said. No engaging. No selfies ... But this was Paul McCartney, asking *me*.

David Stark stepped forward with his mobile. The room seemed silent, as though we were underwater. I turned my face. Felt Paul's breath on my cheek. I dared to stare, into the world's most familiar hazel eyes.

What did I see?

I saw eyes. Millions and millions of pairs of eyes, of every type and hue. Eyes upon eyes staring back at me, the way that they had long stared at him. An illusion, obviously. I was projecting. But it prompted me to wonder, how must that feel? People looking at you all the time, everywhere you go, examining everything you do. Clocking your moves, following you around. And voices, endless voices, old and young, loud and soft, talking at you in every language, babbling over and under each other and calling, crying, sobbing your name. That has been Paul's experience for more than sixty years. How hasn't it driven him mad?

Something else happened that day. In that moment, I caught a glimpse of McCartney's secret: his gift for character splitting. Not in a pathological sense, as can occur in cases of borderline personality and other disorders, but in terms of interpersonal relating. He appears to have the knack to be able to separate his celebrity self from his authentic self. He seems to know when each is appropriate. What a skill that is. What a survival technique.

It dawned on me that I had never met anyone so self-aware. Paul has spent almost 75 per cent of his life flooring the world with his songs, his boyish charm and his beguiling gaucheness. He is like it even now, into his eighties. He seems to need us to believe that he remains untouched by age and unchanged by his influence and fame, that most addictive of all drugs. 'I'm the same as all of you,' is the message. He isn't. He can't be. He knows.

He also knows that things would be different if John were still here. Having to live with the loss of his two most significant others has kept him humble. But he can still make a room, a venue, a global audience believe that he is divine.

Was the real Paul there in his eyes that day? Did I see all the way back to the motherless boy who wrote, sang and played himself out of misery, who loved and lost and loved and lost, who is happily married again, who worships the ground his children and grandchildren walk on, who makes music with anyone he likes, but who will mourn Lin and John to his dying day?

Did I see him, blessed reader?

What a fool believes.

YESTERDAYS

1941
24 September
Linda Louise Eastman born Scarsdale, New York, USA.

1942
18 June
James Paul McCartney born Liverpool, UK.

1956
31 October
Paul's mother Mary Patrician (née Mohin) McCartney dies of embolism/breast cancer, when Paul is fourteen years old.

1957
6 July
Paul meets John Lennon and his band the Quarrymen at St Peter's church fête, Woolton, Liverpool. Paul has just turned fifteen. John is sixteen.

1958
15 July
John Lennon's mother Julia (née Stanley) Lennon knocked down by a car and killed outside his home when John is seventeen.

1960

August

The Beatles come together. On 17 August, they set off for their first residency in Hamburg.

1962

1 March

Linda Eastman's mother Louise Sara Eastman killed in American Airlines Flight 1 crash, Jamaica Bay, New York, USA.

18 June

Linda marries first husband Joseph Melville See Jnr on her future second husband Paul's twentieth birthday. (Linda and See divorce in 1965.)

5 October

The Beatles release their first hit 'Love Me Do' in UK. (27 April 1964 in US.)

31 December

Linda's first daughter Heather Louise born.

1964

The Beatles conquer America.

1965

Paul purchases 7 Cavendish Avenue, St John's Wood, London, for £40,000. (Worth around £17m now.)

Paul begins to take over from John as the dominant force in the band. *Rubber Soul* album marks turning point both creatively and personally. Intra-band tension is on the rise.

1966
17 June
Paul purchases 183-acre High Park Farm, Kintyre, Scotland.

5 August
The Beatles release *Revolver* album.

29 August
The Beatles perform final live tour gig, Candlestick Park, San Francisco, USA.

November
They begin recording the album *Sgt. Pepper's Lonely Hearts Club Band*.

1967
15 May
Paul and Linda meet at the Bag O'Nails Club, London.

26 May
Sgt. Pepper's Lonely Hearts Club Band album released. (2 June in US.)

27 August
The Beatles manager Brian Epstein dies from overdose, aged thirty-two. The band are cut adrift. Paul steps in to fill the void, assuming control.

1969
30 January
The Beatles perform 'farewell' impromptu gig on roof of their London Apple Corps HQ, 3 Savile Row, Mayfair.

12 March

Paul and Linda marry at Marylebone Register Office, London. Linda is carrying their first child together.

Paul purchases modest house in Amagansett, Long Island, New York, with 22 acres. He will later build two further houses there.

28 August

Mary Anna McCartney born at Avenue Clinic, St John's Wood.

September

John Lennon tells Ringo, Paul and George that he is leaving the Beatles. For legal/contractual reasons, he makes no public announcement.

26 September

Abbey Road album released.

1970

10 April

Paul announces publicly that he is leaving the Beatles, infuriating John, who 'said he was leaving first.'

17 April

On the future anniversary of his wife's death (twenty-eight years later), Paul releases eponymous debut solo album *McCartney* on Apple Records. It becomes a US Number One.

8 May

Let It Be album released. 'The Long and Winding Road', the Beatles' final single, is released in US but not in UK. Their *Let It Be* documentary released later that month wins the 1970 Academy Award for Best Original Song.

31 December
Paul files lawsuit pleading for the dissolution of the Beatles. The process will not be completed until four years later.

1971
March
Court appoints Official Receiver to preside over the Beatles' and Apple Corps' disintegrating finances.

17 May
Paul's *Ram* album released on Apple Records.

13 September
Stella Nina McCartney born by emergency C-section at King's College Hospital, Camberwell, London. Her difficult birth threatens the lives of both mother and baby, and inspires the name of Paul's new band: Paul prays during her birth that she would be born 'on the wings of an angel'.

Former Moody Blues singer and guitarist Denny Laine joins Paul and Linda to form Wings.

17 December
Wings' debut album *Wild Life* released on Apple Records.

1972
February
'Give Ireland Back to the Irish' single about Bloody Sunday banned by BBC.

Wings university tour: eleven shows around the UK.

Summer
Wings Over Europe tour: twenty-five shows.

Wings' single 'Mary Had a Little Lamb' reaches Top Ten UK.

19 September
Police raid High Park Farm, Kintyre, and remove suspicious plants.

1 December
'Hi, Hi, Hi/C Moon' single released. Banned by BBC for suspected sexual and drug references. B-side is played instead. Single makes UK Number Five.

1973
Paul purchases 160-acre Blossom Wood Farm, Peasmarsh, near Rye, East Sussex.

8 March
Paul and Linda face court trial in Kintyre for drug possession.

23 March
The single 'My Love' from forthcoming LP *Red Rose Speedway* released. It scores Wings their first US Number One single.

30 April
Red Rose Speedway album released.

1 June
The James Bond film theme 'Live and Let Die' released. US Number One and UK Top Five.

Wings 1973 United Kingdom tour, twenty-one shows.

TV special *James Paul McCartney* panned by critics.

5 December
Band on the Run album released on Apple Records.

1974

Both Paul and John hint publicly at a Beatles reunion that never happens.

Paul records *McGear* album with younger brother Mike.

1975
9 January
The Beatles' partnership legally dissolved.

27 May
Venus and Mars album released.

9 September
Wings embark on sixty-six-date 'Wings Over the World' tour of UK, Australia, Europe, US and Canada. The North American gigs are Paul's first live shows there since Beatles' last in 1966, nine years earlier, and the only time Wings perform live in the US and Canada.

1976
25 March
Wings at the Speed of Sound album released.

10 December
Triple live album *Wings Over America* released.

1977
31 May
Linda's song 'Seaside Woman', which had been recorded for the *Ram* album, is at last released in US, credited to 'Suzy and the Red Stripes'. (UK release 10 August 1979.)

12 September
Paul's only son James Louis McCartney born at Avenue Clinic, St John's Wood, London, eight years after sister Mary and six years after sister Stella.

11 November
'Mull of Kintyre' single released.

1978
31 March
London Town album released.

1979
24 May
Back to the Egg album released.

November–December
Wings 1979 United Kingdom tour, twenty shows.

Wings Over the World documentary released.

19 December
'Rockestra' all-star performance for UNICEF and Kampuchean refugees.

Paul and Linda buy a 151-acre ranch in Tucson, Arizona.

1980
16 January
Paul and Linda, family and band arrive in Tokyo for Japanese tour. Paul arrested for marijuana possession, and spends nine days in jail. Tour cancelled. Wings music banned from Japanese TV and radio.

21 January
All Wings except Linda and their children leave Japan.

25 January
Paul released without charge and deported.

Denny Laine releases *Japanese Tears* single and forms short-lived Denny Laine Band with Steve Holley. In December, releases *Japanese Tears* solo album.

Rockshow cinema film of the tour released.

16 May
Paul releases second solo album *McCartney II*.

8 December
John Lennon is murdered on the street outside his home, the Dakota building in New York City, USA.

1981
Paul records *Tug of War* solo album with Beatles producer George Martin and A-list musicians including Denny Laine, who is later replaced by 10CC's Eric Stewart.

Denny Laine leaves the band, and Wings fold officially. Paul does not confirm their demise until 1982, during *Tug of War* promotion.

1982
November
Paul begins work on his only feature film, *Give My Regards to Broad Street*.

1983
31 October
Paul releases solo album *Pipes of Peace*.

1984

January

Paul and Linda arrested in Barbados during their holiday, and charged with drug possession. They are fined $100 each.

Rupert and the Frog Song animated short film and soundtrack released.

13 July 1985

Paul appears at Live Aid, his first live performance for five years after John Lennon's murder.

1991

April

Linda McCartney Foods launched, selling vegetarian products. Some of the proceeds fund her animal aid charity Animal Line. Her company is approved by the Vegetarian Society.

7 October

Paul releases *Paul McCartney's Liverpool Oratorio* live album in UK, his first major classical work, recorded with Carl Davis. (22 October in US.)

1995

Linda diagnosed with breast cancer.

1997

25 September

Paul's second work of original classical music, *Standing Stone*, released in US. (29 September in UK.)

14 October

World premiere performance of *Standing Stone* at London's Royal Albert Hall.

1998
17 April
Linda dies, aged fifty-six, on the McCartney farm in Tucson, Arizona, USA. Her ashes are said to have been scattered there. Others have since indicated that the family brought her home, and that she was scattered at their home in Peasmarsh.

1999
20 May
Paul meets glamour model and charity campaigner Heather Mills at Pride of Britain Awards, Dorchester Hotel, London.

2001
Paul purchases $4m Beverly Hills home.

7 May
Wingspan: Hits and History compilation album released, a retrospective of Paul's career 1970–1984. A made-for-TV special also released.

23 July
Paul proposes to Heather Mills.

2002
11 June
Paul and Heather marry, four years after Linda's death.

1 November
Statue of Linda unveiled in Campbeltown, Kintyre, Scotland.

2003
24 May
Paul gives his first-ever concert in Russia – in Red Square, Moscow, before 100,000 fans. Vladimir Putin gives Paul and Heather a tour of the Kremlin.

28 October
Paul's fifth child Beatrice Milly McCartney born at the hospital of St John and St Elizabeth, St John's Wood.

2006
17 May
Paul and Heather separate.

2007
Summer
Paul meets American divorcee Nancy Shevell.

2008
12 May
Divorce from Heather declared absolute.

2011
9 October
On what would have been John Lennon's seventy-first birthday, Paul marries Nancy at Marylebone Register Office, London – where he had married Linda in 1969.

2015
Paul purchases $15.5m penthouse in Upper East Side, Manhattan, New York. He later sells it at a loss in 2022, for $8.5m.

2020
18 December
Paul releases the third album in the trilogy: *McCartney III*, recorded during the COVID-19 lockdown.

2023
January
Paul releases 'Why Are They Cutting Down the Rainforest?', his long-lost, never-heard-before musical collaboration with Jeff Beck

recorded nearly thirty years earlier, to mark Beck's death on 10 January at the age of seventy-eight.

June

Paul announces the autumn release of an 'AI-enhanced' recording, describing it as 'the last-ever Beatles release'. Media hysteria focused on the potential of Artificial Intelligence to destroy original music obliges him to release a clarifying statement. 'Been great to see such an exciting response to our forthcoming Beatles project,' he writes. 'No one is more excited than us to be sharing something with you later in the year. We've seen some confusion and speculation about it. Seems to be a lot of guesswork out there. Can't say too much at this stage, but to be clear, nothing has been artificially or synthetically created. It's all real and we all [the four Beatles] play on it. We cleaned up some existing recordings – a process which has gone on for years. We hope you love it as much as we do. More news in due course – Paul.'

The same month, he and Nancy are in the wings for Elton John's first-ever Glastonbury Festival performance. Paul opens an exhibition of his own photography at London's National Portrait Gallery: *Paul McCartney Photographs 1963–64: Eyes of the Storm*. He had taken all the recently rediscovered, never-before-seen images himself between December 1963 and February 1964, during the period when the Beatles soared from British sensation to global phenomenon. An online event, *Paul McCartney in Conversation with Stanley Tucci* is also announced.

CHAPTER NOTES

CHAPTER 1: BEFORE

1 'Here Today', a song composed by Paul in memory of John Lennon in 1981, in which he imagines a frank conversation that the pair never had. He later told the *LA Times* that he cried as he wrote it, reflecting that Northern males are never that open, honest or emotional with each other. He wished they could have been. McCartney wrote and worked up the song at home on High Park Farm, Kintyre, Scotland. George Martin produced it at AIR Studios in London. The track featured on Paul's post-Wings album *Tug of War*, released in 1982.

2 Candlestick Park, home of the San Francisco Giants baseball team, made 42,500 seats available, of which 'only' 25,000 sold. The five-feet-high stage was located directly behind second base on the field, and was protected by a six-feet-high wire fence. On that chilly, gusty night of low visibility due to fog, the support acts were the Remains, Bobby Hebb, the Cyrkle and the Ronettes. The Beatles strolled out late, at around 21:27, and gave the crowd just eleven songs in a standard-for-the-time thirty-minute set: 'Rock and Roll Music', 'She's a Woman', 'If I Needed Someone', 'Day Tripper', 'Baby's in Black', 'I Feel Fine', 'Yesterday', 'I Wanna Be Your Man', 'Nowhere Man', 'Paperback Writer' and 'Long Tall Sally'.

John and Paul snapped the audience and themselves with their own camera, and their PR Tony Barrow made an audio recording of this last-ever gig. He later made a single copy for himself, which he guarded under lock and key, and gave the original to Paul. How a bootleg of the most unique Beatles recording ever made later came to be in global circulation has never been explained. The night was the end of an era. 'That's it,' said George Harrison on the plane home to London, 'I'm not a Beatle anymore.'

3 Paul McCartney, fifteen, was introduced to John Lennon, sixteen, by mutual friend Ivan 'Ivy' Vaughan in the church hall of St Peter's, Woolton, following a garden fête at which John's skiffle band the Quarrymen had performed in a field. Paul had observed John's strange guitar-playing and noticed his habit of peering at the audience, not knowing that John was extremely myopic but hated wearing glasses. Across the road in the church hall afterwards, Paul picked up a guitar and played Eddie Cochran's 'Twenty Flight Rock' and Gene Vincent's 'Be-Bop-A-Lula'. He then tuned John's and fellow Quarryman Eric Griffiths's guitars, and noted down the correct lyrics to songs from their setlist. Unsettled by the younger boy, whom he knew was likely to upstage him, John recognised the need to raise his band's game by inviting Paul on board.

4 Not until 2021, fifty-two years later, would the *Get Back* footage be released. Peter Jackson's ground-breaking 'documentary about a documentary', featuring audio recordings from the *Let It Be* album sessions and sequences from sixty hours of film footage shot by Michael Lindsay-Hogg in January 1969 and formatted as an eight-hour documentary in three long episodes, is a Walt Disney Studios/Apple Corps/WingNut Films production, with Paul McCartney, Ringo Starr, Olivia Harrison and Yoko Ono as co-producers. The segment featuring the rooftop concert was released in IMAX cinemas across the US on 30 January 2022, and throughout the world the following month.

The Beatles: Get Back was released on DVD and Blu-Ray on 12 July 2022. *Get Back*, incidentally, had been the working title of the album that became *Let It Be*. Although the *Abbey Road* album (released 26 September 1969 UK/1 October US) was the final Beatles album to be recorded, it was not the last to be released. *Let It Be* went on sale after it, on 8 May 1970. It has long been disputed among Beatles experts and music fans as to which can be regarded as 'the final Beatles album'. Going by release dates, *Let It Be* is technically the swansong, but because *Abbey Road* features 'The End', recorded on 20 August 1969 – the last time that all four band members were in the studio to record together – *Abbey Road* is widely acknowledged to have been 'the last'.

5 NRK, the Norwegian Broadcasting Corporation: Norway's equivalent of the BBC.

6 Badmain, Keith, *The Beatles: Off the Record: Outrageous Opinions and Unreleased Interviews*, Omnibus Press, 2007.

7 'Just Like Starting Over' from John Lennon and Yoko Ono's 1980 album *Double Fantasy*.

8 Lennon and McCartney composed 'I Wanna Be Your Man' and gifted it to their friends the Rolling Stones, who released it as their second single in November 1963 and chalked up their first Top 20 hit with it. The Beatles subsequently recorded it themselves, for their second studio album *With the Beatles* (also November 1963). It is not too far-fetched to imagine that Paul's inclusion of this song in his Glastonbury set was a direct dig at Mick Jagger, with whom he has enjoyed a long-running feud.

After Paul fobbed off the Stones publicly as a 'blues covers band' in 2021, Jagger hit back with a considered retort: 'There's obviously no competition. The big difference ... is that the Rolling Stones have been a big concert band in other decades and other eras, when the Beatles never even did an arena tour, Madison Square Garden with a decent sound system. They broke up before that business started, the touring business for real.' Touché.

CHAPTER 2: ESCAPE

1 Ringo Starr joined the Beatles in August 1962, cementing the classic line-up that would become the focus of the pop music world. Two months later, they released their first single, 'Love Me Do'.

2 The British National Service (Armed Forces) Act of 1939 imposed conscription on all males aged eighteen to forty-one, who had to register for service. Those deemed medically unfit were exempted, as were men in key industries such as medicine, engineering, farming and baking. In December 1941, Parliament passed a second National Service Act to make all unmarried women and childless widows aged between eighteen and thirty liable for call-up, and to extend the age of eligible men up to age sixty. National Service ended in 1960, with the exception of those with periods of deferred service to complete. The last national servicemen were discharged from the armed forces in 1963.

Only George Harrison was born too late (1943, turned eighteen in 1961) to have to worry about it. Both Ringo Starr, born 7 July 1940, and John Lennon, born 9 October the same year, turned eighteen in 1958. Paul, born 18 June 1942, blew out eighteen candles in 1960. How did they manage to get out of it? Because National Service began to decline from 1957 onwards. It was decreed that those born on or after 1 October 1939 would not be called.

According to former *Daily Express* journalist Ivor Davis, the only British reporter to accompany the band on their first American tour, Lennon said that he planned to dodge any future draft by relocating to his ancestral homeland. 'If I ever get called up to serve in the British army,' Davis quotes Lennon in his book *The Beatles and Me on Tour* (Cockney Kid Publishing, 2014), 'I'm going to emigrate to Ireland.'

3 Stuart Sutcliffe, a gifted painter, was the Beatles' first bass player. He was part of the band on their debut residence in Hamburg,

where they performed at the Kaiserkeller, a rough joint frequented by sailors and prostitutes, and were befriended by local art students Klaus Voormann, Jürgen Vollmer and Astrid Kirchherr. Astrid shot many of the band's early, iconic black and white photographs. The Beatles adopted her short, forward-combed hairstyle and were influenced by her fashion sense. Stuart and Astrid fell in love and got engaged. When the Beatles returned home, Stuart opted to remain in Hamburg and continue his art studies. He died of a brain haemorrhage on 10 April 1962, two months shy of his twenty-second birthday. Astrid died of cancer on 12 May 2020, at the age of eighty-one.

4 In 1965, Paul bought his father a beautiful detached mock-Tudor house called 'Rembrandt' on Baskervyle Road in the village of Gayton, Heswall on the Wirral – a desirable location where similar properties change hands for upwards of £1m today. Jim's crippling arthritis soon necessitated a move to a bungalow. Paul bought 'Rembrandt' back from Jim, and maintains it to this day. He is still spotted there occasionally, driving around locally in an old Mini Cooper S. Jim died on 18 March 1976.

Neither Paul nor his brother Mike were close to their stepmother Angie – nor to their half-sister Ruth, whom Jim legally adopted when she was five years old and who would become an entertainer. After her second husband died, Angie opened her own rock group agency in Liverpool. Paul accused her of misappropriating the family name. She went back to her first married name of Williams, in 1981, after selling the story of her relationship with her famous stepson to the *Sun* newspaper. She relocated to Australia, and later to Munich, Los Angeles and Nashville, launching various ventures such as McCartney Music, McCartney Multimedia Inc. and an online organic tea business called Mrs McCartney's Teas. She also became an ordained Minister of Religion, licensed to perform ceremonies of marriage in all fifty US states.

In 1995 she popped up again in the tabloids, appealing to Paul for financial help. He fobbed her off, flagging up that she had 'sold my original birth certificate without saying anything to me or letting me know that she was putting it up for sale at auction – so some bugger has got my birth certificate and I don't know who it is.' She had sold the document to an American investor for an undisclosed sum.

In 1990 it came up for sale again, and was sold by Simpson's auction house in Houston to 26-year-old Beatles fan Brian Taylor of Washington DC for more than $20,000 – the highest price ever paid for such an item at that time. Taylor announced that he would 'sell it back' to Paul for the right amount. Paul's retort was that he didn't see why he should buy it, given that it was his in the first place. The certificate was auctioned again seven years later for $84,146, making it the most expensive birth certificate in the world.

5 In a curious twist, Margaret Asher had once given oboe lessons to future 'Fifth Beatle' George Martin, who later signed the Beatles to Parlophone and became their producer. Margaret also taught Paul to play the recorder, a skill he demonstrated on 'The Fool on the Hill'. Jane's father was Dr Richard Asher, a pioneering endocrinologist and haematologist. The family lived 'above the shop' on the upper floors of their Wimpole Street house. The doctor fell prey to depression in 1964, gave up his practice, and committed suicide at the age of fifty-seven.

6 *Woman: An Intimate Geography*, Natalie Angier, Houghton Mifflin Co., 1999.

7 *Surrender: 40 Songs, One Story*, Bono/Paul David Hewson, Hutchinson Heinemann, 2022.

8 Winston's Wish bereavement charity: www.winstonswish.org. Helpline: 08088 020021.

9 In reference to the work by Welsh poet Dylan Thomas (1914–1953): *Do Not Go Gentle into That Good Night* (Florence, 1947).

CHAPTER 3: PASSING

1 The family's croft cottage where Lennon stayed is still there. A poem he penned there while on holiday was the original inspiration for the Beatles' song 'In My Life' on the 1965 album *Rubber Soul*. Not for the first time, when he or John were in the mood to discuss who wrote what of their collaborations, Paul set cat among pigeons when he claimed, to the author Barry Miles of his authorised biography *Many Years From Now*, that *he* came up with the lion's share of the melody and lyrics. In fact, the original poem that John wrote still exists. It turned up among John's papers when Yoko charged family friend Elliot Mintz with making an inventory of her late husband's personal effects. It's pretty obvious that John wrote what became the song.

2 Paul's 1997 classical album *Standing Stone* features an image of the ancient monument on its cover. The photograph, shot by Linda, appeared originally on the gatefold spread of snaps of Paul's debut solo album *McCartney*. He described the stone as 'symbolic of long-lastingness and standing and weathering the storms of time.' A famous shot of Paul depicts him sitting with his back against the stone, dressed in short-sleeved white polo shirt, brown slacks and black gumboots. The *Standing Stone* album was commissioned by EMI Classical to commemorate that label's centenary. It was the last album that Paul released before Linda died.

3 'Two Little Dickie Birds', a classic nursery rhyme.

4 In 1974, Argyll was conjoined with the Isle of Bute to become the council and lieutenancy area Argyll and Bute.

5 Scotland's *Sunday Herald*, 16 November 2003, *Truth Behind Ballad that Split Beatles*, Mike Merritt.

'The Long and Winding Road' featuring Paul on lead vocals and piano and John Lennon on bass – unusually and poorly – was recorded originally in January 1969. A track on the 1970 album *Let It Be*, it was released as a single a month after the Beatles went their separate ways. Their last official US single, it

287

became their twentieth and final Number One American hit. The record fell one place short in the UK, where the last Beatles single release was 'Let it Be'.

The song became the subject of huge controversy because producer Phil Spector, brought in after George Martin to do additional work, embellished it with his 'Wall of Sound' techniques including choral and orchestral overdubs. When Paul heard Spector's overdubs, he was beside himself at what he considered to be a desecration of his song. But he could do nothing to halt the album's release. Only days after it appeared, he informed his fellow Beatles that he was quitting the band. Through his lawyers, he later pointed to the 'abominable' arrangement of the track as one of his reasons for calling for the Beatles to be terminated.

Since the track's original release in 1970, McCartney has made six further recordings of it. Having refused to perform Beatles songs with Wings during their early days, he relented and played 'The Long and Winding Road' on their 1975–1976 world tour. A live recording of it features on their 1976 album *Wings Over America*. He also recorded it for the soundtrack of *Give My Regards to Broad Street*, his 1984 film. He made another version for the B-side of single releases from his 1989 album *Flowers in the Dirt*. On the live album of his 1989–1990 world tour, *Tripping the Live Fantastic*, a recording made during his April 1990 Rio de Janeiro show was included. That live version was also offered in the seven-inch Singles Box released in 2022. The Beatles' 1996 outtakes compilation *Anthology 3* features the original January 1969 recording without Phil Spector's overdubs. It was then released again on *Let It Be . . . Naked*, a stripped-back edition of the *Let It Be* album, released in 2003.

McCartney continues to perform the much-loved song live. It has been widely covered by other artists including Ray Charles, Aretha Franklin, Leo Sayer, Peter Frampton, George Michael, Faith Hill, Billy Ocean and Cilla Black – who included it on her 1973 album *Day by Day with Cilla*. Paul singled out this take by his old friend and Epstein stablemate as the definitive version. The Beatles' own recording (one assumes a version without Spector's ornamentation) played out her coffin from the church on the occasion of her funeral in August 2015.

6 Andy Stewart's name was once synonymous with New Year's Eve parties. The kilt-clad entertainer with an international following, thanks to his many recordings celebrating Scottish culture, hosted BBC Scotland's annual television *White Heather Club* knees-up throughout the sixties. His 'heather, haggis and Hogmanay' formula persisted on ITV during the seventies, and on the BBC and Grampian Television into the eighties. Stewart's shortbread-tin image, hugely popular in its day, made the royal favourite one of the most popular Scottish entertainers of the twentieth century. His hits included 'A Scottish Soldier', 'Donald Where's Your Troosers', 'The Road to Dundee' and 'Campbeltown Loch'. He died in Edinburgh on 11 October 1993, aged fifty-nine. He is remembered for his ability to transport his audience back to a time that never will be again, in a Scotland that never really was.

7 There is now also a sustainable gin distillery, Beinn an Tuirc, Gaelic for From the Hill of the Wild Boar – the hill where their water is sourced. Situated on the Torrisdale Estate, the distillery uses its own hydro-electricity. Tours, gin-tasting and classes are offered here: https://www.kintyregin.com.

8 St Columba arrived from Ireland to found a monastery on Iona in AD 563. The Abbey that now stands there is one of the oldest and most important Christian sites in Western Europe.

9 'Helen Wheels' the single was released in 1973, ahead of the *Band on the Run* album. Not included on the UK edition of the album, it appeared on the American version. Its title was taken from the name of Paul and Linda's 1970s green Land Rover, dubbed 'Hell on Wheels' because it was so uncomfortable to travel in. That morphed into 'Helen Wheels'. Paul owns the

vehicle to this day. 'Linda loved Scotland,' he told Paul du Noyer (*Conversations with McCartney*). 'I still love setting off in London, going up the motorway, and you see the land change. It's like going all the way through America. We always cheer as we go over the border, then around Loch Lomond. It's got a lot of memories for me, that Land Rover, with everything in the back, dogs, kids, us all up at the front, and me, driving on this epic journey.'

10 A.P. McGrory's shop on the Main Street, a Campbeltown institution for a hundred years, was hit hard by the new trend for internet mail order. It sold off its remaining stock, bolted its doors for the last time and closed down in July 2007.

11 Stella McCartney, *Daily Telegraph*, 31 August 2022.

CHAPTER 4: EARTH MOTHER

1 Some sources put the date of Hendrix's first gig at the Bag O'Nails back to 11 January 1967. Elsewhere, it is recorded that he first landed in London on 23 September 1966, and made his debut UK performance the following night at the Scotch of St James in Mason's Yard.

2 *Rock and Other Four-Letter Words: Music of the Electric Generation*, J. Marks and Linda Eastman, Bantam Books, 1968.

3 *Paul McCartney: Many Years from Now*, Barry Miles, Secker & Warburg, 1997.

4 In 1972, scriptwriter Francie Schwartz penned a memoir, *Body Count*, about this period of her life.

5 Jane must have been more hurt and damaged by her break-up from McCartney than she let on. She would not marry for almost thirteen more years. Nine months after the engagement collapsed, and twenty days after her twenty-third birthday, her 57-year-old physician father Richard Asher committed suicide. She threw herself into work; met cartoonist, illustrator and graphic artist Gerald Scarfe (famous for Pink Floyd's *The Wall*)

in 1971, who is ten years her senior, and married him a decade later when she was thirty-five. The couple have three children. She has never discussed her relationship with Paul. He has spoken of Jane only rarely and with caution.

Between 1985 and 1987, Jane starred alongside Felicity Kendal in the BBC2 TV sitcom *The Mistress*. Its two series were written by Carla Lane, 'the television writer who dared to make women funny', who co-created *The Liver Birds*, *Butterflies* and *Bread*; and who founded Animal Line with her great friend . . . Linda McCartney.

6 *The Beatles: Off the Record*, Keith Badman.

7 *Linda McCartney: A Portrait*, Danny Fields.

8 *Vanity Fair*, October 1992, Zoë Heller.

9 The Beatles' first EMI Abbey Road session was held in Studio 2 on 6 June 1962, and lasted from 7 p.m. until 10 p.m. George Martin and Ron Richards produced, and Norman Smith was the engineer. They ran through a selection of songs then recorded four: 'Besame Mucho', 'Love Me Do', 'P.S. I Love You' and 'Ask Me Why'. Nothing of John and Paul's songwriting ability and little of the foursome's winning personality, chemistry and flair were evident that day.

10 Peggy Lipton became a quintessential seventies West Coast hippie chick who charmed everyone from Elvis Presley upwards. Her fourteen-year marriage to record producer and musician Quincy Jones gave her two children and a deep depression. She resumed her acting career after the relationship's demise, starring as Norma Jennings in David Lynch's acclaimed *Twin Peaks*. In April 1982, fourteen years after her last encounter with Paul, the almost forty-year-old former Beatle was working in Los Angeles with Michael Jackson on the tracks 'Say Say Say', 'The Man' and 'The Girl is Mine'. Jacko's producer was none other than Quincy Jones, Peggy's husband. The wily music man insisted that the McCartneys and the Joneses have a bygones-be-bygones dinner together. God knows what Linda

made of it. The Joneses divorced in 1990. Peggy died of colon cancer in May 2019. She was seventy-two.

11 'All I Want for Christmas is a Beatle', sung by actress Dora Bryan, words and music by Gladys Benton, was released on Fontana Records and was voted 'the best bad record of 1963'.

12 The Dalton School, founded in 1919 and still widely considered a 'bastion of privilege', is a private co-educational prep school on the Upper East Side of New York City. Sean Lennon and Christian Slater were taught there.

13 *Paul McCartney: Many Years From Now*, Barry Miles.

CHAPTER 5: RENAISSANCE

1 The 14th Annual Rock and Roll Hall of Fame Induction Dinner was held at New York's Waldorf-Astoria Hotel, Park Avenue, on 15 March 1999. It was one of Paul's first public appearances since Linda's death almost a year earlier. He was accompanied by his 27-year-old youngest daughter Stella, who wore a white vest emblazoned with blue lettering: ABOUT FUCKING TIME! Paul's fellow inductees were Bruce Springsteen, Billy Joel, the Staple Singers, Bob Wills and his Texas Playboys, Dusty Springfield, Del Shannon, Curtis Mayfield (who would die nine months later) and the recently deceased Charles Brown.

George Martin, seventy-three, received the Ahmet Ertegun Award, given to 'non-performing industry professionals who, through their dedicated belief and support of artists and their music, have had a major influence on the creative development and growth of rock & roll and music that has impacted youth culture.' www.rockhall.com.

2 Paul McCartney, *Uncut* magazine, January 2021.

3 The follow-ups in the originally unintended trilogy, *McCartney II* and *McCartney III*, were released ten years after the first in 1980, and fifty years after the first in 2020, respectively. 5

August 2022 saw the worldwide release of all three albums as a limited edition three-CD/three-vinyl-albums box set.

4 *Wonderwall* was the title of an obscure 1968 film with a soundtrack album called *Wonderwall Music* recorded by George Harrison. Noel Gallagher purloined the title for Oasis's October 1995 hit, the fourth single release from their second album, also released that year: (*What's the Story) Morning Glory*. 'Wonderwall' became, in October 2020, the first song from the nineties to achieve a billion streams on Spotify.

5 Mickie Most was sixty-four when he died in May 2003, probably from peritoneal mesothelioma: a malignant cancer caused by the ingestion of asbestos fibres. He is believed to have been over-exposed to the substance during the era when vinyl tiles containing it were used routinely in the soundproofing of recording studios.

6 There is no indication that Most remained involved in *The Second Coming of Suzanne*. The film – 'a modern fairytale' with a female Christ figure – inspired, went the studio line, by the lyrics of Leonard Cohen's song 'Suzanne', was released eventually in October 1974, starring Sondra Locke and Jared Martin. A very young Richard Dreyfus put in a blink-and-you'll-miss-it appearance as a production associate. The part of Lee Simon, 'a poet and romantic' intended for McCartney, was played by Paul Sand.

7 Paul, quoted from *Wingspan: Paul McCartney's Band on the Run*, means SS *France*. SS *Île de France* was an earlier, late-1920s cruise liner that saw action during the Second World War as a troop ship and then a prison ship. She returned to luxury-liner service during the late 1940s and was scrapped in 1959.

Launched in 1960, the black-hulled, distinctive red-funnelled SS *France* was, like her predecessor, owned by the Compagnie Générale Transatlantique/the French Line, and was at the time the longest and one of the fastest cruise liners in the world. She made her maiden voyage to New York on 3 February 1962. On

14 December that year, she carried the Mona Lisa to Manhattan, whence the painting was taken on a tour of America. Despite a reputation for elegance and old-world luxury, she was quite the rock'n'roll cruise ship in her day. On 11 April 1974, David Bowie disembarked in New York after a five-day crossing. During the trip, he treated the crew to an impromptu live performance in the canteen, accompanying himself on guitar with backing vocals by a few crew members.

And in September that year, Elton John sailed the Atlantic on her, passing his time writing the music to Bernie Taupin's lyrics for his 1975 *Captain Fantastic and the Brown Dirt Cowboy* album at the ship's piano. Who knows what his fellow first-class passengers made of his outrageous get-ups and bright green hair. It appears that he won them over by playing Bingo with them. The SS *France* was sold to Norwegian Cruise Line, glitzed up for Caribbean jaunts and renamed SS *Norway*, later still the SS *Blue Lady*. She went to the scrapyard in 2005.

8 The Beatles 'took over music forever' via their first of three prime-time Sunday evening appearances on *The Ed Sullivan Show* on 9 February 1964. CBS had received 50,000 requests for 728 tickets, according to the *New York Times*. They performed 'All My Loving', 'Till There Was You' and 'She Loves You', returning after a break to play 'I Saw Her Standing There' and 'I Want to Hold Your Hand'. Sullivan confirmed that the first Beatles show had 'played to the greatest TV audience that's ever been assembled in the history of American TV.' While the Beatles were on air, virtually no crime was reported anywhere in the US.

Contrary to popular belief, their first appearance on *Ed Sullivan* was not their first time on US TV. Although it did count as their first live appearance, they had earlier been featured in *The Huntley–Brinkley Report* on 18 November 1963, in a four-minute piece about Beatlemania. The *CBS Morning News* aired a five-minute item about the band on 22 November, and had planned to repeat it that evening. It was bumped by coverage of the assassination of President John F. Kennedy, and was eventually aired again on 10 December.

On the *Billboard* Hot 100 singles chart of 4 April 1964, the Beatles held all five top slots: 1) 'Can't Buy Me Love'. 2) 'Twist and Shout'. 3) 'She Loves You'. 4) 'I Want to Hold Your Hand'. 5) 'Please Please Me'. It was the first time in *Billboard*'s history that a single artist or group had held all five positions. In addition that week, they claimed another seven places: 31) 'I Saw Her Standing There'. 41) 'From Me to You'. 46) 'Do You Want to Know a Secret?' 58) 'All My Loving'. 65) 'You Can't Do That'. 68) 'Roll Over Beethoven'. 79) 'Thank You Girl'.

Several of these were B-sides. Two more singles were added the following week, 'There's a Place' and 'Love Me Do', totalling fourteen Beatles singles on the Hot 100's 11 April 1964 chart. Source: *Billboard*.

9 *Wingspan: Paul McCartney's Band on the Run.*
10 Max Bell, *Classic Rock.*
11 Eric Carmen's magnum opus was based on Sergei Rachmaninoff's second piano concerto. Celine Dion covered the song in 1996, and scored a gigantic hit. Familiar to many younger fans via the film *Bridget Jones's Diary* (2001).

CHAPTER 6: RAM

1 I examine the death of Rolling Stone Brian Jones at length in my 2022 biography *The Stone Age: 60 Years of the Rolling Stones.*
2 In 2021, Denny Seiwell produced the album *Ram On: The 50th Anniversary Tribute to Paul and Linda McCartney's Ram* with producer, session bassist and guitarist Fernando José Perdomo. It also features David Spinozza.

Now here's a bizarre coincidence: the doorman in his sentry box outside the Dakota building, New York, on the night that John Lennon was murdered was also called José Perdomo. In one of the many post-assassination conspiracy theories, it was alleged that the now-deceased doorman was an anti-Castro

Cuban exile linked to 1961's failed Bay of Pigs military invasion to overthrow Fidel. It was claimed, never proven, that Perdomo was working for the CIA, and that he, not Mark Chapman, was the man who killed John Lennon. No connection to musician Fernando Perdomo is implied.

3 *Making Music*, edited by George Martin (Pan Books, 1983).

4 Andrew Gold's mother was Marni Nixon (1930–2016), who ghost-sang on film for a string of famous actresses, including Natalie Wood in *West Side Story*, Deborah Kerr in *The King and I*, and Audrey Hepburn in *My Fair Lady*.

5 *The Bass Book: A Complete Illustrated History of Bass Guitars*, Tony Bacon and Barry Moorhouse, Backbeat Books, 1995.

6 Beatles historian Mark Lewisohn has obtained documentary evidence, revealed during his autumn 2022 live stage show *Evolver:62* at London's Bloomsbury Theatre, that head of Decca Dick Rowe did not turn down the Beatles. A formal letter from the record company destroys the widely held myth. It shows that they made the group an offer, which was rejected by Brian Epstein. Lewisohn is the author of several books about the Fabs. *Tune In*, which is volume one of his three-part biography *All These Years*, was published in 2013. Work on volume two is ongoing.

7 Geoffrey Giuliano, a prolific if at times controversial Beatles biographer, found second-wind fame via his appearance in the Netflix drama series *Squid Game*. He is the author of *Blackbird: The Unauthorised Biography of Paul McCartney* (Smith Gryphon Ltd, 1991), on which Denny Laine collaborated extensively.

8 'How Do You Sleep?', a track from John Lennon's 1971 solo album *Imagine*, is a blatantly vicious attack on Paul. It is said to have been written in angry response to what John perceived as direct attacks on him made by his former partner on Paul's album *Ram*. George Harrison plays slide guitar on the track, as if to rub it in. Paul would admit down the line that the track 'Too Many People' was indeed a dig at John, but denied that

others such as 'Three Legs' were aimed at him. Lennon later denied that his song was a deliberate act of spite, dismissing it as 'good, clean fun'.

CHAPTER 7: STARTING OVER

1 Kyoko is also name-checked in the intro of John and Yoko/ Plastic Ono Band's 1971 single 'Happy Xmas (War Is Over)', the intended Vietnam protest song turned perennial Christmas favourite. Yoko can be heard whispering 'Happy Christmas, Kyoko', while John murmurs the same greeting to Julian.

2 In October 2022, it was announced that some unused recordings made by British DJ 'Lord' Tim Hudson formerly of Piccadilly Radio during the Beatles' 1965 US tour, never broadcast during his KCBQ San Diego show then rediscovered after Hudson's death in 2019, were to be auctioned together with other related items by Hudson's estate. Lennon is heard 'admitting' that there was nothing he could do to stop the war in Vietnam.

This was presented in the press as a 'revelation', overlooking the fact that conflict in Southeast Asia could never rationally have been considered a 25-year-old pop star's responsibility. The recording was made four years ahead of his and Yoko's launch of their bed-in for peace movement – by which time, John had clearly grown confident in the notion that he might be able to exert influence in that direction. During their campaign, John and Yoko refused to rise from their hotel bed for days at a time while the war raged on. The auction lot, together with copyright of the Beatles' recordings, was sold by Omega Auctions Merseyside, hammer price £2,000, on 11 October 2022.

3 Neil Young's own personal life could not have been more troubled. Himself the product of a broken home, his first wife was Susan Acevedo, to whom he was married for two years. His relationship with actress Carrie Snodgress produced one son.

He married his second wife, singer-songwriter Pegi, in 1978. The couple had two children. He left her after thirty-six years for actress Daryl Hannah, whom he married in 2018. Pegi died in 2019. Two of Young's offspring have cerebral palsy and one has epilepsy.

4 Data, Office for National Statistics: www.ons.gov.uk.

5 The Lennons lost their first child together, whom they named John Ono Lennon II, at Queen Charlotte's Hospital in London. They recorded the foetal heartbeat before the baby died, and used it on their 1969 album *Life With the Lions*. He was buried by the couple in a secret location.

6 Kyoko Chan Cox, now sixty, was married to financial attorney James (Jim) Helfrich. They had two children, Yoko's grandchildren Emi Ono Helfrich, born 4 September 1997, and John (Jack) David Yeisuke Helfrich, born 9 January 2000, both in Denver, Colorado. The couple subsequently divorced. Emi, now twenty-six, graduated from New York University with a major in East Asian Visual Media and a minor in Japanese language. She then studied Japanese in Tokyo, returning to the US in 2020. She is a screenwriter and filmmaker, sometimes collaborating with her 23-year-old brother Jack, who has composed music for her film pieces. He also has a band called Good for Health.

Yoko's son Sean, forty-eight, is not married, but has been in a relationship for fifteen years with singer Charlotte Kemp Muhl; they do not have children. John's first son Julian, sixty, never married, and has not had children. Yoko and Sean were John's only beneficiaries. The estate is believed to be worth around $700m (£557m) currently. Julian sued successfully for a share after his father died. The drawn-out battle was not settled until 1996, sixteen years after John's death.

7 John had a 1968 conviction for possession of marijuana. During the same trial, Yoko was cleared of possessing cannabis and of obstructing police officers.

CHAPTER 8: WILD LIFE

1 *Linda McCartney: A Portrait*, Danny Field, 2000.
2 Holy Bible, Matthew 10: 16–22.
3 South African-born photographer Barry Lategan 'discovered' sixties fashion model Twiggy. His iconic portraits of her, and a study of Princess Anne, hang in London's National Portrait Gallery and in the V&A. In 2015, when he was eighty years old, he stood trial accused of sexually assaulting several women after 'scouting' them on buses and in cafés. He was found to be suffering from evolving dementia.
4 *Paul McCartney: In His Own Words*, Paul Gambaccini, Omnibus Press.
5 The *Rupert and the Frog Song* video included two other short films with songs composed by Linda. 'Seaside Woman', credited to 'Suzy and the Red Stripes' and 'The Oriental Nightfish' were both performed by Wings. Adapted for television, further films and video games, Rupert has more than earned McCartney his keep.
6 Not one but three London Transport buses were used for the filming of *Summer Holiday*.

CHAPTER 9: NARCISSISMA

1 *Memories, Dreams and Reflections*, Marianne Faithfull, Fourth Estate, 2007.
2 Sick of Mick's incessant adultery, Jerry Hall dumped the man she thought was her husband after twenty-three years when she discovered he'd had a child with someone else. During their divorce, she learned to her horror that they had never been married legally. Mick used the revelation to screw her down to a pittance of a settlement during the 'divorce'. Lucas Morad Jagger, born 9 December 1997, is the seventh of the rocker's eight children with five different women. Jerry eventually tied the knot again with Rupert Murdoch in 2016. The 92-year-old media tycoon ended their six-year marriage by email in August 2022.

3 Various live recordings were made throughout the Wings 1972 European tour, most of which went on to languish in vaults. Of note are the performances captured by the Rolling Stones Mobile (RSM) studio, also known as 'The Mobile': the recording truck which that band had come up with in 1968, when Mick Jagger wanted to cut extortionate studio expenditure and find a way of recording at his Stargroves country estate. The Stones used it to record some of their *Sticky Fingers* album in 1970 and all of their *Exile on Main Street* double album in Villefranche, South of France in 1971. It was also used by a variety of other artists including the Who, Fleetwood Mac and Bob Marley. Forty-six years after the Mobile captured them, recordings from the 1972 tour were released as part of the boxed set *Paul McCartney and Wings: Wings 1971–73* in December 2018.

4 Yew Corner may have given Alan Alexander Milne the idea for Winnie-the-Pooh, but he wrote all of the stories in East Sussex at Cotchford Farm, a farmhouse dating back to the mid-sixteenth century. Milne died there in 1956. Statues of his son Christopher Robin and his character Owl stand in the garden., which also features a sundial with a base carved with other Pooh characters, including Piglet, Tigger and Roo. Rolling Stone Brian Jones acquired the property in November 1968, and drowned in its pool in July 1969, at the age of twenty-seven. The house gained Grade II listed status in 1982.

5 'Mannish Boy (Manish Boy)' is a blues standard by Muddy Waters, written with Bo Diddley and Mel London and released originally in June 1955. The Manish Boys were the second group with whom David Bowie, as David Jones (his real name) recorded in the mid-1960s; the first having been Davie Jones & the King Bees.

6 Jimmy Miller's second wife Geri Miller died of breast cancer, three years before Jimmy's death at fifty-two from liver failure.

CHAPTER 10: METAMORPHOSIS

1 Paul would move to CBS in 1979, where he remained until 1984. He returned to EMI in 1985. The Universal Music Group acquired the EMI and Capitol brands in 2012, when EMI ceased to exist as an independent major music company. John Lennon signed with Geffen (distributed by Warner Bros) in 1980 after his five-year hiatus, for his and Yoko's 'comeback' album *Double Fantasy*. The posthumous album *Milk and Honey* (January 1984) was released by Polydor.

What goes around, comes around: Polydor was the first label the Beatles ever recorded for, in Hamburg with English guitarist and singer Tony Sheridan in June 1961. The sessions generated several tracks, including 'My Bonnie', which Polydor released as the single that would bring them to the attention of their future manager Brian Epstein. Or did it? Legend held for a long time that it was when a customer by the name of Raymond Jones came into Epstein's NEMS Liverpool music store to request a copy of that single that Brian was prompted to go and see them performing at the Cavern Club, which he did on 9 November 1961. But local journalist and editor Bill Harry had been writing about them in his *Mersey Beat* magazine for some time by then. Brian must already have been aware of the fledgling Beatles.

2 A variation of 'Live and Let Die' sung as a cabaret number by American singer Brenda Arnaud performing as B.J. Arnau appears later in the same film. It earned her a recording contract with RCA, but she was to die of a brain haemorrhage in 1989.

3 The Beatles never played Madison Square Garden, 'the world's most famous arena' and the oldest major sporting facility in New York. They performed at Shea Stadium in Flushing Meadows, Queens, as the William A. Shea Municipal Stadium was known, in August 1965 and during the same month the following year. The stadium was named after William Shea, an American lawyer who was instrumental in returning National League baseball to New York City after the Dodgers and the

Giants relocated to Los Angeles and San Francisco respectively in 1957. The home of the New York Mets baseball team since 1964, Shea Stadium had a far greater audience capacity. It no longer stands. Demolition concluded in February 2009. It was replaced with Citi Field, the Mets' current home stadium.

Madison Square Garden has been called 'the holy temple of rock'n'roll for most touring acts.' Billy Joel holds the record for the highest number of performances there, which stands currently at one hundred and thirty-four gigs. On 30 August 1972, John Lennon gave two concerts there, in support of New York's Willowbrook School. These were his last full public concerts. On Thanksgiving, 28 November 1974, he joined Elton John on stage there as a surprise guest. It turned out to be his last-ever live performance.

Paul McCartney and Wings made it to Madison Square Garden for two concerts during their *Wings Over America* tour, on 24 and 25 May 1976. Paul has also performed at the midtown-Manhattan arena several times as a solo artist: during his Paul McCartney World Tour 1989–90, on 12, 14 and 15 December 1989; on his US Tour 2005, on 1, 4 and 5 October that year; and on his *One to One* Tour 2016–17, on 15 and 17 September 2017.

4 'With a Little Help from My Friends' was written by John and Paul and sung by Ringo performing as Billy Shears. It features as the second track on the *Sgt. Pepper's Lonely Hearts Club Band* album (1967). Starr has performed it live many times since.

5 Craigard House, built by a whisky distiller and requisitioned by the council for use as an emergency maternity hospital in 1942, fell derelict from 1973 for the next twenty years. It was purchased at auction by English model aircraft factory owner Roger Clark, who opened it as a hotel in 1997. Roger also moved his business there, making plastic planes for the world's airlines, including the miniature Concordes that were given to every passenger who flew supersonic. His factory employed between seventy

and ninety local people for thirteen years, until the business went under in 1999. When I stayed at the Craigard House Hotel during my extended visit to Campbeltown, I slept in what had been the maternity hospital's delivery room.

CHAPTER 11: RETURNS

1 Adam Faith was born Terence Nelhams in west London on 23 June 1942. His early pop career, as one of the wave that included Cliff Richard and Billy Fury during the late fifties and early sixties, earned him hits such as 'What Do You Want', 'Someone Else's Baby' and 'Lonely Pup (In a Christmas Shop)', but was effectively killed by the Beatles and other guitar-led bands. He reinvented himself as an actor, notably playing the title role in *Budgie* on television and the manager of David Essex's rock star character in David Puttnam's film *Stardust*. Having invested successfully in property, he became a financial journalist and columnist but managed to lose the family fortune, and left his estranged wife Jackie penniless when he died of a heart attack aged sixty-two while in bed with his much younger mistress.

CHAPTER 12: VELOCITY

1 Clarence 'Frogman' Henry (1937–) was nicknamed on account of the croak in his voice. He is synonymous with his 1961 hits '(I Don't Know Why) But I Do' – remember it from *Forrest Gump*? – and 'You Always Hurt the One You Love'. He opened eighteen concerts for the Beatles across the United States and Canada in 1964. Well into his eighties, he is still performing live.

2 Then again, according to the official Graceland website (www. graceland.com/achievements), more than a billion Elvis records have been sold worldwide, 'more than anyone in record industry history'. Really? One thousand million? Anyway, the Beatles' sales eclipse those of other top-selling artists Elvis, Michael Jackson, Elton John, Queen, Madonna and Led Zeppelin.

3 Elvis Presley also covered 'Lady Madonna' in 1971.

4 Allen Toussaint (1938–2015) was a prolific songwriter, musician, producer, arranger and major figure in New Orleans rhythm and blues. In 1973, the year when he worked with Wings on *Venus and Mars*, he produced the Number One hit 'Lady Marmalade' ('Voulez-vous coucher avec moi?') for Labelle. He wrote 'Fortune Teller', a song covered by many sixties artists including the Rolling Stones, the Who, the Hollies and the Nashville Teens, and much later by Alison Krauss and Robert Plant. During the seventies he began working with artists outside the New Orleans scene, such as Robert Palmer, Sandy Denny, Solomon Burke and Frankie Miller, and eventually Bonnie Raitt, Eric Clapton and Elvis Costello.

He launched his studio in eastern New Orleans in 1973, where McCartney and Wings were among the first to record. His studio and home were destroyed by Hurricane Katrina in 2005, after which he relocated, first to Baton Rouge and then to New York. In 2007, he sang a duet with Paul of the Fats Domino song 'I Want to Walk You Home' for the album *Goin' Home: A Tribute to Fats Domino*. He did return to New Orleans to live, but died from a heart attack in Madrid while on tour in November 2015, aged seventy-seven.

5 Twenty years later, during his New World tour, Paul returned to New Orleans to headline the Superdome on 24 April 1993. Tickets were priced at only $32, but sold so poorly that they were given away before the show to 'paper the room'. Paul and Linda were interviewed backstage by local filmmaker Stevenson Palfi for a documentary on Allen Toussaint. They had been asked for five minutes but Paul talked for almost an hour, and gave an a cappella rendition of Toussaint's song 'Working in the Coal Mine'. The following day, Toussaint returned the compliment by singing to the McCartney sisters at the New Orleans Jazz and Heritage Festival.

On 21 October the following year, he and Linda were back for a retrospective exhibition of her photographs. Ahead of the private opening, the couple visited the French Quarter, where Linda took pictures of unusual doorways and street musicians.

On 3 February 2002, during the year of his marriage to Heather, Paul performed there at Super Bowl XXXVI (U2 played at half-time). He and his fiancée adjourned to the Polo Lounge at the Windsor Court Hotel, where Paul asked the pianist, Charlie Dennard, to play 'The Very Thought of You'. 'Play it again, Charlie,' said Paul, and this time he sang the song, dedicating it to Heather. That October while on tour for the first time in almost ten years, Paul performed at the old New Orleans Arena. During the encore, he introduced local saxophonist Thaddeus Richard, a former member of the Wings horn section, who performed soprano sax lines in 'Lady Madonna'. Intriguingly, during that trip, Paul hired another local saxophonist by the name of Rebecca Barry to give Heather a sax lesson. If the second Lady McCartney was inspired to 'do a Linda', the idea didn't last long.

In February 2013, Paul attended Super Bowl XLVII, and was a guest at the *Rolling Stone* and *GQ* parties. He also attended DIRECTV'S bash featuring Justin Timberlake. He also took a ride on a streetcar along Canal Street, which was considered such an event that it was reported around the world.

In October 2014, Paul was back in the city to sing at the Smoothie King Center. Five years later, the 76-year-old was back at the same venue, performing on his *Freshen Up* tour. His daughter, photographer and mother-of-four Mary, was in attendance at one of the shows. She was in town for an exhibition of her photographs at the same gallery, A Gallery for Fine Photography, where her mother had shown her own collection twenty-five years earlier.

6 It has been suggested that Paul wrote 'Girlfriend' for Michael Jackson ahead of their first meeting on the *Queen Mary* in 1975. Also, that producer Quincy Jones advised Michael to cover the track, recorded by Wings for their 1978 album

London Town. Which he did, and then included it on his 1979 album *Off the Wall*. In 1982 the two duetted together on Michael's song 'The Girl is Mine', which appeared on Jacko's career-defining album *Thriller.* The following year they collaborated on two songs for Macca's fourth solo studio album, *Pipes of Peace*: the lead, hit single 'Say Say Say' and the track 'The Man'.

But there was betrayal in the air and on the horizon. When Paul advised MJ to invest in music publishing, the latter took him at his word. On 14 August 1985, he snapped up the rights to most of the Beatles' back catalogue from parent company ATV for $47m. He did it before Macca could get a look-in. Paul was incensed. It was like, he said, being 'someone's friend, and then buy[ing] the rug they're standing on.' They 'kind of drifted apart after that'. Michael died in 2009. Eight years later in 2017, McCartney's lawyers filed a lawsuit in New York against what is now Sony/ATV, to regain his share of the Beatles' back catalogue. The company settled.

7 Jack Douglas interview: https://www.pbs.org/wnet/american-masters/lennonyc-beyond-broadcast-episode-1-jack-douglas/1623.

CHAPTER 13: OVER AMERICA

1 The old Regent Cinema in Rye was bombed during the Second World War, and was rebuilt and relaunched in 1948. EMI took it over in 1967. It closed down in September 1973, after which it stood empty for several years. In 1975, the band rehearsed their *Wings Over America* and world tour there. The building was eventually demolished, and the Regent Motel was built and opened on the site in 1984. It is a lovely location, is open to this day and makes a fine destination for Wings fans: Regent Motel, 42 Cinque Ports Street, Rye, TN31 7AN. It is often mentioned in books that the band rehearsed in an old 'theatre'. Linda gave an interview without naming the venue (for obvious reasons)

and describing it as such; as an American, she referred to a cinema as a 'movie theatre'.

2   Or perhaps Paul was inspired by the British sound effect comedy film *San Ferry Ann* (without the 'e') when he wrote this. The 1965 picture about a group of elderly British travellers on a trip to France starred Joan Sims, Ron Moody and Wilfred Brambell – who at fifty-two starred alongside Paul, twenty-two, playing his 'Grandad' in the Beatles' film *A Hard Day's Night*. Brambell also immortalised rag and bone man Albert Steptoe in television's *Steptoe and Son*, alongside Harry H. Corbett and Hercules the horse.

3   A reference to the Ye Cracke pub on Rice Street off Hope Street, Liverpool, close to what was Paul's and George's grammar school, Liverpool Institute, now the Liverpool Institute of Performing Arts (LIPA). John, his future wife Cynthia (mother of Julian) and other fellow art students began drinking at the unassuming establishment in October 1957.

CHAPTER 14: SONS OF KINTYRE

1   Michael Lindsay-Hogg is an American-born British television and film director. He worked on TV's pop series *Ready Steady Go!*, was a pioneer of music film production, and directed promos for both the Beatles and the Rolling Stones. He created *The Rolling Stones Rock and Roll Circus* in 1968, but the band were not happy with it. It did not see the light of day for nearly thirty years. He was then engaged by the Beatles to make a television special, *Get Back*, which would depict them recording their new album and rehearsing for a performance. But after the 1969 rooftop concert, both album and film were shelved. The album emerged in 1970, as *Let It Be*. Director Peter Jackson used some of Lindsay-Hogg's footage for his 2021 documentary series *The Beatles: Get Back*. Lindsay-Hogg became Sir Michael Lindsay-Hogg, 5th Baronet of Rotherfield Hall, East Sussex, after the death of his father in 1999.

2 Ailsa Craig in the Firth of Clyde is one of the only two sources in the world for curling stones. The quartz-free, low-water-absorption granite is quarried there and at the Trefor Quarry on the North Wales coast just west of Caenarfon. They're funny, aren't they, the bedpan-like stones. But they are highly prized. A single curling stone certified for World Curling Federation contests and the Winter Olympic Games costs nearly £480; a full set of sixteen stones sells for about £7,600.

3 *The Lyrics: 1956 to the Present*, Paul McCartney.

4 During the 1970s, the UK Christmas Number One became a national obsession. *Top of the Pops* was partly to blame. It created a clash between Slade and Wizzard, 'Merry Xmas Everybody' versus 'I Wish it Could be Christmas Everyday' (*sic*). The book-makers saw an opportunity and got in on the act. The public has been betting on the Christmas chart-topper and on whether it will snow on the big day ever since. Some notable Yuletide records never made it to the top at the time, including Wham!'s 'Last Christmas' and Mariah Carey's 'All I Want for Christmas is You', although Carey's song finally reached the summit in 2022, twenty-six years after its release.

Band Aid's 1984 effort 'Do They Know It's Christmas' was a good year. The three consecutive years in the nineties when the Spice Girls bagged it, not so much. By the 2000s, Simon Cowell's *X Factor* winners were dominant. Many objected to that, and campaigns arose to support alternatives all the way to the top. We have lately seen charitable fund-raisers by military wives and NHS choirs. Let's not do LadBaby, and thank good-ness for streaming.

5 Top ten musician earners in the UK according to www.statista. com: 1) Sir Paul McCartney, £865m. 2) U2, £625m. 3) Lord Andrew Lloyd-Webber, £495m. 4) Sir Elton John, £395m. 5) Sting, £320m. 6) Sir Mick Jagger, £318m. 7) Keith Richards, £303m. 8) Olivia & Dhani Harrison, £295m. 9) Sir Ringo Starr, £285m. 10) Ed Sheeran, £168m.

6 McEwan's Export is Scotland's biggest-selling tinned ale.

7 *Let the Good Times Roll*, Kenney Jones, Blink Publishing, 2018.

CHAPTER 15: SAYONARA

1 ... although I've always winced at the line about 'orthopaedic shoes'.

2 *Moses and Monotheism*, Sigmund Freud, Hogarth Press and the Institute of Psycho-Analysis, 1939.

3 The Concerts for the People of Kampuchea staged over four nights at London's Hammersmith Odeon featured, in addition to Wings, Queen, the Who, the Pretenders, Elvis Costello, the Clash and more, to raise money for victims of war in Cambodia. Paul organised the benefits with Austrian politician and diplomat Kurt Waldheim, who at the time was Secretary-General of the United Nations. A live album, EP and film were later released, further funding the cause.

4 Would they ever learn? Linda and Paul were arrested again on 16 January 1984, four years to the day since Paul's arrest in Tokyo, when their holiday villa in Barbados was raided after a tip-off to police. Hauled before the Beak, they pleaded guilty to possession. They were fined $100 each and were free to go. They were not deported, but flew home on schedule shortly afterwards.

5 Paul was interviewed by *Nights with Alice Cooper*, a radio show hosted by 'the godfather of shock rock' himself. It is syndicated to dozens of stations across the US and Canada, in Australia and New Zealand, Germany and Denmark, and in the UK can be accessed via digital radio station Planet Rock.

CHAPTER 16: DEAR FRIEND

1 Dr Stephen Lynn gave many press interviews in the aftermath, his recollections becoming more elaborate with each re-telling. In 2015, having listened to his lies for years, Dr David Halleran came forward 'for the sake of historical accuracy' and gave an

interview to Fox TV. In it, he said that neither Dr Lynn nor another physician who claimed to be involved by the name of Richard Marks had even touched John's body that night. His revelations were supported by two nurses, Dea Sato and Barbara Kammerer, who had worked alongside him in Room 115 that night. Yoko has supported Dr Halleran's version of events. Why didn't he say anything sooner? 'It just seems unseemly for professionals to go out and say, "Hi, I'm David Halleran, I took care of John Lennon,"' he said. 'At the time, I just wanted to go home. I was distraught, I was upset, you feel somewhat responsible, on what you could have done different.'

CHAPTER 17: ALL YOU NEED

1 'The newspapers said, "She's gone to his head"' is a lyric line from 'The Ballad of John and Yoko', a song written by John and credited to Lennon–McCartney. It charted the experiences of John and Yoko that led to their wedding in Gibraltar on 20 March 1969. Released on 30 May 1969, it was the Beatles' seventeenth and final Number One single.

2 Professor of Sociology Deborah Carr conducted a 2004 study on the subject for Rutgers, the state university of New Jersey.

3 New York lawyer turned politician Bruce Blakeman was married to Nancy Shevell for twenty-three years. The couple were legally separated in December 2008. Their son Arlen, born in December 1991, is thirty-two years old at the time of writing. Paul McCartney is his step-father, and Heather, Mary, Stella, Beatrice and James are his step-sisters and step-brother. Arlen graduated from Rollins College, Winter Park, Florida and later attended the private Orthodox Jewish Yeshiva University in New York City. He graduated from their Benjamin N. Cardozo School of Law in 2019, and started his professional career as an intern at the Universal Music Group. Bruce Blakeman remarried in 2015. His second wife is lawyer Segal Magori.

4 'My Valentine', one of the two original songs on Paul's 2012

album *Kisses on the Bottom,* was penned on a rainy day on holiday in Morocco, and recorded with Eric Clapton at Abbey Road. It is one of the 154 songs discussed by Paul in his book *The Lyrics: 1956 to the Present,* written for him by Irish poet Paul Muldoon and published in November 2021.

5 Paul's official title is now 'Sir James Paul McCartney CH MBE'. be accessed via digital radio station Planet Rock.

P.S. I LOVE YOU

1 '6,889,524 people have died so far from the coronavirus COVID-19 outbreak as of June 09, 2023, 13:45 GMT. There are currently 690,078,591 confirmed cases in 229 countries. The fatality rate is still being assessed': Worldometers: https://www.worldometers.info/coronavirus/coronavirus-death-toll. World Health Organization: https://www.who.int/data/stories/the-true-death-toll-of-covid-19-estimating-global-excess-mortality.

IN OTHER WORDS

It was like a tug of war. Imagine two people pulling on a rope smiling at each other and pulling all the time with all their might. The tension between the two of them made for the bond.
Sir George Martin on Paul and John

The Beatles was the best band in the world. It's difficult to follow that. It's like following God. Very difficult, unless you're Buddha. Anything Wings did had to be viewed in the light of The Beatles. And the comparisons were always very harsh. Denny Laine wasn't John Lennon. Henry McCullough wasn't George Harrison. That was inevitable. The interesting thing is that, looking back on some of the work, some of the stuff, it's better than you think it was, but . . . it got such harsh criticism . . . from me.
Sir Paul McCartney

Even Dad found it hard living up to the Beatles.
James McCartney

I don't follow Wings, you know. I don't give a shit what Wings are doing, or what George's new album is doing, or what Ringo is doing . . . It's not callousness. It's just that I'm too busy living my own life to be following what other people are doing.
John Lennon

I had no confidence in myself as a guitar player having spent so many years with Paul McCartney. He ruined me as a guitar player. I think it [Wings] is inoffensive. I've always preferred Paul's good melodies to his screaming rock and roll tunes.

George Harrison

He's an incredible musician. He's incredible at singing too and as a writer, but for me, as a bass player, he is the finest and the most melodic. It's always fun when we're playing together. I've played on several of his records, mainly in the '90s. People keep saying, 'Oh, it's been so long.' It's not been that long . . . we are still pals, but we don't live in each other's pocket.

Ringo Starr

He is not in the least arrogant. The last album was written in a room in Sussex. He was like a mad professor, spending all day writing and then coming out with brilliant tunes.

Linda McCartney

Me and him had this kind of feel together musically. We slotted in well together. We could read each other, and that came from growing up on the same musical influences. Paul's got a good sense of rhythm, and he doesn't overplay, which I like.

Denny Laine

My claim to fame is I was the first drummer Paul McCartney asked to make music with after The Beatles. The last drummer he'd played with before that was a guy named Ringo! I used to be a jazz drummer until I played with a Beatle, and it really screws up your jazz career (laughs). After leaving Wings, I wanted to get away from bands and some of the madness that goes with them, and get back to being a legitimate session guy, playing in a 120 piece orchestra that does movie soundtracks, where I'm just one of eight guys playing percussion, and I did this for a lot of years, with some jazz on the side – but when you play with one Beatle, that's what you're known for.

People don't know about my fun projects with James Brown and Billy Joel and Rick Danko, but they know I played on *Ram* and that's the one they talk about. In a career spanning fifty years, I've played on 200-plus albums, but if I had to pick the most cherished one, it'd be *Ram*.
Denny Seiwell

It was a real happy time, apart from the hiccup in the middle of it, when I suggested that maybe we could get in a better piano player than Linda – I had to back off real quick. She learnt how to work with the band. I was sorry that I'd actually brought it up. She was such a beautiful woman, I felt really sorry about it. But I wanted a fuckin' Jerry Lee Lewis!
Henry McCullough

After leaving Wings, the media hounded me and asked me why I left Wings, well here you go. 'With Wings I was virtually an employed musician, working mainly in the studio. With the birth of the McCartneys' son I realised it would be some time before we ever toured again and that's the side of a musician's life I like best. I left amicably. I don't think anyone was too upset about the parting. We had some very good times together. Though Linda doesn't know much about music, she's a really nice chick and I certainly learned a lot over the past three years.

I joined the reformed Small Faces and we went on a small tour. After the tour, we recorded an album called *78 In The Shade*. After that, things didn't really work out for me with the Small Faces, so I left the band. After leaving the Small Faces, I realised how much I missed Wings. The years I spent with Wings were some of the best years of my life. I now regretted leaving Wings. I wanted to call Paul and beg him to let me back in the band. I miss them.
Jimmy McCulloch

I gotta tell you when we were in Nashville for six weeks living together, rehearsing and recording, I'd be right behind him, touch[ing] him. I'd seen the Beatles live, and like everybody that era . . . they were just so enormous. For example, in the headlines on the paper, the nationals would be [on] their backs, and you knew who they were referring to. They were just gigantic. So, I'm sitting there playing drums, and I'm looking at the back of Paul McCartney, and I gotta say it was a real kind of reality check, I think.
Geoff Britton

It was a real band situation. It wasn't like, 'Hey, I'm Paul McCartney. I know more than you.' It wasn't like that. If people had good suggestions it was used. It was a real learning experience just to be in that situation. Working at Abbey Road with good engineers, actually watching the recording process go down. I soaked in as much as possible. To this day, when I'm in the studio getting into some production stuff, some things will come out that I'd learned back then and forgotten about. I couldn't even put a dollar value on what that experience was worth.
Joe English

There is no question that Wings as a core group is the Paul, Linda and Denny ensemble. This is where it carries over into getting Wings into the Rock and Roll Hall of Fame. Wings was not just Paul McCartney post-Beatles. Wings was Paul McCartney's group post-Beatles, if that makes sense. If you go see Paul now and when he does a Wings song in his set, it's great but there is something missing. You're not hearing Linda's voice; you're not hearing Denny's voice; you're not getting the qualities that they brought to Paul's work. It was a tempering. I think Paul recognised that he needed a foil, without John being around.

Obviously, no one could fill in for John Lennon, but Denny has his own eclecticism with his gypsy/folk sensibilities with an R&B voice and rock guitar prowess. And Linda was kinda the glue. Things

just worked better with Linda there in the room, because she was Paul's soulmate and the female balancing part of his creative energy. There was a dynamic that happened and, as much as Paul will perform a Wings song and you tap your foot and sing along with it and think, what a great song, it doesn't sound like Wings. I do appreciate the fact that he plays some of those tunes though.
Laurence Juber

Sir Paul McCartney taught me many things. One was to trust my instincts. I also remember him saying, 'If you can't hide it, paint it red.' He has given my career longevity just by our association.
Steve Holley

The big difference, though, is . . . that the Rolling Stones have been a big concert band in other decades and other eras when the Beatles never even did an arena tour, Madison Square Garden with a decent sound system. They broke up before that business started, the touring business for real.
Mick Jagger

No McCartney, No Beatles, No 10cc.
Graham Gouldman

Paul McCartney's on another level completely.
Lol Creme

Do you know the story about Paul's first solo album? I was working on my first solo album, *Who Came First*, at Olympic. He was in the studio doing something as well and came in to listen to the whole album. Paul said: 'How did you do this?' I said that I recorded it at home. I said, 'I've got a little mixing desk and an eight-track tape machine.' He went, 'F***! And you did it yourself?' I said, 'Yeah, you should do it.'
Pete Townshend

One day I was recording with the Barron Knights [the novelty rock/pop group] when Paul McCartney suddenly walked into the studio. He sat in the control room and listened for a while. Then he went to the piano, announced that this was what he was doing in a studio nearby, and played 'Hey Jude' for eight minutes.
Elton John

Paul and I used to hang about quite a bit – more than Dad and I did. We had a great friendship going and there seems to be far more pictures of me and Paul playing together at that age than there are pictures of me and my dad.
Julian Lennon

Paul is the father of my child and whatever he's done, whatever has happened, I can never speak badly about the father of my child. We'll have a relationship forever. And I still love him. But you can love somebody and you're not right for each other and you have to move on. Paul is a really, really good father.
Heather Mills

My blood father has had a lifelong influence on me. He trained as a geologist and now, as an artist, I'm very interested in crystals, quartz and turquoise. Mel's a lovely man, but I don't phone him and say, 'Hi, Dad.' That's what I say to Paul. He adopted me and took responsibility for me.
Heather See McCartney

Clearly, there isn't as big a pressure on me as there is on my dad, I just have never looked at him and his name in the way everyone else does. I distinctly remember when we were kids, and he'd play his guitar and we would say, 'Dad, can you shut up, we are trying to watch television.' And he would then say: 'Do you kids know how many people out there actually appreciate my playing?' Naturally,

he's not Sir Paul McCartney to me, but just my dad who makes me laugh and smile.
Mary McCartney

I think, oh my God, he's one of the few living icons. I'm struck by that quite often, but not in an obsessed way. I mean, he's my dad, it would be weird if I was like, 'Oh wow' all the time. But I'm not blind. I am incredibly proud.
Stella McCartney

He's a genius, he's beyond genius, and he's a big inspiration. Very intellectual and obviously amazing at what he does, so it's great fun. He helps me get in tune with myself and be the best person that I can be.
James McCartney

I'm just so excited when I'm around him. It's like when you see a white buffalo and you just hold your breath – you're just hoping that it's not going to end. Because it's the closest I can come to hanging out with my dad. Every second I've ever spent with Paul has been really meaningful to me. He was my dad's best mate for a long time. And my dad didn't have many friends, you know?
Sean Lennon

I guarantee he'll be back home doing the school-run on Friday. Wherever Paul is in the world, it'll be planes, trains and automobiles, just to pick Beatrice up. I've seen him come off stage in Brazil, 100,000 people, get on a plane, fly straight to London, helicopter to Sussex, get in the car, drive, school-run. That, for me, is the mark of the man. And age doesn't come into it. He keeps us all going.
Scott Rodger, Paul's manager

I went down to the South of France to see Wings on the 1972 European tour. It was a lovely warm evening, I was backstage, and I sat down and had a long chat with Linda about reggae. I told her to get the Jimmy Cliff [compilation soundtrack] album *The Harder They Come*, and we talked about Paul Simon's 'Mother and Child Reunion'. She knew a lot more about music than people might have thought.

Paul tried very hard to, but I don't think he ever quite managed to, eclipse himself as a Beatle. Nowadays on tour, he seems to play 75 per cent Beatles numbers. There are a few Wings songs that match what he did with his first band; but overall, he created a better body of work with the Beatles than as Wings. Even if what he's doing now is not as good as it used to be, he is still having a go. Which is to be applauded, because so many of his vintage just give up. If you only rely on your old stuff, you become stagnant. A cabaret act. Externalising your inner emotions is a foundation of rock'n'roll. It's to not dry up. It's to feel in yourself that you can still do it. That's why he does it.

Chris Charlesworth, music journalist, author and former managing editor, Omnibus Press

The massive year-long *Wings Over the World* tour started in the UK in September 1975 ... this was when the band was at its finest in my opinion, with masterful playing by Paul, Denny Laine and Jimmy McCulloch, together with new addition Joe English on drums, a superb player. Plus, Tony Dorsey, Howie Casey, Thaddeus Richard and Steve Howard on saxes, brass and percussion; and last but not least, the lovely Linda on keyboards and backing vocals. I remember the brilliant gig at Wembley for all the wrong reasons: my car got stolen that night.

David Stark, Songlink publisher, author and drummer

Everyone covers Beatles songs. No one covers Wings. Apart from when Guns N' Roses did 'Live and Let Die'.

A fifty-year career is some going. He's not competing against anyone. He's competing *with* everyone, for space and bandwidth. He knows he's already won Gold for England a zillion times. He'd never admit it, but he knows he's been there and done that. Why keep doing it? It's what he does and it's what he knows. He's a musician. It's the way he expresses himself. He can't voice an opinion about anything political, he'd get shot down.
Mike Batt

He is still who he is . . . despite the fact that, for the past fifty years, he hasn't produced an album that anybody cares about.
David Ambrose

He is famously thrifty, which I find very endearing. I did my solo album *First Day* at AIR Studios, and recorded a hundred-piece orchestra at Abbey Road, co-produced by Andrew Powell. 'Paul's in the other studio,' they said. 'Ok,' I said, 'I'll pop in.' 'Oh, 'allo,' he said, 'how are you? Have you got a cigarette, mate?' He took the Dunhill I offered him and put it behind his ear, 'for later!' On the train up from Peasmarsh, he'll go second class and take a packed lunch.

Has he come to terms with the inevitability that this is all going to end? In his mind, he probably consoles himself with the legacy. With the thought that people will speak about him in say a hundred years' time, the way they speak about Beethoven, Picasso, Mozart, Leonardo da Vinci. 99.9 per cent of people get born, live and go. Only a fraction elevate it to the level of greatness that rare human beings can achieve. God selects only the chosen few.
David Courtney

I am reminded of one of my favourite lines from the 'News on the March' sequence in the film *Citizen Kane*: 'All of these years he covered, many of these he was.' For a very few people in music, this statement is applicable. Think of Elvis (1956–57), Elton John

(1973–74) and Michael Jackson (1983–84) at [their] peak: they were so dominant in popular music with their own records and their guest appearances that they 'were' these years. Paul held this status for a long time, but couldn't hold it forever. Although he held on to his own esteem and occasional great success, the trends of music moved to territory he did not occupy.

This is why we remember Paul in what the Pet Shop Boys call his 'imperial phase' (the period in which a musical artist is regarded as being at their commercial and creative peak simultaneously). He was naturally more important when his work was the dominant style in music than when punk and disco were introduced. No one can control the taste of the public, no matter the quality of their own work.

Paul Gambaccini

Would you say that Paul reached his zenith, vocally and as a songwriter, during the Wings decade?
Possibly. Taking it all the way back to the 'White Album', and all the way through to *Back to the Egg*, Paul's songwriting and vocals are on another level. I'm not sure there's another singer/songwriter who can write and perform in so many different styles. Did he and John match the magic they conjured together as Beatles? I think they both had moments. There are a lot of what-if moments. John's 'Cold Turkey' with a McCartney bass line, for instance. I also think that, thank goodness, neither of them tried to recreate the Beatles too much. I believe John was always listening to what Paul did. I'm sure Paul listened out for John, but I think John's paranoia followed him everywhere.

Is it fair to say that, with the exception of 2018's Egypt Station, *little of Paul's vast output over the past fifty years since* Band on the Run *has come anywhere close?*
Again, possibly. He sort of writes half or three-quarters of a good album. I really love a lot of tracks from all the albums, but I'm more

likely to play the early solo works as a whole. He's a bad editor of his own work. Some of his B-sides (when B-sides existed) are far better than some of the tracks that made the albums.

The live setlist is basically the same every time with some great stuff thrown in every now and then. He should expand it – but can he be bothered to learn it? Can he sing it? I'd love to hear him do 'No More Lonely Nights' and so many others. But I don't think he can without changing key, and he obviously won't. Maybe his voice is just gone. Personally, I don't mind it. He's Beatle Paul. He can do it how he wants, I'll be there!

The thing is, for me, the solo output of Paul, John and George – and some Ringo – is just an extension of the story that I love. It's supposed to be separate, but it's all one long journey. Would it have come full circle? Who knows.

Warren Bennett, musician and composer

For Beatlemaniacs, Wings was a jolt. At the time, fans just didn't get it, and foolishly thought that without Lennon's acerbic gaze, Paul would give in too much to his whimsical nature. Only from some distance can we see just how amazing that band was. There was plenty of gibberish and whimsy for sure; and later there was the 'Frog Chorus' and other indulgences. But hidden in all that pent-up creativity was arguably a cache of McCartney's greatest compositions – such as 'Live and Let Die', 'Maybe I'm Amazed', and my two favourites 'My Love' and 'No More Lonely Nights'.

Moving forward in the McCartney solo era, he continues to remind each pop generation that not only is he 'still here', but he's the one to beat for sheer popular song perfection via songs like 'Little Willow' and 'My Valentine'. Any one of his post-Beatles hits would have been enough to cement him as a genius. But he kept on creating these gems so we have almost an excess of riches.

Only now do I 'get it' with Wings. Paul was only thirty when he formed Wings. Having had to start all over again, he created a world-beating combo. That's astounding. If the Beatles had never happened and Wings had been Paul's first band, they would have become what the Beatles became. No question.

Tim Fraser, songwriter, producer, multi-instrumentalist and co-writer of Tina Turner's 'Falling'

SELECT BIBLIOGRAPHY

Allan, Adrian, *Wings Live: On Tour in the 70s*, Meadow Music Publishing, 2020

Altman, John, *Hidden Man, My Many Musical Lives*, Equinox Publishing Ltd, 2022

The Beatles, *Lyrics*, Futura, 1974

The Beatles, *Anthology*, Chronicle Books LLC, 2000

Brown, Peter and Gaines, Steven, *The Love You Make, An Insider's Story of the Beatles*, Macmillan London Ltd, 1984

Courtney, David, *Oh Wot a Life: My Autobiography*, Courtney World Music Ltd, 2020

Doyle, Tom, *Man on the Run: Paul McCartney in the 1970s*, Ballantine Books/Random House LLC, 2013

Fields, Danny, *Linda McCartney: A Portrait*, Renaissance Books Los Angeles, 2000

Gambaccini, Paul, *Paul McCartney In His Own Words*, Omnibus Press, 1976

Giuliano, Geoffrey, *Blackbird: The Unauthorised Biography of Paul McCartney*, Smith   Gryphon Ltd, 1991

Goldman, Albert, *The Lives of John Lennon*, Bantam Press/Transworld Publishers Ltd, 1988

Goodden, Joe, *Riding So High: The Beatles and Drugs*, Pepper & Pearl, 2017

Harry, Bill, *The McCartney File*, Virgin Books Ltd, 1986

MacDonald, Ian, *Revolution in the Head: The Beatles' Records and the Sixties*, Fourth Estate Ltd, 1994

Martin, George, *All You Need is Ears*, MacMillan London Ltd, 1979

Martin, George, *Making Music*, Pan Books Ltd, 1983

McCartney, Paul, *Blackbird Singing: Poems and Lyrics 1965–1999*, Faber and Faber Ltd, 2001

McCartney, Paul; McCartney Donald, Mary; Lewisohn, Mark, *Wingspan: Paul McCartney's Band on the Run*, Little, Brown, 2002

McCartney, Paul, Muldoon, Paul (Ed.), *The Lyrics: 1956 to the Present*, Allen Lane, 2021

McGee, Garry, *Band on the Run: A History of Paul McCartney and Wings*, Taylor Trade Publishing, 2003

McNab, Ken, *And in the End: The Last Days of the Beatles*, Polygon/Birlinn Ltd, 2019

Miles, Barry, *Many Years from Now*, Secker & Warburg, 1997

Napier-Bell, Simon, *Black Vinyl, White Powder*, Ebury Press, 2002

Napier-Bell, Simon, *The Business: A History of Popular Music from Sheet Music to Streaming*, Unbound, 2022

Norman, Philip, *Shout! The True Story of The Beatles*, Hamish Hamilton Ltd, 1981

Norman, Philip, *Paul McCartney: The Biography*, Weidenfeld & Nicolson, 2016

Peebles, Andy, *The Lennon Tapes*, BBC Publications, 1981

Shotton, Pete, with Schaffner, Nicholas, *John Lennon in My Life*, Stein and Day New York, 1983

Sounes, Howard, *Fab: An Intimate Life of Paul McCartney*, Harper Collins, 2010

Spitzer, Michael, *The Musical Human: A History of Life on Earth*, Bloomsbury Publishing, 2021

Stark, David, *It's All Too Much: Adventures of a Teenage Beatles Fan in the '60s and Beyond*, This Day in Music Books/Songlink International, 2020

ACKNOWLEDGEMENTS

I was there, and I was not there. Too young to have experienced the Beatles in real time, I came in at Wings and discovered the Fabs backwards. The following were here, there and everywhere. Without their recollections, reflections and connections; their talent, their knowledge of the business and their enduring love of music; and without the patience and support of my family and friends, I could not have written this book. I am indebted, too, to a significant number of 'insiders' who agreed to see and talk to me on the assurance of anonymity.

What a difference you made. Thank you all.

Thanks to Keith Altham, John Altman, David Ambrose, Mike Batt, Brian Bennett, Warren Bennett, John Brown, Lorna Brown, Clem Cattini, Chris Charlesworth, David Courtney, Robin Denselow, Mark Ellen, Tim Fraser, Steve Gadd, Paul Gambaccini, Bob Harris, David Hepworth, Richard Hughes, Jill Jackson, Allan James, The Revd Canon Dr Alison Joyce, Cynthia Lennon RIP, Lady Linda McCartney RIP, Zandra McGougan, Ian McKerral, Johnny MacKinnon, Sir George Martin, The Revd Steve Morris, Earl Okin, May Pang, Mike Parry, Andy Peebles, Ed Phillips, John Pidgeon, James Saez, David Stark, Michael Watts, Richard Williams, Jane Wroe Wright.

The Craigard House Hotel, Campbeltown, Kintyre; Saddell Bay, Kintyre/The Landmark Trust; Gravetye Manor, West Hoathly,

Sussex; The Fountain Inn, Ashurst, West Sussex; Lympne Castle, Hythe, Kent; Loews, Ventana Canyon, Tucson, Arizona; The Hedges Inn, East Hampton, Long Island, N.Y.

Thank you, Hannah Black, Erika Koljonen, Tom Atkins and the dream team at Coronet/Hodder & Stoughton, and to Barry Johnston.

Thank you, Clare Hulton.
Thank you, Mum and Dad.

To Mia, Henry and Bridie,
Adam and Matthew, Nick, Alex and Christian, Cleo and Jesse.

PICTURE CREDITS

INDEX

'#9 Dream' 108, 179

Abbey Road 8, 34, 157
Adams, Gilly 146
Adler, Lou 59
All the Best! 212
All Things Must Pass 77
Altman, John 176–8
Ambrose, David 151–5, 321
Anderson, Rusty 242
Angier, Natalie 25
'Another Day' 76–7
Anthology 11, 50, 81, 181
Apple Corps 8, 11, 56–7
Asher, Jane 8, 21–2, 32, 50–3, 131, 223–4
Asher, Margaret 21, 22
Asher, Peter 21
Aspinall, Neil 1, 57, 59, 84, 122, 181, 196, 257
Atkinson, Rowan 263
'Attention' 189

'Baby's Request' 230–1
Bach, Barbara 56, 261
Back to the Egg 15, 224–5, 230–1
'Back Seat of My Car, The' 108
Back in the US 205
Baez, Joan 7
Baker, Geoff 137, 255
Baker, Ginger 142
'Ballad of Bonnie and Clyde, The' 85

Balls 92–3
Band on the Run (album) 15, 43, 109, 124, 164, 165–8
'Band on the Run' (song) 16
Barry, John 157
Batt, Julianne 263
Batt, Mike 171–3, 263, 320–1
Beatles, The
  impact of 3
  rise of 5–6
  break-up of 7–12, 19–20, 72
  comparison with Wings 88–9
  possible reunion 110, 163, 189
  'Red' and 'Blue' albums released 162–3
  formal dissolution of 181–2
  influence of Fats Domino on 183–4
Beattie, Charles Noël 31–2
Beethoven, Ludwig van 28, 29
Beethoven, Maria Magdalena van 28
Bennett, Warren 322–3
Best, Mona 6
Best, Pete 6
'Beware My Love' 196
Blackberry Train, The 227
Blaine, Hal 68, 85
Blair, Tony 77
Blakeman, Arlen 257, 259
Blakeman, Bruce 257, 259
'Blueberry Hill' 184
'Bluebird' 167
Bolan, Marc 93

'Jet' 16, 167
John, Elton 179, 204, 318
John Lennon at 80 (radio programme) 5
John Lennon/Plastic Ono Band 23, 77, 97, 107
Johns, Glyn 158–9
Johnson, Angella 145
Johnson, Wilko 1
Johnston, Tom 39
Jones, Brian 79
Jones, Kenney 221–2
Juber, Laurence 224, 230, 231, 239, 316–17
'Julia' 23
'Junk' 66
'Just Fun' (Lennon & McCartney) 5

Kass, Ron 57
Keltner, Jim 87
Kendall, Melinda 96, 101
Keys, Bobby 175
King, Jonathan 84–5
Klein, Allen 9, 162, 163, 181

Laboriel, Abraham 'Abe' 242
Lady Linda McCartney Memorial Garden 46
Lagos 164–7
Laine, Denny
  in Wings 15, 89, 93–4, 115–16
  and 'Mull of Kintyre' 39
  in Campbeltown 44
  early musical career 90–3
  on Linda McCartney 118
  and *Wild Life* 120–1
  recommends Henry McCullough 122
  and 'Mary Had a Little Lamb' 127
  and Joanne Alice LaPatrie 142, 143–4, 145–6, 147, 164, 232
  David Ambrose on 153
  and *Red Rose Speedway* 159
  in Lagos 165–6
  and *Band on the Run* 166

  and *Wings at the Speed of Sound* 196–7
  and 'Mull of Kintyre' 212
  and *Back to the Egg* 224, 230
  on Wings last tour 232–3
  and cancellation of Japanese tour 236–7
  and break-up of Wings 239
  solo career 239–40
  quotes from 314
Laine-Adams, Ainsley 146
Lane, Carla 138
Lane, Ronnie 159
LaPatrie, Joanne Alice (Jo Jo) 141–3, 145–6, 147–9, 164, 232
Lategan, Barry 121
Lee, Christopher 167
Lennon, Alf 3, 198
Lennon, Cynthia 8, 9, 21, 22, 50, 100
Lennon, John
  death of 1, 79–80, 103, 108–9, 241, 243–8, 250
  childhood of 3–4, 20–1
  meets Paul McCartney 4
  and Ringo Starr 6
  song-writing with Paul McCartney 6, 86–7, 89–90, 241–2
  meets and marries Yoko Ono 6–7, 50
  and break-up of the Beatles 8, 9, 10
  marriage to Yoko Ono 9, 98, 104, 106, 178–9, 186–7, 188
  swipes at Paul McCartney 12
  loss of mother 20–1, 23, 24, 27–8, 30
  experience as parent 25–6, 100–2, 139, 188–9
  links to Scotland 33–4
  in New York 62
  Andy Peebles on 73
  and *John Lennon/Plastic Ono Band* 77, 97
  after break-up of the Beatles 95–9
  relationship with May Pang 101, 104–7, 174, 179, 188–9, 200–1
  albums recorded 108–9

334

and break-up of the Beatles 19–20, 72

experience as parent 25–6, 100–2

in Scotland 33, 34

after break-up of the Beatles 95–9

albums recorded 108–9

and use of John Lennon's songs 205

and death of John Lennon 242–3

'Oo You' 66

Orbison, Roy 175–6

Out on a Limb (Mills) 254

'P.S. I Love You' 6, 82

Page, Jimmy 83, 147

Pang, May 101, 104–7, 174–5, 178–9, 187, 188–9, 200–1

Parkinson, Michael 167

Parsons, Alan 159

Past Masters 81

Peebles, Andy 72–4, 90, 91, 243, 244, 245–6

Peel, John 246

Perkins, Carl 250

Perry, Richard 185

Pessoa, Fernando 114

Petty, Katherine 28

Petty, Tom 28

'Photograph' 161

'Picasso's Last Words' 167

Pidgeon, John 159

Pinder, Mike 90

Plastic Ono Band 9

Please Please Me 82

Preston, Billy 9–10, 162

Pure McCartney 212

Quarrymen, The 5

Ram 69, 74, 75–6, 77, 84, 108, 109, 116, 158

Rarities 81

Ray, Brian 242

Red Rose Speedway 15, 109, 124, 129, 157–61, 163

Resurrection (documentary) 29–30

Revolver 7, 8

Rhoads, Randy 147

Ringo 161–2

Robbins, Jane 46

'Rockestra Theme' 230

Rock'n'Roll 107, 108

Rodger, Scott 319

Rolling Stones, The 83

Rory Storm and the Hurricanes 6

Rose, Axl 157

Rupert the Bear 128–9

Rupert and the Frog Song 129

Saltzman, Harry 157

'San Ferry Anne' 197

Sargent, Bill 200

Sayer, Leo 169

Schwartz, Francie 51, 53

Scott, Tom 187

Secunda, Tony 92, 93

See, Mel 55

Seiwell, Denny 15, 74–5, 76, 80, 93–4, 111–13, 120, 122, 155, 164–5, 314–15

Seiwell, Monique 111–13

Seymour, Jane 157

Sgt. Pepper's Lonely Hearts Club Band 7, 8, 50, 52

Sharif, Omar 232

Sheridan, Tony 5–6

Shevall, Jon 257

Shevall, Mike 257–8

Shevall, Nancy 256–61

'She's My Baby' 197

'Silly Love Songs' 16, 197

Simon and Garfunkel 109–10

Slick, Earl 189

Some Time in New York City 96, 108

Spector, Phil 77, 10

Spector, Ronnie 1

Spinozza, Dave 74, 75, 80

Springsteen, Bruce 18

Stark, David 263, 264, 320

Starkey, Zak 227

Starr, Ringo

joins the Beatles 6

and break-up of the Beatles 8

338